28 DAYS DATA

ENGLAND'S TROUBLED RELATIONSHIP WITH ONE-DAY CRICKET

PETER MILLER AND DAVE TICKNER
FOREWORD BY GEORGE DOBELL

First published by Pitch Publishing, 2016

Pitch Publishing
A2 Yeoman Gate
Yeoman Way
Worthing
Sussex
BN13 3QZ
www.pitchpublishing.co.uk

A CIP catalogue record is available for this book from the British Library.

ISBN 978-1-78531-150-5

Typesetting and origination by Pitch Publishing

Printed by Bell & Bain, Glasgow, Scotland

Contents

Authors' Note

THE story of one-day cricket starts long before the focus of this book, but this is an attempt to understand why England went from almost winning the 1992 World Cup to consistent underachievers for the next two decades. We have tried to speak to as many of those who played for or coached England as possible, but it was difficult to speak to those who are still within the England set-up. Access is, perhaps understandably, closely guarded. We hope that we have been able to tell as accurate a version of events surrounding the most recent tournaments as possible. We are extremely grateful to all of those who took the time to speak to us on the record, and those that were able to fill in the gaps off the record. We could not have done this without them. When we have spoken to someone for the book we have tried to make it clear they are speaking directly to us by using the present tense "says"; quotes that we have collated from elsewhere are attributed to their original source. We would like to thank the following interviewees for sparing the time to speak to us: Jonathan Agnew,

Mike Atherton, Lawrence Booth, Ali Brown, Robert Croft, Phil DeFreitas, Mark Ealham, John Etheridge, Angus Fraser, David Fulton, Ashley Giles, Graham Gooch, Adam Hollioake, Nick Hoult, Nasser Hussain, Raymond Illingworth, Steve James, Nick Knight, Andrew Miller, Lord MacLaurin, Peter Moores, Alan Mullally, Paul Nixon, Kevin O'Brien, Kevin Pietersen, Derek Pringle, Jack Russell, Owais Shah, Neil Smith, Alec Stewart, Andrew Strauss, and Graham Thorpe.

Thank you to Pitch Publishing for agreeing to let us tell an unloved story. We hope the chance you have taken is worth it.

Also, thanks to those of you who were a sounding board for ideas, and to proofreaders and transcribers. You know who you are and you know you are appreciated.

Foreword

By George Dobell, Senior
Correspondent, *ESPNCricinfo*

AN optimist, they say, describes the glass as half-full. A pessimist describes it as half-empty. And a regular supporter of England at cricket World Cups expects the glass to fragment, explode and kill everyone in the near vicinity.

It is, psychologists would tell us, a conditioned response. We've experienced so much disappointment associated with World Cups that we should, by now, consider it a success if the team arrive at the venue on the right day (beyond them in 2003, albeit with mitigating factors), sober (the 2007 tournament was like Woodstock; if you remember it, you probably weren't there) and looking smart in their blazers (something they didn't manage until 1987).

So this book should probably come with a health warning. It will bring back memories of long-buried traumas. There's the Wasim Akram spell in 1992, Andy Bichel beating England all on his own in 2003,

Kevin O'Brien producing an innings so incredible he should probably have worn a cape (2011), the day-night loss in Wellington that was completed before there was any need to turn on the lights (2015) and, maybe grimmest of all, the 1999 elimination that occurred before the event's theme song was released. A theme song whose video suggested that only the insane attended cricket.

There are recurring themes in the catalogue of failures contained here. Most of all there is the prioritising of Test cricket to the detriment of the ODI side and the habit of abandoning long-held plans on the eve of the tournament. Invariably, England have gone into World Cups a bizarre mixture of the exhausted and the inexperienced.

For that reason, England's debacle at the 2015 World Cup has a strong claim to be ranked the most disappointing performance of all. They had, you see, been extended every advantage heading into it. The Ashes had been moved – we had three Ashes series within two years to ensure England could spend the whole winter of 2014/15 honing the relevant skills – and, in eight months between August 18, 2014 and March 14, 2015, they played 23 matches in all formats and 22 of them were ODIs. Yet, having persevered with Alastair Cook long after the point when it became clear to most that he was – in ODIs at least – part of the problem rather than part of the solution, they then changed the identity of their opening bowler and No. 3 batsman on the eve of the tournament. In a format where role identity and familiarity is so important, it was a self-defeating move.

It might be tempting to conclude that England have always been hopeless at ODI cricket, but that would be simplistic. They have been, in their own conditions at least, the best in the world on several occasions and should have won the Champions Trophy in 2004 and 2013. It often seems to be the way that England's successes are explained away but, in 2012, when they beat Australia 4-0 at home and Pakistan 4-0 away, they were rated the best ODI side in the world for a reason. Let's not forget that. Even after they lost the Champions Trophy Final in 2013, there was no reason to think that, with Graeme Swann, Jonathan Trott and Kevin Pietersen available, they would not challenge in the 2015 World Cup.

Peter Moores carried the can for that failure. And it is only right that the coach should take some of the responsibility. But he didn't inherit a handful of aces when he took the job about 12 months earlier. Instead, he took over a team in transition, an administration committed to a captain not worth his place in the side and found himself representing a board whose behaviour has left many supporters disillusioned. He became the focal point for their anger and the scapegoat for the failure. Lampooned for a phrase he didn't say and a method in which he didn't believe, he became more piñata than coach. He wasn't the problem.

He may not have been the solution, either, though. It is true that results improved, in ODI cricket at least, once he left. But he wasn't the only departure. England also discarded several of their senior players – all of whom had failed at the World Cup – and instead embraced younger, fresher talent developed in the county game. Almost immediately, they started to enjoy better results.

There might be a lesson there.

For while some blame the standard of the ECB's domestic competitions for England's failing in World Cups – they argue that players are disadvantaged by developing in that environment – it is not an argument that stands up to much scrutiny.

Consider Ian Bell, for example. Bell was chosen to open the batting in the World Cup in 2015. But he had not played a domestic T20 match between June 25, 2010 and August 23, 2014.

It was a similar story with the man who was to lead England's bowling attack in the event, James Anderson. He has, at the time of writing in May 2016, played five T20 games since June 2010 and didn't play any in 2012 or 2013.

And, at the time Cook was selected in the England squad to play in the Stanford series in late 2008, he had a career-best T20 score of 15.

The problem wasn't so much county cricket as the fact the top players had stopped playing in it. As a result, they failed to keep up to date with the latest developments in the game. It showed in Australia and New Zealand.

We shouldn't be surprised. The one global limited-overs tournament that England have won – the World T20 in the Caribbean in 2010 – came when England discarded several players on the brink of the tournament and embraced players fresh out of the county game. So Craig Kieswetter, man of the match in the final, made his T20 international debut in the first game of the tournament. So did his opening partner, Michael Lumb, while Michael Yardy was playing just his fourth such game and his first for three years.

The point of all this?

The key to improvement is not to radically overhaul our county system. It is to embrace it.

There is plenty of talent out there. And the domestic game still offers the opportunity to learn and develop new skills. We need to ensure our international players have the opportunity to play enough county cricket to ensure they remain in touch with changes within the game much as even an experienced doctor will benefit from regular training sessions to ensure they remain up to date with medical advances.

Remember, Australia have never won the World T20 and India haven't won it since the IPL was formed. It's not the cricket we tend to admire in those competitions. It is the marketing.

Domestic cricket has a PR problem, for sure, but it remains the foundation for all that is good in England cricket. We need to build upon it, not knock it away.

I hope you enjoy the book as much as I did. It is written by guys who really care and who have shared the pain of disappointment. And, come what may, they will be hoping for an improvement in 2019.

Prologue

We'll have to look at the data

MONDAY, 9 March 2015. England have just lost to Bangladesh to be eliminated from the ICC World Cup at the group stage with a game still to play.

They had only managed to beat Scotland at that point, and even then it was not a forceful performance. They did enough to beat their lowly neighbour, but nothing more. They would go on to defeat Afghanistan in their last game four days later, but by then their tournament was already over. In a bloated schedule, England's World Cup – and with it another four years of axed players and discarded plans – had come to an end after just 28 days.

Peter Moores, in his second stint as England coach, was speaking to the BBC. He was talking about what

England could learn from this performance, from this defeat, from this humiliation.

"We'll have to look at the data."

The quote exploded. The word "data" was already one loaded with negative connotations. It was an example of England's obsession with numbers and rejection of spirited cricket. They were spoken of as cricket-playing automatons who had all the joy and expression programmed out of them. Back in the English summer before this World Cup, as England succumbed to an embarrassing 3-1 defeat to India, it had become the *cause célèbre*. The first ODI at Bristol was a complete washout. The journalists in the makeshift press box in the Nevil Road pavilion were scrambling around for something to write about. Former England spinner turned commentator Graeme Swann helped them out.

Speaking on the BBC's *Test Match Special* Swann did not hold back, exclaiming that England had "a cat in hell's chance" of winning the World Cup. He was vicious about England's "old fashioned" approach and their game that was a decade out of date.

Swann saved some of his fiercest criticism for Alastair Cook, whose position as both opening batsman and captain of the side had come under increased scrutiny. Cook had been having a torrid time in all forms of the game and had only just rediscovered some form during the Test series victory over the Indians.

"I love Alastair Cook dearly but I don't think he should be bothering playing ODI cricket anymore," Swann told *TMS*. "He doesn't need to. He has proved a very good point in Tests. Enjoy being England Test captain. Let young people play, people who want to smash it everywhere and win you the World Cup."

Swann could not have been more correct, as events bore out. Cook would not make it as far as the World Cup. Swann went on to speak in detail about England's data driven approach, how the numbers men would help them set their game plan. Swann's attention turned back to the previous World Cup in 2011, and England's meek quarter-final exit.

"I remember sitting in a team meeting – before the new fielding restrictions were brought in – and we were told that if we scored 239 we will win 72 per cent of games. That meant the whole game was built on having so many runs by a certain stage and having so many partnerships. I used to shake my head, thinking 'this is crazy'. I remember Jonathan Trott getting close to a hundred in Colombo. We had batted to our plan almost perfectly and scored 229. Trotty got 86 in 115 balls. Everyone said 'brilliant', then Sri Lanka knocked them off in 39.3 overs."

This stuck. For the rest of that summer and the winter that followed the tag of England as numbers-obsessed conservatives stuck.

When Moores said what he said in the aftermath of that defeat to Bangladesh it was confirmation of that critique. Data was to blame.

There was only one problem: Moores didn't say data to the BBC. A crackly radio line had led to him being misheard. He had said, "We will have to look at it later." An attempt to avoid saying anything, to wait and analyse what had gone wrong once emotions had settled. The BBC issued an official apology to Moores for the suggestion that he had used the word data. He had in fact mentioned data in a different interview, with Sky Sports, but not in such a damning context: "We'll have to analyse the game data a bit later". It still wasn't a great thing to say, but in both interviews what Moores was attempting to do was to avoid passing judgement in the immediate aftermath of England's defeat.

The rot had set in, though. Paul Downton, the Managing Director of England Cricket, was also under serious pressure. As the man who appointed Moores, he was seen by many to be as culpable as the coach. Downton's interviews in the days following that World Cup exit suggested that he was a man out of his depth, although his handling of the sacking of Kevin Pietersen had already indicated he was not the man for a crisis.

It was when Downton mentioned the influence of T20 cricket on the most recent World Cup that those listening to him nearly choked on their cup of coffee.

"My perception is that what has happened in the last year or two is that the crossover between Twenty20 and 50-over cricket has accelerated enormously," Downton told the press at the time.

The last year or two! Twenty20 had been rocking white ball cricket to its core since its inception. If the man running cricket at an elite level in England had only just realised the influence that Twenty20 had made in the last ten years in the wake of this World Cup exit the problems were even worse than feared.

Downton's days were numbered. A year in which the England and Wales Cricket Board (ECB) had failed spectacularly in almost everything it had done that he had overseen. The sacking of Kevin Pietersen divided cricket and left the board looking detached and vindictive. While many supported the jettisoning of Pietersen few were happy when a press release described criticism coming from "outside cricket". The term was actually directed towards former tabloid editor and media motormouth Piers Morgan, who had been using his Twitter account to make visceral attacks on the ECB in general and Downton and Cook in particular.

In reality that "outside cricket" jibe left many to wonder if it referred to fans in general. It was a spectacularly ill-advised turn of phrase that summed up a brand that was becoming "toxic" – there was even talk of changing the name to something other than ECB such was the depth to which attitudes towards it had sunk.

Within a month of England's World Cup exit Downton had been fired. His role was done away with, replaced by a Director of England Cricket whose remit was to focus solely on the men's team at the highest level. When making the announcement of Downton's departure the ECB's new chief executive, Tom Harrison, said: "This doesn't impact on Peter Moores' position at all. This is with respect to delivering an environment for the future."

Few believed that, and, once Andrew Strauss had been given the newly created role, the firing of Moores was his first significant move. Strauss had been due to appear as a pundit for Sky Sports' coverage of England's ODI against Ireland. Suddenly his involvement was cancelled and it soon became clear that the reason he was no longer appearing on TV was because he was the man the ECB had placed in charge of the England team.

This increased speculation about Moores' position and very quickly attention turned away from a rain-affected and low-intensity ODI in Dublin and to discussions of the coach's position. Sat at the other end of the picturesque Malahide ground, those sat in the press box seemed to know that Moores had been sacked before he did.

Moores might not have said "we will have to look at the data", but he never shook the perception that he had.

※ ※ ※

The British have a fine sporting tradition. They create a sport, give it to the world, and are then very quickly surpassed at it.

Football is the best-known example, but these small islands have been responsible for creating three formats of cricket. The first England vs Australia Test match took place in 1877. By 1882 there was an obituary commemorating the death of the sport in *The Sporting Times* giving birth to the Ashes.

While the antecedents of limited overs can be found in the Indian province of Kerala in the 1950s, it became a professional pursuit in England in 1962 when the "Midlands Knock-Out Cup" took place between Leicestershire, Northamptonshire, Derbyshire and Nottinghamshire. It was 65 overs a side and Northamptonshire beat Leicestershire in the final.

By the following season the Gillette Cup was born and all of the then 17 first-class counties took part. The tournament was created because there was a concern of falling attendances at county matches and administrators were keen to create something that resonated with the public; a sentiment that has led to almost every change in cricket in its history. For most of its existence the sport has been trying to find a way to stay relevant.

It was a massive success and the knockout cup along the lines of that first Gillette Cup existed in some format or another from 1963 up until 2009. It was reduced to 60 overs a side for the 1964 season and it stayed that way until 1999 when it became a 50-over competition. With Lord's hosting a final late in the season every year for 46 years the tournament was seen as the jewel in the county cricket crown almost from its inception. A day out for a final at the "home of cricket" in front of a full house is the closest many professional cricketers ever get to international cricket.

By 1969, the idea that one-day cricket was the way to attract new fans was well and truly entrenched. At the time County Championship games were three-day affairs with a day off on Sunday. For that season the decision was made to play a 40-over league competition instead of giving the players a day off, prompted by a change in the law that allowed more sporting activities to take place on a Sunday. It was massively popular with the BBC broadcasting at least one game a week all the way into the 1990s. Many fans first got into cricket thanks to these games, chancing upon the action on TV or watching it with an already cricket-obsessed relative.

Some great finishes, an early afternoon start and a quick game aided by the fast bowlers only being allowed a short run-up made it a very family friendly affair.

Raymond Illingworth played in the very first year of the Sunday League. He has happy memories of it.

"I thought the Sunday League was an excellent competition, everybody was playing on the Sunday, you could see how the matches were going," Illingworth told us. "I know we were pushing to win the title a few times, we finished early once or twice and we watched the end of the matches at Yorkshire playing Essex and things like that which was affecting our games. We got good crowds. Once or twice we had 12,000 at Leicester. They only get 4,500 in now so where we put 12,000 I don't know."

That is not to say it was perfect for the players. It wasn't always the same teams playing each other on a Sunday and in the Championship match that it interrupted. There were times when play would finish in the Championship match on a Saturday night and the players would have to travel long distances that night for the Sunday League game, making the same arduous trip in reverse for the resumption of the three-day game on Monday morning. Illingworth recalls one Bank Holiday weekend where the 100 miles on back roads from Kent to Hampshire took well over four hours.

Illingworth says that, despite the travel, and despite the amount of cricket they played in those days, the players liked it. The sponsors looked after the cricketers, with John Player making sure any smokers had all the cigarettes they wanted, and one would imagine those that didn't smoke may have asked for one or two boxes to sell on.

Another competition, the Benson & Hedges Cup, made its first appearance in 1972, with a regional aspect that allowed a number of local derbies that drew big crowds. Cricket had gone from having the one county competition to having four in a few short years. One-day cricket was here and here to stay.

※ ※ ※

The league format created by the Sunday League existed all the way until 2009, although with two divisions from 1999 with it renamed the National League with a 45-over format introduced. It later became the NatWest Pro40 with the overs back down to 40-a-side.

Into the 21st century and the public's love affair with the format was fading and the introduction of snazzy nicknames like Middlesex Crusaders and Lancashire Lightning did not stop the rot. The Benson & Hedges Cup had come to an end and there was space in the calendar. There was a concern that having three limited-overs competitions with broadly the same format was overkill. Combined with the introduction of legislation that restricted tobacco companies advertising at sporting events, the fate of the third one-day cup was sealed and it was done away with. In the sort of neat symmetry that sport can throw up the last Benson & Hedges Cup Final between Warwickshire and Essex was umpired by John Hampshire and Barry Dudleston. They had faced each other in the very first final 30 years earlier as players. Barrie Leadbeater, third umpire for the 2002 final, had also appeared in 1972.

What replaced the Benson & Hedges Cup was about as radical as cricket gets, and has changed the face of the sport to such an extent that at times it is no longer recognisable. The Twenty20 Cup was an attempt to inject some fun into proceedings. It is unlikely that anyone involved in the decision knew what they were unleashing, that "Twenty20" cricket would become such a behemoth of change.

In fact, Adam Hollioake, the man who captained Surrey to victory in the inaugural event, told us that he couldn't quite believe what was being planned. Players, county chairmen and fans were far from convinced. Hollioake thought the ECB was joking when he first heard of the plans. He thought the ECB had "lost their mind". He soon changed his mind, but with all the success that T20 has brought it is strange to think it was not uniformly welcomed at the time.

By 2010 the T20 Cup was such a feature of the fixture list that the Sunday League and NatWest Trophy had been rolled into one event, a 40-over affair that had a league phase followed by semi-finals and a Lord's final. There were 21 teams taking part, with Scotland, the Netherlands and the Unicorns, a side made up of minor county players, in addition to the 18 first-class counties.

This, too, was short-lived, with a move to a 50-over-a-side mid-season event taking place from 2014. For many the move to a format that mirrored that played in one-day internationals was long overdue.

At the time of writing, that 50-over mid-season event is still how one-day cricket is played, with T20 spread throughout the season, but that is up for debate yet again. Even though one-day cricket has been a mainstay of English cricket for 50 years the sport still struggles to work out where the format fits, how it should be played and how long it should take.

※ ※ ※

England failing to *get* limited-overs cricket is nothing new. Of all the people we spoke to for this project, not one felt that England have focused on one-day cricket. Some were more forthright than others, but the message was the same. Tests are best.

The argument that has long been made about England and ODI cricket is that it was an unloved and poor relation of Test cricket. If a player needs to be rested it will be from the ODI side, if a series needs to be tacked on to the summer at the beginning or the end it will be the ODIs. Jonathan Agnew, the BBC's cricket correspondent, told us this is part of the issue with the white-ball game in the mind of the public. They could buy their ticket for the game months in advance and end up not seeing the best players available and be sat shivering in the stands in late September.

"I've always felt that England have missed a trick by degrading the one-day internationals. In some ways that's sort of understandable as there is so much international cricket. Generally now, usually but not always, the ODIs follow the Test series, players have played back-to-back Tests, they are usually spent, they have a tour coming up almost immediately," Agnew says.

Nor do ODIs have the same level of coverage as Tests. The big names in the press corps disappear when it is time for the ODIs, the 2,000-word features are replaced by 500-word quote pieces. Part of that is to do with the narrative that Test cricket creates and part of it is to do with the pervading belief that cricket fans in England just like Test cricket more. This was a point that was made by *Wisden* editor Lawrence Booth; the secondary nature of ODIs in the Almanack reflects its readers and what they want.

"To a degree you're reflecting the readership but you're also reflecting the prejudice inherent within English cricket, which is that Test cricket matters more than one-day cricket. And I think that was always the case even when England were reasonable at one-day cricket," Booth says. "The other point, there's more to write about in a Test match than a one-day international – five days, things can change more. In terms of narrative, Test cricket does offer more potential. But that's not to say that what we're doing isn't indicative of a wider prejudice."

This suspicion of white-ball cricket isn't just restricted to the press; even players that have been seen as specialists in the limited-overs game have struggled to maintain a steady place in the ODI team, with England continually going back to the Test boys whenever the going gets tough.

One of those that has suffered is Owais Shah, who never really found a place in England teams. He did well for the ODI side but never found a way in Tests and, in the end, he was dropped from both sides.

"I scored the most runs in the 12 months for England in one-day cricket prior to being dropped. That almost makes you think 'OK, well because I'm dropped out of the Test team, looks like I have to make way out of the one-day squad even though I'm one of the highest scorers'. When that happens you ask do we really care about one-day cricket, then? It's all about Test cricket, that you have to be a regular Test player to hold a spot in the one-day team. That's what it felt like," Shah says.

Every player we spoke to was very keen to point out that they cared, that playing for England mattered to them more than anything, no matter the format or the opponent.

"There certainly wasn't a lack of intensity about how we went about our cricket when I was playing," Graham Thorpe says. But for Thorpe the biggest problem during his time in the team was that there wasn't enough one-day cricket, something that Mike Atherton also raised as an issue. That has changed over the years but England still do not play as many ODIs as other teams.

Then there are the fans. The assumption has always been that if you were to ask an England supporter to choose between an Ashes win and a World Cup victory, almost to a man they would say they want to beat Australia in a Test series.

Whether fans would feel different if they did win the World Cup is up for debate, but chances are there would be no open-top bus parades like we had after the Ashes win in 2005. The English cricket-watching public just don't really seem to care quite so much about one-day cricket, even when it's the World Cup. "I've covered every World Cup since 1996," says *The Sun* cricket correspondent John Etheridge. "And unquestionably the World Cup is not the pinnacle of the sport. The Ashes is considered in England certainly as the pinnacle of the sport."

There is a traditionalist bent in the heart of the English cricket fan that even all these years after limited-overs cricket became a central part of the calendar, it still comes second to wonderful Test cricket.

When former England captain Michael Vaughan carried out an extremely unscientific "RT or Fav" Twitter poll in September 2014 some 89 per cent of those that responded said they wanted an Ashes win more. In April 2016, as England were on their way to the final of the World T20, we asked the same question. While Vaughan had 1,685 responses our slightly less flawed but still far from scientific Twitter poll had 873. It was a simple question: Which would you rather see England win, the Ashes or the World Cup?

The result was surprising, and perhaps reflected of the success that England had during 2015 and 2016 in white-ball cricket: 51 per cent said they would rather England won the World Cup. Maybe a shift in fan attitude is happening, but that change is nascent.

It is only really in the last year that the limited-overs game and the Test game have been given anything close to an equal footing by the England management, and that it took close to 50 years after the first ever one-day international for that to happen says a lot about England's love for the format.

※ ※ ※

That first one-day international happened by accident. England were touring Australia for the Ashes in 1970/71. There had already been two deadly dull draws in the first two matches. When the teams arrived in Melbourne for the third Test the series was in need of an excitement injection. What it got was two days of heavy rain. It was suggested that the game should start on the Sunday so there was a chance something approaching a meaningful contest could take place. The boards refused. Playing Test cricket on a Sunday would "set a dangerous precedent" it was said.

There was a hastily arranged seventh Test as a replacement when the inevitable abandonment happened, something that the England players were furious about. There was some talk of that new fixture not taking place and in an attempt for the Melbourne Cricket Ground to recoup some of its potential losses from the abandoned Test a one-day game was arranged between the two teams.

No one was particularly sold on the idea, and even the public reception was lukewarm. There was no official "status" at the time – that only came later. Instead the game was billed as Australia XI vs England XI. Raymond Illingworth, the England captain, said the players themselves weren't massively interested. Speaking in 1994 he said, "It was obvious it would be commercially successful, but I couldn't say we played with the same intensity as today."

When we caught up with Illingworth, he went into a bit more detail about how the players felt about the match.

"To be honest I don't think we were too keen on [the game]. It was just slipped in and, as we were going to play five Test matches in six weeks after Christmas, we weren't too keen on having that slipped in. We weren't getting paid for it, either. It wasn't in the contract," Illingworth told us. "I think we played it because we had to play it but it was just a matter of 'well, let's get on with it' because we had to. That was the attitude we had to that particular match. Nobody was very keen on it."

By 1975 the format nobody was very keen on had a World Cup. England even made the semi-final in the first one, losing when they were bowled out for 93 by Australia. At the next World Cup four years later, England made it all the way to the final, losing only after a Viv Richards masterclass took the game beyond them – the great West Indies bowlers of the day finished the job.

England came closer in 1987, their first World Cup away from home. India and Pakistan were the hosts, both eliminated in the semi-finals. England made the final, but lost to Australia by seven runs. Graham Gooch was the leading run-scorer in the tournament and England were unlucky not to have got their first win.

The fact that England had a longer history than anyone else in the one-day game domestically allowed them to compete well in those first four World Cups. In many ways it is surprising that they didn't win at least one of them. By 1992 the rest of the world had caught up, although England still went into that tournament as one of the favourites. That was a great tournament for England but things have got progressively worse since then.

Alec Stewart, a veteran of four World Cups for England, summed it up when he spoke to us: "As I say to everyone, the 1992 World Cup is one of my fondest memories, though not winning the final hurt, and the next three World Cups were very miserable experiences for various reasons."

It is in Australia and New Zealand in 1992 that our story begins.

1992 World Cup

Front runners, almost winners

THE 1992 World Cup was a tournament of firsts and lasts. It was the first World Cup for Brian Lara, Sachin Tendulkar, Inzamam-ul-Haq and Alec Stewart; the last for Imran Khan, Ian Botham and Kapil Dev. It was the first to feature coloured clothing and the first to use white balls – they even used two per innings, one at each end, as per the regulations at the most recent World Cup – and floodlights. And 24 years later it remains the last time England have avoided an ignominious early exit.

This was a far larger event than the four previous World Cups – in every way. More teams, more spectators, more matches, more money. This was a modern, large-scale sporting event and actually looked like a modern, large-scale sporting event. Although the fifth World Cup took place only 24 years ago, it is the first that would be instantly recognisable to the modern fan as one-day cricket.

It was the first to feature South Africa after 21 years in the international sporting wilderness and therefore the first with a full complement of the then eight Test nations present. Kepler Wessels' effervescent and exciting side, featuring the outrageous fielding of Jonty Rhodes and the explosive pace of Allan Donald, would more than play their part in the tournament's success, as well as being centre-stage for its biggest controversy.

Zimbabwe – still a few months away from being granted a seat at the top table – earned the final place in a nine-team event by easing to victory in the 1990 ICC Trophy, replicating their previous successes of 1982 and 1986 to reach the World Cups of 1983 and 1987. That 1990 tournament, staged in Holland, was open to all 19 associate members of the International Cricket Council, and Zimbabwe won all six of their matches across two group stages before beating Bangladesh in the last four and the hosts in the final.

In a gloriously crickety way, Zimbabwe were the only team who had to actually earn their place in the World Cup and they did so by winning a tournament played over 60 overs a side rather than 50, and in white clothing with red balls. No ICC Trophy matches at that time had official one-day international status – indeed, Zimbabwe's 20 matches across the 1983, 1987 and 1992 World Cups represented their only 'official' international cricket before their first Test against India in October 1992.

While Zimbabwe may have qualified in whites, the coloured clothing for the main event was an enormous success, with the iconic 1992 outfits surely never bettered in the years before or since. Even today, originals and more recent reproductions for all nine participating nations are still seen in the stands at international matches.

You're not even reading this, are you? Not properly. You're still thinking about the kits.

Take a moment…

The pastel shades of England, New Zealand and Pakistan, the bright red of Zimbabwe. The classy dark blue of the Indians. Even Australia's canary yellow looked great. Each country's name printed in bold type across the front. Dave Houghton ruining the otherwise flawless and iconic captains' photograph in front of the Sydney Opera House by outrageously breaking ranks with the other skippers and choosing to wear the rather less striking sweater.

The genius of the kits lay in the simplicity of a design which made them instant and enduring classics. While each country wore their own colours with players' names on the back (but no numbers, which wouldn't make an appearance until 1999) each kit was made to the same template and featured the same blue, green, red and white stripes across the shoulders. This, and the fact that none of the nine colours chosen clashed with any other, made each team stand out while retaining a pleasingly consistent aesthetic. The overall effect managed to seem both modern yet in keeping with the grand old sport's traditions of uniform, well, uniforms. Everyone just looked good.

Such is the 1992 kit's status, even the basic description above is surely unnecessary. Can there be a cricket fan anywhere – even one born years after the event – who cannot instantly now conjure up in their mind's eye Martin Crowe in light grey or Allan Border in canary yellow? Or a blur of dark and light green and splattered stumps as Jonty Rhodes channels Superman to run out Inzamam-ul-Haq? They are part of the fabric of the tournament. It's as hard to imagine the 1992 World Cup without those kits as it is to imagine it without stumps or bats or Wasim Akram's delivery to dismiss Allan Lamb in the final. If the ICC announced the much-maligned ten-team 2019 World Cup were to copy the 1992 kits as well as its format, almost all opposition would surely disappear overnight. They could probably even bring back the 1992 rain rules without too much fuss, as long as promises were kept about the kits.

The return of South Africa created a nine-team tournament and gave organisers their first headache. All four previous World Cups had featured eight teams split into two groups of four. The only alteration in the format during the first four World Cups had been a change from teams playing other sides in their group once in 1975 and 1979 to twice in 1983 and 1987.

Instead of lopsided groups or an awkward three-group structure, the nine teams were placed into one big superpool where everyone would play everyone with the top four progressing to the semi-finals. Everyone at the tournament was thus guaranteed at least eight games – up from six at the previous two World Cups and just three in the two before that.

This continued the trend for a larger tournament, the total number of games having already risen from 15 in 1975 to 27 in 1983 and here to 39 in an event that would last 33 days. This marks another way in which the 1992 event acts as a touchstone in the tournament's development, a bridge between the early events with too few matches and the unwieldy, over-long modern-day behemoths.

As well as being the ideal length for a World Cup, this Goldilocks' bed of a format was just right for the teams of the time. There was not the same clamour then for greater associate participation that has seen the ten-team 2019 World Cup – following the same format as 1992 but with one extra side – so widely criticised. And the 1992 format did at least guarantee one associate participant, albeit one on the brink of Full Member status.

While the 2019 World Cup achieves the neat trick of having both too few teams and too many matches, the 1992 World Cup was just right for the time and the format, for the most part, worked.

How much that owed to happenstance and a unique place and time in cricket's development can be debated endlessly. We will perhaps only know for sure after the 2019 edition, but there is an argument that the 1992 World Cup succeeded in spite of its format, not because of it.

But what is clear is that this World Cup came at an optimum moment for such a format to work. There was no dominant side, and arguably no event since has been as tough to predict. The great West Indies side of the 1980s was beginning its descent. Australia, though defending champions, were not quite yet the world-beating greatest-of-all-time contenders they were to become. England have never been better before or since, and the same was true of New Zealand until the World Cup's return to their shores 23 years later.

While the weakest sides, Sri Lanka and Zimbabwe, won only three games between them, they were competitive. Sri Lanka's squad contained a core of the team that would go on to shock the world by winning the 1996 event four years later: Jayasuriya, De Silva, Ranatunga, Mahanama, Tillakaratne, Wickramasinghe.

Ultimately any tournament, any format, any sport, relies on entertaining contests where the best teams thrive but the unexpected can never be ruled out. The 1992 World Cup had that. And the kits. We really cannot overstate the importance of the kits.

The most consistent sides in the group stage were rewarded, while the late surge of Pakistan's 'Cornered Tigers' highlighted the virtue of peaking at the right time for the biggest matches. India, West Indies and – most surprisingly – the primary hosts and pre-tournament favourites Australia were all consistently inconsistent, which meant the exact make-up of the semi-finalists was not known until the final day of the round robin, when Pakistan's win over New Zealand and West Indies' defeat to Australia allowed Imran Khan's side to sneak into the final qualifying position.

If results had gone according to the form book, rather than the wildly fluctuating efforts the 1992 World Cup produced, then the four semi-finalists could have been decided much, much earlier. In that way the nine-team group format got really lucky.

For New Zealand, that loss to Pakistan was a first defeat after seven straight wins had comfortably secured their last-four spot. Even defeat came with a victory of sorts, ensuring as it did that Australia could not progress. As a result, trans-Tasman bragging rights and, more importantly, a home semi-final were theirs.

Martin Crowe's side had prospered in their own conditions. Having been well beaten by England in the one-day series before the World Cup, New Zealand changed their approach at the World Cup and prepared slow decks for their games.

In what was at the time still a hugely original departure from the norm, the Kiwis successfully deployed batsman-turned-off-spinner Dipak Patel as an opening bowler, with a variety of medium-pace trundlers following him to further deceive and discombobulate their opponents. Chris Harris and Gavin Larsen were cast as unlikely world-beaters. They were as inventive at the top of the batting order as well, with Mark Greatbatch deployed as a sort of proto-Jayasuriya pinch hitter to exploit the 15 overs of fielding restrictions. With Crowe's inventive captaincy allied to his world-class batting, the co-hosts quickly stamped their mark on the tournament with a stunning victory over Australia on the opening night. Crowe made an unbeaten century.

If New Zealand were the standout side of the group stage, winning their first seven games, it was Graham Gooch's England who adopted the mantle of favourites once Australia's fallibility became clear.

This really was a fine England one-day side. No playing catch-up here, no being surprised at what the rest of the world was doing and how the game was changing. In one-day cricket as it was played at the start of the final decade of the 20th century, England had it pretty much cracked. They even had Ian Botham pinch-hitting, sort of.

There was close to a perfect blend of youth and experience, and a side packed with all-rounders batted deep. And for that era, England were as well-equipped as anyone. They had stroke-makers, nudgers, nurdlers – and plenty of players who could give it a whack.

Alec Stewart would play at four World Cups and amass 170 ODI caps in a near 15-year career. He is in no doubt where that 1992 side ranks.

"Since I retired, I've always said that that side, or that squad of players, was the best squad of players that I've played with, for all-round cricketing ability and experience, as the game was played back then," Stewart says. "We worked out, with the regulations how they were back then, how best to play. And right up until the final I'd have said we were the best team in the tournament."

For the captain, Gooch, it was all about the balance of the squad. "We had a good mixture. Lots of all-rounders like Phil DeFreitas, Chris Lewis, Dermot Reeve, Derek Pringle, Ian Botham. Also with younger players in Graeme Hick and Alec Stewart and Neil Fairbrother, and experienced batsmen like myself and Allan Lamb."

Like New Zealand, England only tasted defeat after their semi-final spot was secured – although a rain-ruined no result against Pakistan would prove decisive in the final reckoning as the point gained allowed the eventual champions to sneak into the last four via the back door.

※ ※ ※

It was when rain come into play that the biggest downside to the tournament become obvious. The 1992 World Cup rain rules have entered cricket infamy and were truly farcical.

While the acknowledgement that a straight recalculation based solely on run-rate was inadequate in games featuring shortened innings, the solution the organising committee arrived at was surely even worse.

The system, devised at least in part by Richie Benaud, meant that the required reduction in the target when overs were lost would be equivalent to the lowest-scoring overs from the side batting first. So if the team batting second lost five overs from their innings, their target would be reduced by however many runs the team batting first had made in their five lowest-scoring overs.

In other words, if you bowled five maidens and then your innings was reduced by five overs, your target would be unchanged; you'd have five fewer overs to get the same number of runs. Conversely, if your innings was reduced to 20 overs then your target would be equivalent to the opposition's best 20 overs, even if you'd bowled them out in 25. It's incredible that nobody seemed to have spotted the obvious potential for nonsense.

While this manifested itself most famously – or infamously – in England's "22 runs off one ball" semi-final victory over South Africa, there were arguably two far more egregious examples that went against Gooch's men earlier in the tournament.

Against South Africa in Melbourne, England lost nine overs of their run-chase but saw their original target of 237 in 50 overs reduced by only 11 runs to 226 off 41. They would eventually win off the last ball. No harm done. The right result was achieved, albeit far closer than it should have been.

The no-result against Pakistan, though, was to prove far more significant. Having dismissed their opponents for just 74, England suddenly found themselves chasing 63 off 16 overs. The rules made no allowance for the fact Pakistan had been bowled out with ten overs of their innings unused.

"If you bowled ten maidens, they got taken out," says England bowler Derek Pringle. "So it didn't actually pay you to bowl well if it was going to rain."

Against Pakistan, England were 24-1 after eight overs and, ridiculously, actually in danger of defeat. They still needed almost 40 from the remaining eight overs when further rain brought an ultimate end to the farce. With 15 overs per side needed to constitute a game, the points were shared.

After the humiliation of their 74 all out, Imran Khan told his side to "fight like cornered tigers". They won their last two group games and scraped into the semi-finals by that one point secured against England when rain fell in Adelaide for the first time in 14 months.

%. %. %.

England started their campaign with a vaguely underwhelming victory over India. Gooch's side had been expected to win comfortably in Perth.

They had spent the previous six weeks winning handsomely in New Zealand, and they struggled with the extra pace and bounce that suddenly confronted them. In the end they were indebted to Robin Smith's 91 and four run-outs in India's innings – the last clinching victory in the final over – to get over the line by nine runs.

Get over the line they did, though, to extend a winning run that would reach eight straight ODI successes with a comfortable six-wicket victory over the West Indies. Gooch and Hick made fifties as England overhauled 157 with more than ten overs to spare in Melbourne.

It was close to the ideal display from this team. Derek Pringle kept things tight with the new ball, Phil DeFreitas and Chris Lewis picked up three wickets each, before a comfortable run-chase.

Momentum was building, and there was even better to come. After the no-result against Pakistan came the high point of England's World Cup campaign. Perhaps their high point of any World Cup campaign.

Under the lights at the SCG, faltering pre-tournament favourites Australia were ruthlessly dispatched. Ian Botham, whose weapons by now amounted to little more than personality, a name and some gentle outswing, ended with ODI career-best figures of 4-31 as the Aussies subsided from the promise of 106-2 to 171 all out against their old nemesis. Botham bowled Allan Border and then, in his next over, removed Ian Healy, Peter Taylor and Craig McDermott. Four wickets, seven balls, no runs.

Botham was not done there. He followed that extraordinary bowling tour de force with a half-century in a hundred partnership alongside Gooch that made a chase of just 172 for victory look very simple.

Here, for one last time, was Botham the great all-rounder, ripping apart the old enemy on their own turf. Even if he was doing it in slow motion.

Next, a game Sri Lanka side were eventually blown away by a ferocious last ten overs of batting that brought England over 100 runs and a final total of 280. That target was always beyond the islanders despite some batting that served notice for four years later to kick off a run-chase that eventually petered out for 174.

With the rain-affected victory over South Africa, England had played six, won five, and done more than enough to secure passage to the last four.

Despite the on-field success, problems were beginning to mount. England had begun picking up injuries to key players. Gooch had damaged his hamstring against Sri Lanka. When England fell victim to New Zealand's new tactics in Wellington, they lost not only the match – Patel conceding just seven runs and dismissing Botham in a five-over new-ball spell – but more importantly the increasingly influential Derek Pringle to injury. Gooch and Fairbrother missed that game altogether. Dermot Reeve and Phil DeFreitas were carrying knocks. Chris Lewis was unable to bowl. The return of Allan Lamb was the only good news as

England's 17-match unbeaten run in all formats since departing for New Zealand at the start of the year came to an end.

"We played them in games away from the Basin Reserve," remembers Derek Pringle. "Then we played that one at the Basin and they got the perfect pitch that they'd obviously been planning all along, it was just so slow, it just gripped a little bit for Harris and Larsen and the spinners. They did a number on us, no doubt about it."

※ ※ ※

England's build-up to the World Cup was crucial to the way their campaign would pan out – for better and worse. While their meticulous planning and preparation surely played a key role in taking them to the latter stages, it may also be why they ran out of steam once they got there.

On the face of it, an England squad can rarely have been better prepared for a winter's cricket than they were for 1991/92.

A tour of New Zealand ahead of the World Cup had the potential to be helpful, placing the squad as it did in the right part of the world for six weeks ahead of the global showpiece without the extra glare, attention and stress of facing the Australians.

The coach Micky Stewart and captain Graham Gooch were no-nonsense characters and nothing was left to chance. First, the England players were given six weeks of complete rest at the end of the 1991 summer. Their schedule to that point had been exhausting, with key men having played with barely a break for 18 months. England started 1990 with five Tests and five ODIs in the West Indies, and ended the year in Australia for the Ashes before heading to New Zealand at the start of 1991 for more one-dayers. With two full domestic summers in there as well, a break was needed.

That was followed by six weeks of intensive coaching at Lilleshall and elsewhere. Players were able to hone techniques and prepare for New Zealand under the gaze of a coaching staff made up of former internationals.

A similar approach was taken before the 1990 tour of the Caribbean, and this time was bankrolled by sponsorship. It meant England were refreshed yet ready to hit the ground running when they arrived in New Zealand.

England didn't lose a single match in New Zealand, and rarely looked like doing so, winning two of the three Tests to go with three ODI wins and three wins from five in practice matches.

Even Ian Botham's arrival for the tour being delayed by his pantomime commitments could not derail England's preparation. As England began their tour in New Zealand, Botham was in Bournemouth, starring in *Jack and the Beanstalk* alongside Max Boyce.

"No, that had no impact at all," insists Gooch. Botham was only due to be involved in the two one-day internationals after the Test series. But with only two days between the second and third Tests, Chris Lewis and Derek Pringle missed the final match of the series through injury. Botham was drafted in for his

100th Test. He took three wickets in a drawn match remembered primarily for the horrific knee injury that ended Sid Lawrence's international career.

With confidence growing as success followed success, everything began falling into place. Even bad fortune was turned to the side's advantage. At the World Cup, Derek Pringle's long spells with the new ball were a key factor in England's passage to the final. Botham named Pringle as the tournament's best bowler.

But Pringle with the new ball was not always the plan. The first one-day international was played before the Test matches. Chris Lewis and Phil DeFreitas opened the bowling, with Pringle coming on first change.

By the time of the second almost a month later, DeFreitas was injured. Pringle stepped up to open the bowling, and didn't look back.

"Daffy got injured, and then I opened the bowling and swung it all round corners and that gave me the idea to bowl like that in the World Cup," Pringle says. "I don't think that was the plan to start with. I hadn't opened the bowling before."

In the third ODI, after England had racked up 255-7 in a match reduced to 40 overs a side by overnight rain, Pringle took 2-11 in six overs.

When DeFreitas returned for the start of the World Cup, he was relegated to first change.

By the end of the group stage the effects of this long run in were being felt. Alec Stewart admits England "ran out of gas a little bit" as the injuries took their toll.

But defeat to a New Zealand side enjoying home conditions and boasting a one hundred per cent record was of little concern. Both sides were already assured of semi-final spots. New Zealand had given themselves some happier memories of facing England should they meet again in the knockouts, but no more than that. And with the two sides on course to finish first and second in the group, their next meeting – if any – would be in the final at Melbourne where New Zealand's tactics were at best unproven.

No, this was a defeat that could be taken in stride. What came next was the first big entry in the lengthening list of England World Cup embarrassments.

"This is the problem with you amateur sides, you don't know how to rotate the strike and take singles," Geoffrey Boycott told Zimbabwe captain Dave Houghton after England had dismissed his side for just 134 in 46.2 overs. "You watch the professionals come out after lunch. They'll just knock the ball into the gaps and run their ones and twos and win this game easily."

A short while later, Eddo Brandes removed Graham Gooch lbw first ball with an inswinging yorker that beat the England captain for pace. Brandes could be erratic, but was always slippery. He had worked on his accuracy and bowled his ten overs off the reel for figures of 4-21, cleaning up first Robin Smith and then bowling best friend Graeme Hick for nought. England were 43-5 and a very long way from winning the game easily or otherwise. Despite a painstaking stand of 52 in 24 overs between Alec Stewart and Neil Fairbrother – suffering from illness and spending two ultimately futile hours at the crease without hitting a boundary – England were nine runs short when the tenth wicket fell to the first ball of the final over.

In fairness to the outspoken professional York-shireman, Boycott would hardly have been alone in holding such a view at the halfway stage. Although he may have been alone in expressing it. But still. England had won five and lost just one of their first seven matches and were safely through to the last four having played some excellent cricket. With Australia struggling, England were the tournament favourites. Zimbabwe, still an associate side over six months away from their first Test match, had lost all seven of their matches at the event and 18 in a row at World Cups since stunning Australia in 1983.

Even Houghton was doubtful that Zimbabwe could defend such a total, telling *ESPNcricinfo* years later that his last words before setting about England's batsmen had been: "There are about 8,000 people out here who still need some entertainment and the only way we can entertain is to make this game go as long as possible."

Pringle had injured himself in the previous game, a defeat to New Zealand, and was working as a commentator. "I couldn't quite believe what I was seeing, but there we are. The white Kookaburra swung, and when it swung, Brandes – he was a useful bowler. I find it strange that we couldn't quite somehow get the runs together, but we didn't."

Even a superb England side enjoying a superb tournament were able to offer a taste of what was to come over the following 20 years – and counting.

※ ※ ※

On the back of two contrasting defeats, England faced South Africa in the semi-final in Sydney. It remains one of the World Cup's most memorable matches.

"It's a calculated risk," said Kepler Wessels immediately after opting to bowl first despite the threat of evening rain in Sydney. "The problem comes," he added, "if you're batting tonight and it rains."

Long before that infamous precipitation drama was to play out, though, South Africa had started well. Ian Botham got a couple of early boundaries away before chopping onto his stumps off Meyrick Pringle. England had already lost Gooch to a dubious caught-behind decision off Allan Donald, the ball appearing to brush only thigh after missing the bat.

Then came the first of the day's crucial moments. Twice South Africa thought they had dismissed Graeme Hick before he was off the mark. The first was the latest of the tournament's string of rejected lbw shouts that looks ever more astonishing in the era of DRS, the second a regulation catch at slip off a Pringle no-ball.

Hick would go on to make a decisive 83 from 90 balls, sharing significant stands with first Alec Stewart and then Neil Fairbrother.

By the end of the 73-run alliance with Fairbrother, England were already watching the clock. South Africa were slowing things down, exploiting another of the tournament's odd rules. If South Africa couldn't or, more accurately, wouldn't bowl their overs in the time allotted, those overs would simply be lost. The bowling side would lose the overs too when they came to bat, but it was a worthwhile gamble if the batting side was going well. Shorten the chase, and reduce the run-rate by avoiding the late-innings carnage that appeared likely. Dermot Reeve had raced to 25 from 14 balls and taken Allan Donald for 18 in an over before the innings was cut short with five overs unbowled.

South Africa were later fined for their slow over-rate, but had surely made their task easier with the bat. Unless, of course, it rained.

They made a quick start. With the miserly Derek Pringle still injured, Botham and Lewis took the new ball and were expensive. The first ten overs went for 58 runs. South Africa were up with the required rate.

Wickets fell regularly, but South Africa were always doing just enough to stay in the game. Adrian Kuiper hit Gladstone Small for three consecutive boundaries. Jonty Rhodes made a typically enterprising 43 off 38 balls to reduce the target to 47 off five overs. McMillan and Richardson took that to 22 runs from 13 balls when the fun really started.

The shower was brief, but heavy. In all, 12 minutes were lost. South Africa's first-innings antics meant there was no spare time.

The rules stipulated the reserve day could only be used for a new match, not the conclusion of one that had already passed the point where it could be considered a completed match.

The target was 'reduced' twice: first to 22 off seven, and then, as the players watched on, to 22 off one ball. And even that wasn't actually correct. It should have been 21 from one ball. It could have made all the difference.

The daftness of the situation is somehow amplified by seeing the deadpan, bald facts emblazoned on the big screen. SOUTH AFRICA NEEDS 22 RUNS FROM 1 BALL.

The one delivery that remained for Brian McMillan to try and hit for 21, or 22 just to be on the safe side, provided a strange, almost bleakly comic spectacle as sheepish players in powder blue went through the motions, ticking the boxes. Chris Lewis jogged in and bowled the gentlest of medium-pacers. It was half-hearted. Lewis appeared almost embarrassed to have to do it. McMillan's emotions were rather stronger as he tapped it away for a sarcastic trudged single that said more than any heave out of the ground ever could, before shaking the England players by the hand and stalking off the field in high dudgeon.

It was a stunning anti-climax and unsatisfactory conclusion to such a fine cricket match. But while South Africa's anger in the heat of that moment is entirely understandable, the lingering sense of injustice was, and is, misplaced.

The regulations were a horrendous and unworkable mess, the product of a simple failure to think things through. While on the face of it a rather neat and straightforward way to counter the inherent advantage in chasing rather than setting a reduced target over a shortened period, neither Benaud nor anyone else involved in these rules' conception appears to have stopped for even a second to consider the potential absurdities.

Instances like this semi-final, or England against Pakistan in Adelaide, were not far-fetched or unlikely scenarios. It remains mystifying and an utter embarrassment that nobody had considered the obvious flaws. Nobody stopped to consider what might happen when this back-of-a-fag-packet calculation was applied to either a low all-out total or in the last few overs of a chase. It left an indelible black mark on a tournament that had so, so much going for it.

Yet whatever misfortune South Africa suffered in those final minutes, they had manufactured for themselves. South Africa had taken that "calculated risk" at the toss. South Africa had bowled their overs slowly. The rain rules had been a disaster, however well-intentioned, and however flawed all other systems at that time might have been – but this was well-known. England v South Africa was the 38th game of the tournament. Both sides had already played in matches where the rain rules' flaws had been laid bare. Wessels was literally asked about it at the toss. He had even said exactly what could go wrong for his side. "The problem comes if you're batting tonight and it rains."

South Africa could have done no more to tempt fate that day in Sydney.

"They brought it on themselves," says Alec Stewart. "They used the tactic to slow the over-rate down, we were thumping them everywhere. Dermot Reeve at the end was whacking Donald back over his head, and people, unless they analyse the game, and analyse the rain rules and regulations, would just see that 22 off one ball, when actually we thoroughly deserved to win that game. They put themselves in that position where it was impossible to win."

%. %. %.

A now red-hot Pakistan had already secured their place in the final with a second victory in quick succession over a hitherto untouchable New Zealand side.

In Auckland, the hosts racked up 262-7 on the back of Martin Crowe's 83-ball 91. It was another masterclass from Crowe, who had been named player of the tournament and ended with 456 runs at a three-figure average and a decidedly 21st-century strike-rate of 91 runs per hundred balls. The only other man in the top six run-scorers at the tournament to even crack a strike-rate of 70 was a 22-year-old West Indian left-hander called Brian Lara. Crowe had not only led his side superbly, but had been playing a different game to every other leading batsman.

He may have been in outrageous batting form but he was powerless to save his team. A hamstring injury during his innings meant he was nothing more than a frustrated spectator as Pakistan chased the target down from the unlikeliest of positions.

Pakistan needed 123 from 15.2 overs with six wickets in hand when Inzamam-ul-Haq strode to the crease. Eight an over in 1992 was a very different prospect from eight an over in 2016. But Inzamam made it look easy. He smashed 60 off 37 balls, adding 87 in ten overs with Javed Miandad before Wasim Akram and Moin Khan applied the finishing touches.

※ ※ ※

And so to Melbourne, 22 March 1992. England, the most consistent side across the month of competition, against a rampant Pakistan, peaking at the right time

and hitting the final on a run of four straight wins –
three of them against the two tournament hosts. The
memories of a ten-wicket defeat to the West Indies
and that 74 all out against England were now long
forgotten.

Certainly, England were not reading much into the
74 all out. "Pakistan only got stronger and stronger as
the tournament went on," says Stewart. "We might just
have dropped off a fraction, through injuries, a bit of
tiredness. But Imran, basically, took it upon himself to
make sure, after that Adelaide game, that they went on
to win that tournament."

The night before the final there was a gala dinner
for the two sides and assorted dignitaries. Quite why
players are being asked to get suited and booted for
such an event the night before a World Cup Final is
another matter, but the evening would not pass without
controversy.

In the middle of dinner, comedian Gerry Connolly
came on stage in drag and, in Gooch's words, began
"taking the mick out of the Queen". Neither Gooch
nor Ian Botham were happy. "We all turned up in
our blazers and everything," says Gooch. "Pakistan in
their national dress, and they had a sort of comedian
that started taking the mick out of the Queen halfway
through the dinner. We thought it was completely in
bad taste, myself and Ian just got up in the middle of
the dinner when everyone was sitting down and just
walked out. The rest of the team didn't, but we did."

Botham was more strident still, with feelings still
running high years later when he told *sportasylum.com*:
"World Cup final, 1992, last game I'm going to play,

big game in a big arena, retire the following summer ... and I'm there and I've got some poofter gay guy comes on stage in drag with a stuffed corgi under his arm and takes the piss out of the Queen. Why should I put up with that? If it was done the other way around and he came in with a turban on his head and took the mickey out of the Pakistan team it would be called racism."

An unrepentant Connolly was quoted as saying: "They left before I got to the really mean bits."

With a good meal, anti-royal sledging, some homophobia and the delicate questions of white privilege and racism covered, it was time for the main event.

Imran Khan won the toss and chose to bat and Pakistan were soon in trouble. Derek Pringle was back from injury. Having taken 3-8 in the 74 all out game, he set about Pakistan once more. A nervous Aamir Sohail fended a low catch to Alec Stewart.

Ramiz Raja survived once due to another of the tournament's esoteric laws which declared any ball that passed or would pass the batsman above shoulder height was a no-ball, regardless of what the batsman did with it. On this occasion, Ramiz clothed the short ball from Lewis straight to Hick at point.

Umpire Bucknor signalled the no-ball at square-leg, before having to signal dead ball as Hick tried to run out a batsman who mistakenly believed he had already been dismissed.

It was a temporary reprieve, Pringle striking again as Ramiz walked across his stumps and was lbw. Pakistan were a tentative 26-2 after ten overs.

Not for the first time in the tournament, umpiring decisions would play a huge part. The officiating throughout the tournament was not good. England had been on the right end of a mistake in the semi-final when Hick was spared by New Zealand umpire Brian Aldridge before he had scored the first of his 83 runs.

Now the same umpire would again deny a Pringle. It was Derek rather than Meyrick this time, as England's opening bowler saw two huge lbw shouts against Javed Miandad turned down.

The first was almost identical to Ramiz's earlier dismissal, the batsman walking across his stumps and trying to work to leg. The second was, if anything, an even clearer shout. A touch fuller, and hitting the batsman on the move below the knee-roll and in front of off stump. Aldridge shook his head; Pringle threw his arms in the air in frustration.

Imran Khan and Miandad were slowly repairing the early damage, but they were eating up plenty of deliveries. By the time Imran slapped Botham over mid-off for four in the 18th over the score had still barely crept past 40.

At 57-2, another crucial moment. Imran top-edged a short ball from DeFreitas. Gooch, running back from midwicket, could not hold the half-chance.

While the partnership was growing, England still appeared in control. "They were something like 80 or 90-2 after 30 overs and I think we just got a little bit complacent," says Pringle. Steadily, the pace of the partnership increased. The MCG was playing to its full size, sightscreens positioned inside the fences, but the outfield was quick. Imran and Miandad began to find the boundary.

Miandad, having played in all five tournaments, became the first man to reach 1,000 World Cup runs. The hundred partnership came up. Miandad got to 50 off 91 balls, and Imran reached the same milestone a short while later from 88 with a thumping drive for four down the ground.

The run-rate was increasing, but Miandad was struggling. Apparently ill, he needed a runner for the last part of his innings and it's no surprise when, exhausted, he top-edged a reverse-sweep off Richard Illingworth on 58.

But the platform had been set, and semi-final hero Inzamam showed his class once again. Swaggering, helmetless, he dabbed a late cut for four off the spinner before dismissively flicking a leg-stump half-volley from Botham to the fence. Imran fell for 70.

Inzamam, though, kept going. Wasim Akram, too. The boundary boards were taking a pounding. The run-rate, for so long meandering along below three an over was suddenly up over five as two powerful Wasim fours took Pakistan to 247-4 off 49 overs.

Pringle bowled a superb final over. A yorker cleaned up Inzamam for a 35-ball 42 and remarkably Pakistan could scramble only a pair of singles to finish 249-6.

"When they had that total I thought we'd have to bat really well to get it," says Pringle. "I didn't think it was going to be a formality. Some people seem to think, 'Oh, 249, these days, formality.' Someone once described it as a 'low-scoring game'. I said 'Not then, mate! That was quite a good score!'"

Like Pakistan before them, England got off to a poor start. Botham was caught behind off a Wasim

Akram special without scoring before anyone even had the chance to make off-colour remarks about the royal family. Wasim's later dismissals of Lamb and Lewis may be the highlight reel favourites, but this was just as good. Round the wicket and angling away to find the outside edge of Beefy's big Duncan Fearnley. Alec Stewart followed soon after, playing away from his body.

Hick and Gooch attempted to rebuild the innings. Hick, though, was having a torrid time against leg-spinner Mushtaq Ahmed. Hick couldn't pick him. The googly did for him, lbw for a slow and unconvincing 17.

When Gooch followed soon after, top-edging a sweep shot off Mushtaq to be superbly caught by Aqib Javed running in from deep square-leg, England were 69-4 and staring into the abyss.

Neil Fairbrother and Allan Lamb, though, set about trying to replicate Imran and Miandad's efforts from the first innings. First steadily, then more aggressively, they got England back on course.

England were 141-4 in the 35th over. Wasim Akram had the ball in his hand and destruction in his mind. The memory plays tricks, and with brains conditioned to modern one-day cricket it's easy to think England were on top of things. "I still think we were chasing the game at that stage. It still had to go absolutely right for us," says Pringle.

Two balls later – two of the best ever bowled in any game, never mind a World Cup Final – and things were going very far from absolutely right.

First Lamb was bowled by another miracle ball from round the wicket. Squaring the batsman up before nipping away to kiss the outside of off stump, it was to all intents an unplayable delivery.

The next ball hooped from outside off towards the stumps as if it was drawn by a magnetic force. The new batsman, Chris Lewis, got something in the way. But this was beyond his control. That ball was hitting the stumps, and no bat or pad would prevent it. It was too fast, and moving too far to be stopped by conventional methods. Lewis was out for a golden duck, and England were 141-6.

"When Waz suddenly starts to get the ball reverse swinging and bowls those two balls to Lamby and Chris Lewis," says Stewart, "that in a way epitomised what Pakistan were all about. They could change a game in a very short period of time, with a number of match-winners."

Fairbrother gamely continued the fight. The hat-trick ball at the start of the 37th over was a no-ball. Soon Fairbrother needed a runner as the endeavours of the last two months took their toll.

A couple of fours and a comical misfield from Mushtaq on the boundary briefly raised England's hopes. "You're never safe if you back Pakistan," observed Ian Chappell on Channel 9's commentary, a truism for the ages.

The equation was down to a tantalisingly manageable 70 from 44 balls when Fairbrother, exhausted and with nothing left to give, top-edged a pull and sent the ball spiralling into the Melbourne sky. Moin Khan ran 30 yards from behind the stumps to complete the catch.

There was no way back for England. Reeve and Pringle gave it their best, but fittingly it was Imran

Khan who took the final wicket of Richard Illingworth to give his Cornered Tigers victory by 22 runs.

England were left to dwell on a missed opportunity for perhaps their greatest ever one-day side, in undoubtedly their greatest ever one-day kit. "We had a very good side, and a very good mix of players," says Gooch. "And I would say we have been pretty poor at one-day cricket since."

1996 World Cup

From finalists to also-rans

ENGLAND made it through to the knockout stage of the 1996 World Cup. This in itself should not be a surprise. They had done that at all the previous five World Cups. Their opponents were Sri Lanka, who had breezed through to the qualifying stage undefeated. However, that flawless record does come with a caveat.

The 1996 World Cup was jointly hosted by India, Pakistan and Sri Lanka. At the time, Sri Lanka was in the midst of brutal civil war between the government and Tamil separatists. The Liberation Tigers of Tamil Eelam (LTTE) were carrying out a guerrilla campaign and on 31 January 1996 they perpetrated their deadliest attack to date. Three suicide bombers set off explosives at the Central Bank in Colombo killing 91 people and injuring around 1,400 others.

While cricket is of no consequence in comparison with such devastation, this attack did have an impact on the sport. Australia and the West Indies both decided they would not travel to Sri Lanka for their group matches against the co-hosts. The ICC was insistent that the country was safe and that the LTTE posed no threat. The tournament organisers made it very clear; if teams did not travel to Sri Lanka the hosts would be awarded a victory by "walkover".

Australia and the West Indies would not budge and as a result Sri Lanka were given the points from those games and had no real problem in brushing aside the other teams in the group. Kenya and Zimbabwe were never going to present them with too many problems, but it was a surprise that Sri Lanka defeated India with such ease. Even after Sachin Tendulkar had made an undefeated 137 it was not enough to stop them. It may have been that they would have defeated those teams that refused to travel as easily, but it would be naïve to say it didn't help to skip matches against two of the strongest teams in the group. Sri Lanka finished the group stage 'undefeated' in five matches and were the highest qualifying quarter-finalist.

England, on the other hand, had limped to the quarter-finals on the back of beating the two associate sides in their group – the UAE and Holland. These were not professional cricketers, and in the UAE's case it was a team led by a guy that was little more than a club player. Anything other than victory against these teams would have sent shockwaves through

England cricket. Against the other opponents in the group England were soundly beaten, only getting close against New Zealand.

The mood in the English and Sri Lankan camps could not have been more contrasting, and neither could the approach. England's one-day cricket was based around building a base on the back of Mike Atherton's solidity and Alec Stewart's slightly more attacking solidity.

For this World Cup, Sri Lanka paired Sanath Jayasuriya with Romesh Kaluwitharana at the top of the order and told them to go batshit mental from ball one. In the world of Twenty20 cricket, ODI double hundreds and DLF Maximums it is difficult to imagine just how revolutionary this was. Between 1993 and 1995, every single international team had an average ODI run rate of less than five an over, giving teams an average score of less than 250 in 50 overs. Now 250 runs is considered an easy task to chase down on almost every surface. That change began at this World Cup with Sri Lanka.

Teams had made attempts at "pinch-hitting" roles before, but never with this level of commitment or with this amount of success. The Sri Lankan approach was the story of the 1996 tournament and there was no better example of it than in the quarter-final against England.

The English side batted first, making a reasonable total of 235 thanks primarily to a better-than-a-run-a-ball 67 from Phil DeFreitas. Sri Lanka made an absolute mockery of that target. Kaluwitharana fell early, but Jayasuriya blasted England's bowlers to all parts.

England opened the bowling with Richard Illingworth in an attempt to counter this all-out attack – it didn't work. Illingworth conceded 72 runs from his ten overs claiming just that one early wicket of Kaluwitharana along the way. Jayasuriya used his feet to the spinner and medium-pace bowlers, he stood upright and carved the quicker men over extra cover. It was an innings fitting of the Mumbai Indians from a decade before they were even a concept.

England's coach at the time was the indomitable Raymond Illingworth, the archetypal prickly Yorkshireman. He told us that had Atherton listened to him about field placings then Jayasuriya would have been out caught at third man twice in the first over.

Atherton says that he was expecting an attacking mindset from Sri Lanka, but the full-on nature of it was surprising.

"Abroad, teams approached the one-day game more aggressively than in England. We still didn't have the fielding restrictions in England and tended to play a different type of game. Keeping wickets intact and scoring heavily at the end," Atherton says. "So there was no surprise that teams looked to play aggressively at the start in India.

"What surprised everyone was just how aggressive Sri Lanka were. They took it to a different level and that surprised everyone – not just England. Back then, teams tended to have one pinch hitter maybe, but Sri Lanka took that to a different level, by blasting at the start for the entirety of the PowerPlay overs, and then batting deep enough so that it didn't matter if they lost wickets."

When Jayasuriya fell in the 13th over he had made 82 runs from 44 balls, Sri Lanka were 113-2 and the game was over as a contest. Things slowed down a little bit after that, but Sri Lanka still won with just under ten overs to spare.

England were despatched from the World Cup having not beaten a single Full Member side. It was the end of Raymond Illingworth as the "supremo" of England cricket, and for many it was the first time that they had realised just how far behind the rest of the world England had fallen in limited-overs cricket. On these shores Tests have always been best, but up until this World Cup England had competed on the global stage in ODIs. It was the wake-up call that England needed, but one they would fail to heed for the next two decades.

※ ※ ※

England's lead-up to the 1996 World Cup was far from ideal. In fact, England's approach to limited-overs cricket in anywhere other than England was woeful. They played very few one-day internationals at home and treated those that took place overseas as an unnecessary addition to Test tours, as an encumbrance to be endured. Between the end of the 1992 World Cup and the beginning of the 1996 version England played 38 ODIs.

Every Full Member nation apart from Zimbabwe played at least twice that number in that period. Pakistan played 87 matches in that time, and the West Indies 78.

Graham Thorpe is quick to point out this discrepancy in experience. "Probably our attention to detail in one-day cricket just wasn't as well thought out in terms of how we were playing it. Were we playing enough one-day cricket at the time? Probably not, compared to the other sides around the world. Test cricket sat ahead of it, for a lot of the players. I enjoyed one-day cricket, but people alongside me in other countries were probably a lot further down the line in terms of their development because of the amount of cricket they were actually playing. They were playing around 30 one-day internationals a year when at times we were playing six to ten."

In the years before the tournament England had virtually no experience of the conditions in which they were to play. They had played eight ODIs in early 1993 in India and Sri Lanka, but three years later when they arrived for the World Cup less than half of those in the squad had been on those 1993 tours. They were novices in comparison to most of the other teams, both in the number of matches played and in understanding of the conditions they would face.

"In terms of playing ODI cricket in the sub-continent, we hardly played in India or Pakistan in the 1990s, for various reasons," Atherton says. "We went in 1993 and then apart from the World Cup we didn't go back to India until 2001/02. Out of 115 Tests I played one Test in India and a handful of ODIs during the World Cup, so we were pretty inexperienced in terms of cricket out there. That obviously has changed now, given how big a financial drawcard India is, but back then England hardly played India at all. Of course, at the time you don't think about those things, you just go out and expect to do well as at any tournament."

The time that England had to adapt to cricket in India was short and they were learning during the event not before it. "We just had to get out there and get on with it," Jack Russell said to *The Cricketer*. "It was like playing on another planet. You had to readjust your timing, your lengths change, the type of bowling skills you needed were different. If you weren't there long enough before the games started, it could be tough."

Thorpe also highlighted the issue of England's limited experience when he spoke to us. "Our squad lacked skill and knowledge of playing on the sub-continent. In that time, we didn't tour the sub-continent a great deal. It wasn't really until about 2000, or just before that, when the Future Tours Programme started to come in. And then we really started touring Pakistan and Sri Lanka a lot more. So I would say the skill of our players was not of the same level of some of the Asian sides, and they really put us to the sword. That skill as a bowling unit, and also the batsmen, we certainly weren't playing the kind of cricket that was likely to win a World Cup in sub-continental conditions."

The cricket they played at home wasn't even the same as that played elsewhere in the world. The fielding restrictions were not the same. They had never played a floodlit ODI at home before the 1996 event; the first competitive match under lights in England took place a year later. The first ODI in England under lights wasn't until July 2000. England played ODIs at home in white clothing with a red ball in the daytime. At the 1996 World Cup they would be expected to play in coloured clothing with a white ball under lights with differing fielding conditions having played half as much cricket as the best sides. While good cricketers can adapt, and England had good cricketers, to expect them to succeed with all of that going against them was too much to ask.

Phil DeFreitas, a man who had played a pivotal role in getting England to the final of the last two World Cups, admits that England were a long way behind where they should have been. "In the summer we hardly played a great deal [of one-day cricket] apart from at county level. Internationally if I am correct there was only about two or three [games]. I think we were just a little bit behind in the 1996 World Cup. I think the game had moved on a bit and it definitely moved on in that World Cup."

Atherton admits these massive differences in how the game was played at home and elsewhere were on his mind, but he was unconvinced that those with the power to change things had the same worries.

"Well, I was concerned but I don't know about the administrators," he says. "It seemed ridiculous to me that we were playing a different game at home in ODIs to that which the rest of the world were playing and different regulations to international cricket. To give one small example: at home we were still playing with the regulation that allowed off-spinners six men on the legside, so Shaun Udal was very successful in domestic one-day cricket and at home in ODIs. But then away from home he could only bowl with five on the legside.

"That was one reason why we picked Neil Smith from Warwickshire, because in domestic ODI cricket he would generally bowl a slightly wider line with an extra man on the offside," Atherton says. "We were wearing whites, using a red ball, had fewer fielding restrictions, different regulations. It was all slightly ridiculous when you think about it. Obviously, today it wouldn't be acceptable that domestic cricket and ODI cricket at home was played to completely different regulations as in international cricket."

England had lots going against them in one-day cricket, but they did have some success, especially at home. Every player we have spoken to made it very clear that appearing for England in any format was a deadly serious pursuit and it was clear that they weren't lying. They cared. Losses hurt. In order to become a professional sportsman you have to own a winning mentality. There are so many hurdles in your way, so many others competing for a tiny number of spaces in very few teams. To suggest that they didn't play to win would be as foolish as it would be insulting.

Despite all of these things going against them Atherton and his team were confident at the end of the summer of 1995. "We had done exceptionally well in ODI cricket in England during my time as captain. We were unbeaten at home."

Atherton's record as captain is indeed outstanding. He led England against New Zealand, West Indies, India, Pakistan, South Africa and Australia on home soil and won every single one of those series. His record as an England captain at home reads played 15, won 12, lost two with one no result. This contrasts with how England performed overseas under Atherton. Including the 1996 World Cup, Atherton led England in 28 overseas ODIs: he won only eight, losing 19, with one match against New Zealand finishing as a tie.

Perhaps the success England had achieved at home in the years following the 1992 World Cup Final appearance allowed those in charge to believe they were keeping pace with the rest of the cricketing world. The matches that were played overseas had very little visibility at home. Sky Sports had only just started showing overseas tours live, and the focus was always on Test matches, both from the broadcasters and from the authorities. There were no one-day specialists selected, just a team for the Tests that played some ODIs at the end of the tour as well.

Even if those in charge of the national team wanted to change things they couldn't. The governance of the game in England was such that the counties were the ones that called the shots on player availability, England fixtures and playing regulations – the battle to change that would come after the 1996 World Cup and beyond.

Dennis Silk, the then chairman of the English board, was certainly aware of these issues. Speaking to the *Mail on Sunday* in the weeks before the 1996 tournament he was scathing in his assessment of where England stood. "We do not appear to be making any progress. Rather, we are dropping further behind those with whom we are competing. We have no batsmen ranked in the top five, no bowler in the top ten, and no world-class spinner. That is a worry when you consider that we have the only fully professional structure in world cricket... the standard of county cricket is perhaps lower than it has been in most people's memory."

Even with the confidence in their ability that success in one-day cricket at home had given them, the South African tour that preceded the World Cup was a gruelling one that took a toll on the team. Atherton told us just how exhausting that was. "We had been in South Africa for three months beforehand, playing a five-Test series, plus all the other provincial games that you had to play in those days and then a seven-match ODI series so we, or at least I, was pretty knackered by the time we got to the World Cup. We only had a week at home in between [the South Africa tour and the World Cup]."

"It wasn't a great winter, full stop," Alec Stewart told *The Cricketer* magazine. "We were a shambles back then because we didn't know what our best team was, what the best squad was, what the batting order should be, the bowling... anything. We didn't give ourselves a chance of being successful all those years ago because, if you compare the 1996 preparation, or lack of, with the preparation that goes now with the England team, it's chalk and cheese."

The 1995/96 tour of South Africa was certainly very different to the ones we have today. In addition to the full internationals on that tour England had played 11 warm-up matches, five one-day games and six first-class matches, while they were in South Africa. These days teams regularly have one two-day match against weak opposition before a Test series, not a month-long lead-in and then regular matches in between. Combined with that long tour against tough opposition, there was the fact that England were being led by Raymond Illingworth, an increasingly divisive figure.

%% %% %%

Raymond Illingworth, former captain of Yorkshire, Leicestershire and England, was given the job of England coach and selector in 1994. Combative and opinionated, Illingworth became the chairman of selectors as well as the man responsible for day-to-day management of the side, a role that was dubbed the "one-man committee".

In the period between his retirement from playing and his ascent to his all-powerful role with England, Illingworth was an outspoken media pundit who could be brutal about the national team when they did badly. For many this no-nonsense Yorkshire grit was exactly what an underperforming England team needed to whip them into shape.

Illingworth had an unerring faith in his opinion, and in fairness to the man he had the cricketing pedigree to back it up. Success had followed him throughout his career. The issues stemmed from Illingworth's approach to dealing with players. He had what Darren Gough described as "the man-management skills of Basil Fawlty".

Illingworth lost the England team during the tour of South Africa, with his treatment of Devon Malcolm the focal point for the squad's biggest problems. Gough wrote in the *Daily Mail* that the issues seemed to begin when newly elected South African president Nelson Mandela highlighted Malcolm as "the dark destroyer".

"[Illingworth] and his subordinates decided that Devon had got too big for his boots. Maybe it did go to his head a little. But who could blame him? As the black player in the England side he was seen as a hero in South Africa," Gough wrote. "One of the worst clashes came when I was bowling in the nets in Port Elizabeth. A little black kid asked Devon something and he was trying to help coach the youngster when Illy bellowed: 'Devon, fuck off out of the way until it's your turn to bowl.'"

Derek Pringle wrote at the time that the way Malcolm was treated as a man and as a bowler was "brutal".

"To tinker with [Malcolm] now, as Peter Lever has attempted to technically and Ray Illingworth has psychologically with his ill-judged remarks, is to court disaster. Malcolm, like many with a roughly hewn technique, is a mood bowler whose best comes when confidence is high and rhythm good. Far better to encourage these two fleeting and fickle qualities by giving him his head in the middle than to attempt a technical overhaul in the nets," Pringle wrote in *The Independent*.

Worse was to come. England were playing in the final Test in Cape Town. The series was still 0-0 after four matches of brutal and attritional cricket. England had succumbed to 153 all out but had managed to get South Africa nine down for 171. Malcolm returned with the new ball and got blasted by the final-wicket pair. South Africa ended up with a first-innings total of 244, a match-winning lead. England lost the series 1-0.

At the presentation after the game it emerged that Illingworth had arranged for England to play an extra ODI at the end of a tour that had already seen the England team away from home for three months.

The mood was black, and Atherton confronted Illingworth to find out who had given the OK to this extra match. Gough described Atherton as "itching for a fight". According to Gough, Illingworth lost his cool completely and focused almost all of his anger at Malcolm. Jabbing Malcolm in the chest, Illingworth screamed: "You've lost us the fucking Test match."

Gough wrote that he was expecting Malcolm to take a swing at the England supremo, and said he wouldn't have blamed him for doing so. Just then Illingworth went red and started to choke, having to run across the dressing room for a glass of water. "The whole episode showed how Illy had lost touch with his players," Gough wrote. That England would go on to lose that hastily extended one-day series 6-1 should not come as a surprise.

With typical wry understatement, Atherton concedes that the "South Africa series dented our confidence a bit".

※ ※ ※

It was with this still simmering away in the background that England selected the squad to go to the World Cup, and this was not without incident. At the time it was suggested that Atherton wanted Alec Stewart as the wicketkeeper; Illingworth preferred Jack Russell. Illingworth won the argument and Russell was selected as the keeper for the tournament.

Despite these rumours of discontent Atherton insists he was, broadly speaking, happy with the squad that was chosen. "By that stage I wasn't a formal selector I don't think. But I can't remember feeling disgruntled with the squad to be honest."

When we asked Illingworth if England had the best side they could have going into the 1996 tournament his response was emphatic.

"I don't think we did for the one-day stuff, without a doubt. I think we could have had a better team than that for the one-dayers," Illingworth says. "From the captaincy point of view and things like that. You [could] get somebody a bit more inventive with the thing. That's the thing we hadn't got to at that stage. We were still picking the one-day cricket more or less thinking of it as a Test match thing more than a one-day game. I think it came from bowlers and everything. I think we were a bit behind the times without a doubt.

"We had one or two people who were probably just adaptable but we didn't have enough of them who really could play one-day cricket well. If you look at most of the people that went as batsmen none of them really developed into great one-day players."

Alec Stewart echoed this sentiment when he spoke to *The Cricketer* about the 1996 tournament: "These days England can pick from 16, 17, 18 players, and still be a very good side. Whereas when I was playing, we probably had only seven or eight top-class players. The rest was guesswork with guys who had had a good fortnight in county cricket."

When we spoke to Stewart about 1996 he was scathing about the build-up. "I'll be honest, it was a shambles of a selection, not just of the squad, but of the eleven and batting orders. It was a tournament where if we could do everything wrong, we basically did, I would say. It was – as you can tell – it was a frustrated, confused England that went to that World Cup."

For Stewart, a lot of that stemmed from Illingworth and how the side was run. "He was the dominant man, obviously. Athers was captain, but Athers didn't get everything he wanted during that period of time, but we were almost doing things off the cuff – from selection of the eleven, to batting orders and type of bowling. It was a bad World Cup. You get what you deserve and we deserved to go out early."

As it was, the 14-man squad for the World Cup had all played in that series in South Africa beforehand. On balance it was probably the best squad England could have taken. The issue was not so much talent as it was preparation and experience – of both the conditions they would face and the format in which they would play. Surrey's Ali Brown was unlucky not to make the grade and there was perhaps a suggestion that Nick Knight could have been picked, but other than that it is difficult to think who would have improved England's fortunes.

※ ※ ※

The opening game was against New Zealand and could hardly have got off to a worse start. England won the toss and elected to field. Very early in the New Zealand innings Graham Thorpe dropped Nathan Astle. It proved costly, Astle scoring 101 as New Zealand set England 240 to win. The next highest score for the Kiwis was Chris Cairns' 36. It was this Astle innings that set up a challenging total.

With the bat England started poorly once again, losing Atherton in the second over when he was bowled by Dion Nash. Graeme Hick fought manfully during his 85 but England never really came close to winning the game. When Hick departed with 96 runs still needed for victory the game was effectively over. Some sloppy fielding had cost them the game but England still looked a long way off the pace.

After that New Zealand defeat England racked up their two wins of the tournament. After the nine-team tournament in 1992 the 1996 event had 12 teams. There were the nine Full Members, which by this stage included Zimbabwe, and three associate sides. The teams were divided into two groups of six, of which the top four in each would make the quarter-finals. England had two associate sides in their group, so all they had to do was beat them both and they were all but guaranteed a quarter-final.

The first win was against a UAE side led by Sultan Zarawani, a cult figure but no better than a club player and who would never play for his nation again after the World Cup when he had a massive falling out with the cricketing authorities on his return from the tournament. He is best remembered for facing Allan Donald without a helmet and being struck on the head second ball. In this game he bowled six wicketless overs and scored two runs from ten balls. His side were bowled out by England in the 49th over for 136 – Neil Smith was the star bowler with three wickets for just 29 runs.

Just as Zarawani is best remembered for a moment that he would rather forget, so Smith too is associated with an unpleasant incident for him personally. Having not played in the opening match, Smith was given the job of opening the batting with Alec Stewart, a classic England move. It was the second game of the World Cup and they were trying out a new opening partnership. They had four years from the end of the 1992 final until the start of this event and they were trying out a new plan in the middle of the biggest cricket tournament in the world. Smith was doing a decent job when illness struck; it was quite the sight for those back home in England watching over a late breakfast. England had made it to 59-1 in 12.3 overs when a second vomiting episode forced him to retire ill. In a brilliant example of Ray Illingworth's no-nonsense press conference technique he told the assembled media: "He had a pizza last night. Now it's on the field out there."

While how sensible or otherwise it is to be eating pizza in Peshawar is open for debate, what is certain is that remembering Smith just for his lack of intestinal fortitude when it comes to sub-continental Italian food is unfair.

Smith was a vital member of the all-conquering Warwickshire side of the mid-1990s that was led to so many trophies by Dermot Reeve. He finished his List A career with 306 wickets at an average of 27. His effective bowling combined with his ability to hit a long ball made him a very effective one-day player. He finished his career with two one-day hundreds and he was regularly opening the batting for Warwickshire in the season ahead of the World Cup. He was a very solid selection, making the squad based on consistent performance. He was as good a one-day spinner as England had available – and he could bat.

Warwickshire were the side that were setting the standard in county cricket and Smith was part of that excellent team.

"We'd obviously had a couple of very successful years at Warwickshire where we'd made a conscious effort in one-day cricket to look at areas where we could improve our game. And on the back of that we won trophies and I'd started opening the batting therefore that led towards my selection to be in the one-day squad at the end of the '95 South Africa tour," Smith says. "There were a few of them that flew out specifically for the one-dayers and we got out to Cape Town after the last Test match, with the one-day series due to begin in the new year. From those seven ODIs they were going to finalise the World Cup squad to go to India and Pakistan in the New Year."

While Smith ended up as an opener at the World Cup that was not the role he was selected to do. Richard Illingworth, no relation to Raymond, was the first-choice spinner at the time and Smith was brought into the side as his backup. England were going to be playing the World Cup in India and Pakistan after all. Not that Smith had ever been to either of those countries before. In fact according to Smith the plan had been for Craig White to do the pinch-hitting job, but the plans changed. As they always seemed to.

For Smith it wasn't really the best plan anyway. "One of the reasons for having a pinch hitter is that it elongates your batting order more than anything else and I just happened to fit into that role, and I think the downside for myself was not having the experience; Craig [White] had more experience at that level than me," Smith says. "As a non-frontline batter it's hard to suddenly get thrown in when you're facing the South African attack at the time with Fanie de Villiers and Allan Donald and people like that, so it was a big ask to crash them around the park, and I didn't succeed at it. I played two of the lesser nations and then South Africa, and we were probably two or three down early in that game, so it changes the context of how I needed to bat. I think there was an eye on being more positive, but again the other nations were far more positive."

While the picture of Smith plastering the outfield with the contents of his stomach in Peshawar is the most memorable moment of this match, something more important also happened. England lost the services of White altogether thanks to a side strain during that UAE game that ended his World Cup involvement. White was considered an integral part of the one-day team by the management leading into the World Cup. Having made just one ODI appearance in late 1994, White came back into the side during the ODIs in South Africa and was ever present in the team leading up to that injury. He would be missed.

The next assignment for England was against the Netherlands, who had made their first World Cup and would be playing in just their second ODI. It was an opportunity for England to make it two wins in a row against the associate nations in their group and a chance to finally get their tournament going ahead of the tougher tasks that lay ahead. The *Wisden* report from the time highlights that the side that England put out for this game still had an "experimental" feel to it.

England had planned to play three spinners on a wearing Peshawar surface but Richard Illingworth became the next player to fall ill and could not be selected. England batted first and Graeme Hick made a hundred, the only century that an England batsman made during the tournament. Hick and Thorpe put on a partnership of 143 in an England total of 279.

That should have been more than enough against a Dutch side whose only batsman that had come close to competing at this level before was the then 46-year-old Barbados-born Nolan Clarke. As it was the Dutch took the game a lot deeper than they should have. England's fielding continued to look ragged and the excellent running of Bas Zuiderent and Klaas-Jan van Noortwijk made it look even more rough around the edges. Those two Dutch batsmen put together a partnership of 114 that had England worried. Neither man could see it through, but it was another accurate reflection of just where England stood. They were being pushed by a team of amateur cricketers playing in their first World Cup. Both Darren Gough and Dominic Cork went at more than a run a ball. The Netherlands made it to 230-6. The only other side that conceded more than 200 runs against the Dutch was their fellow associates, UAE. It was a win for England, but it won't have given much succour to a weary squad lacking in confidence.

England had made their way into the quarter-finals of the World Cup thanks to these two wins against part-time cricketers but still had no real idea what their best team was and those that were automatic picks were not performing. It was bleak and the next game was against

South Africa – a side that had just beaten them 6-1 in an ODI series.

There was yet more tinkering from England – Atherton returned to the opening role having batted in the middle order in England's two wins. He would have to wait for the second innings of the game to do so as South Africa won the toss and elected to bat. This match was played at Rawalpindi and it was a much better surface than the one England had played on in Peshawar. Not that it was easy, and England did a decent job at restricting their opponents to just 230 off their 50 overs, Peter Martin the pick of the bowlers with figures of 3-33. There were more dropped catches from England, Dominic Cork the worst culprit when he shelled what should have been a high but simple chance to remove Steve Palframan early on.

At the halfway stage England would have been confident of chasing the total down, but they got nowhere near it.

South Africa bowled England out for 152, Atherton making a four-ball duck on his return to the opening spot. Thorpe's 46 was the only noteworthy contribution in yet another embarrassing defeat. 152 was the same total that the lowly UAE had made against the South Africans the week before.

Things got worse for England in the post-match press conference. Pretty much everywhere that the English cricket team travel they are far from popular tourists. They represent the former colonial masters and all too often came across as haughty and superior. Relations between England and Pakistan had not been great for a while. The ugly on-field row between

Pakistani umpire Shakoor Rana and Mike Gatting in 1987 was still very fresh in the minds of the people of Pakistan, even though it had happened almost a decade beforehand. Perhaps the fact this incident happened the last time England had deigned to tour Pakistan was a reason for it still resonating.

Then there were allegations of ball-tampering on the Pakistan tour of England in 1992. Then it emerged that Imran Khan had written magazine articles that accused the England team of doing some similarly aggressive ball management. Allan Lamb and Ian Botham decided to sue, a case they would go on to lose.

Mike Gatting had also been caught up in that court case, but news of an out-of-court settlement in Gatting's favour was in the Pakistani press in the days ahead of this game against South Africa.

England were due to play Pakistan next and the local journalists were keen to get the thoughts of the England captain on the upcoming fixture. Atherton lost his patience. He felt he was being asked the same question for a second time.

"Er, I think I already answered that," Atherton replied in a somewhat tetchy manner. The journalist asked the same question again. "I'm lost," said Atherton. On the third try Atherton gave a firm answer. "We're playing Pakistan next week in Karachi." He then turned to the side and said, "Will someone get rid of this buffoon?"

It was an attempt at a joke, not a truly angry outburst, but it was a foolish thing to say. Reporting in *The Independent* at the time, Robert Winder said that the room "froze". There were immediate calls for an apology, and Atherton duly obliged the next day.

It was not delivered by Atherton; instead it was read to the assembled media by the tour manager, John Barclay. "At yesterday's press conference, after the match against South Africa, I am very sorry if I caused offence to a local journalist and local journalists during questions."

Derek Pringle described it well in his report from the time. "Mind you, Barclay's glib tone, as he read out the words by the hotel pool did not exactly smack of humility on a grand scale," Pringle wrote. "The curtness and brevity made it reminiscent of the apology Mike Gatting begrudgingly delivered to Shakoor Rana here in 1987, after their infamous finger-jabbing argument during the second Test."

In the match itself England would use their third different opening partnership in five group matches. Robin Smith had been struggling with a groin strain that had kept him on the sidelines for the whole of the tournament until now. The change at the top worked – Atherton finally scoring some runs as he and Smith combined to put together a then record opening stand for England against Pakistan. They put on 147 to leave their team ideally placed to push on to a truly dominant total and gain some much needed confidence ahead of the quarter-finals. A big enough win could have seen them finish high enough in the group to avoid Sri Lanka in the quarter-final.

Smith's 75 at a strike-rate of 81 gave England a glimpse of the stability at the top of the order that had been missing so far. It was a powerful innings that also contained a deft touch, especially when sweeping the spinners. He had given England a chance. As was the case with England throughout this World Cup, on the rare occasions that they found themselves in a decent position they threw it away. Atherton and Smith departed within nine runs of each other, and Graeme Hick was dismissed for just one in between. England went from 147-0 in the 29th over to 156-3 in the 32nd. The momentum they had built up disappeared as quickly as it had arrived.

Thorpe once again did a decent job at steadying the ship, but no one could stay with him as England limped to 249-9 off their 50 overs. Thorpe playing a lone hand was becoming a theme; he finished the tournament as England's leading run-scorer and top of the averages, but he never had anybody see the job through with him.

The Karachi pitch for this match was an absolute belter, far better for batting than even the best of the Peshawar surfaces, and Pakistan showed that. They never looked troubled throughout their chase, and while there were half-centuries from Saeed Anwar, Ijaz Ahmed and Inzamam-ul-Haq, the innings that got the loudest cheer from a packed National Stadium was Javed Miandad's 11 not out in what was to be his last game in front of his home crowd in Karachi.

Pakistan scored the winning runs in the 48th over, but in truth the game was not as close as the scorecard led you to believe. There were few alarms and no surprises in Pakistan's chase.

%. %. %.

So England had arrived at the quarter-final to play a side that were engaging in the cricketing equivalent of Anthony Burgess's *ultra-violence*. England were short of confidence, with little idea of their best team and led by a man who was the "Basil Fawlty" of man management. Those that set their alarm for the early morning start to watch this match in England could be forgiven for viewing it while hiding behind their sofa. It was a case of the old and the new, and tradition was set to get an ass-whooping.

Sri Lanka and their revolutionary opening partnership were the opponents, but the idea of a pinch hitter at the top of the order was nothing new; after all, England had experimented with Neil Smith as an opener in this very tournament. What Sri Lanka were doing was different.

In the past, teams had willingly sacrificed a lower-order batsman who was capable of connecting with a few big attacking shots in the hope that he would pull off a quick-fire effort during the fielding restrictions at the beginning of the innings. If they failed, which they usually did, the top-order batsmen coming in below them could rebuild and revert to the traditional approach.

Sri Lanka committed to it completely with top-order batsmen told to attack for the entire PowerPlay regardless of early wickets.

"I think it's what we were expecting," Thorpe says. "We'd obviously seen them play that way all tournament already. The style in which they played, you sort of always felt you had a chance because of the way they were playing so aggressively up top, if you could pick up early wickets. I think in that game actually we did."

And he was right. England dismissed Kaluwitharana very early on, bowled by Richard Illingworth off the ninth ball of the match. He had hit the first two balls he faced for four and went for another big shot and failed to pull it off. Sri Lanka were 12-1. This may have made other sides rein in their attacking instincts, but that was not the Sri Lankan approach.

England had batted first and stumbled and stuttered their way to 235, a score they only achieved thanks to a record eighth-wicket stand between Dermot Reeve and Darren Gough. Phil DeFreitas top-scored as the top order failed again. The batting performances couldn't have been more of a contrast. All of England's specialist batsmen went at a strike-rate of less than 80. Hick scored eight runs from 27 balls, Thorpe managed 14 off 31. The Sri Lankan spinners tied England in knots, with Kumar Dharmasena and Muttiah Muralitharan finishing with combined figures of four wickets for 67 runs from their 20 overs. England had no answers and for the most part didn't appear to be entirely sure what questions they were even being asked.

"Sri Lanka set the standard, with what was back then known as pinch hitters, with Kaluwitharana up top with Jayasuriya, it took everyone by surprise," Stewart says. "New Zealand opened with Dipak Patel the off-spinner in 92, that was something new. In the 96 World Cup Sri Lanka pulled a little ace out of the pack with how they played there and how it came off. And obviously being in the sub-continent conditions suited them."

Sri Lanka didn't need to play the way they did to beat England, it was a sub-par total that could be chased by batting "normally", but they had total commitment to this new approach. Jayasuriya just kept swinging. He passed 50 from 30 balls, the equal fastest half-century in World Cup history.

Perhaps the most remarkable thing about that innings is it wasn't even that quick compared to the effort that Jayasuriya put together later in 1996. Less than a month after the World Cup Jayasuriya set a new record for the fastest ever ODI fifty when he plundered runs from Pakistan, bringing up his half-century from 17 balls on his way to 76 off 28. He had found a method and he was sticking to it. It took 19 years for that 17-ball record to be beaten, AB de Villiers managing it when he reached 50 off 16 balls on his way to 149 off 44 deliveries against the West Indies in January 2015.

In that 1996 quarter-final, Jayasuriya was dismissed when he went for yet another big shot off Dermot Reeve and was well stumped by Jack Russell. He was dismissed in the 14th over by which time Sri Lanka had made 113 runs and were just about halfway to victory.

Richard Illingworth was given especially brutal treatment, with Jayasuriya hitting him for four boundaries in four balls at one point. Phil DeFreitas had been smashed for 32 runs in two overs before he was removed from the attack. He came back a bit later in the innings, bowling off-spin! He conceded just six runs in ten balls of very part-time tweakers before the winning runs were struck.

"Daffy" DeFreitas bowling spin was England at the World Cup writ large. "The thing was, out there the wickets were so flat and we had a lot of all-rounders and a lot of seamers and to be honest that stage of my career where I've lost that yard or two of pace, bowling seamers on those flat wickets hardly anything happened," DeFreitas says.

"Funnily enough the day before the quarter-finals we practised and I was trying to practise a few off-cutters, trying to practise change-ups like you do and we spoke about it and we said we 'might as well' because we only had one spinner in the side. I tried to practise all day the day before. The surface we were practising on was turning but the wicket we got on to for the game it didn't move an inch. Jayasuriya just put his hands through it – on those flat surfaces you are not going to trouble anyone. But it shows you where we were really as a one-day side, literally I am practising those the day before and then I am being told you can bowl those in the quarter-finals."

The game was an unedifying mess, but it was no more than England deserved. Sri Lanka went on to win the World Cup, and they were worthy victors. For England the whole thing was just awful. A disaster. An embarrassment.

※ ※ ※

England really tried. They were working really hard to make a success of their efforts. The issue was that they had the wrong players, the wrong tactics, no experience of the conditions in which the tournament was to be played, and little experience of the format itself. Whereas in the past they had used their county experience and quality one-day players to make a success at World Cups, come 1996 they had just been left behind, covered in the dust generated by the swinging bats of the Sri Lankan openers.

"We tried different things, we tried to look at it," Thorpe says. "But it was the quality of the side, of the personnel, that becomes quite important. To just put someone up from number eight to open the batting, it's probably not well thought out. It's a nice idea. But it's preparation. Someone like Ali Brown who was doing that in the county game, he would've been far more suited. Although on a bouncier surface Browny might have struggled a little bit more, I don't think in the subcontinent it would've been a problem for him."

For Stewart this tournament is remembered for all the wrong reasons. "1996 stands out as a shambles because of the mixed messages and mixed decisions," he says. "We had very mixed selections, batting orders, bowling. We had Phil DeFreitas bowling off-spin against Sri Lanka! We had Neil Smith opening the batting, which he'd done a little bit for Warwickshire."

Raymond Illingworth sees it slightly differently. "I think we probably made the most of what we had. I used to have arguments with Atherton on the field placings. To be fair, I played a lot more one-day cricket than Mike Atherton had having played in the leagues. He never really played in the leagues to mean anything. I had a bit more of an idea where to put the fields when people were giving it a bit of a goose and slogging.

"The point was, for my money, we didn't get the bowlers to bowl in the right place and what lengths to bowl. You know we sometimes had them bowling a bit short. If you're bowling short you can hit the ball from third man to fine leg. It is a lot easier to set a field for someone pitching the ball right up there than it is for someone bowling short," Illingworth continues. "You can't set a field for short bowling. And we didn't do things like that well, and that is disappointing as we could have made better use of what we had than what we did."

While Illingworth may have laid the blame squarely with the skills, and execution thereof, of the England bowlers, the fallout from the failure would see the end of his reign as England's "supremo". He had lost the players. That much was clear even from the outside looking in.

He had probably lost them before the World Cup, but in this tournament all the existing problems bubbling under the surface were writ large. Whatever messages he was trying to pass on to the players they were not being received and the frequency with which the approach changed showed he wasn't convinced they were doing the right thing either.

Neil Smith referred to Illingworth as "old school" and said it was apparent that he "was not going to have foresight and imagination – with the cricket he wanted and the person he was – to really expand the boundaries of one-day cricket." Almost universally it was decided that a change was needed. Illingworth had to go.

All those involved in the England set-up were keen to turn the national team into a "19th county", and with that in mind the enthusiastic David "Bumble" Lloyd was given the job as coach. He was a players' coach, a man who could instil that idea of team identity that the players so craved. Atherton was a hugely strong advocate of centrally contracting England players, but that was a way off. In the meantime Lloyd was given the job of creating "Team England".

While Lloyd's appointment was seen as a positive, the problems ran far deeper than the way Illingworth was running the show. The counties' dominance of the English game had reached a point that it was damaging the chances of England succeeding – in ODIs or in Tests. The system was in need of a radical overhaul, and this World Cup failure was actually a catalyst that started that change, but it would be the equally embarrassing 1999 World Cup that made the real difference in getting people to see that things needed a shake-up.

"I felt that most of the people with whom I was dealing would rather win the County Championship than England win a Test match," Dennis Silk, chairman of the Test and County Cricket Board at the time, told *The Cricketer*.

Things needed to change. The money that cricket created was generated by the national team, not by the counties where cricket was badly attended and, according to most, played at a poor standard.

"The counties wanted what they wanted, and we didn't have the power at the centre to say no, you can't have it," AC Smith, the TCCB chief executive, told *The Cricketer*. "It was one of the exasperations of being at the centre and wanting the England team to do better, because the counties would say, we are paying their basic salaries, we want them to do our bidding!"

The cold economics meant the counties were losing their ability to dictate terms, as AC Smith described to *The Cricketer*. "It became increasingly obvious through the 1980s and early '90s that international cricket was what funded the game. We had to do as much as we could for the international team because it was only the England team that could create the heroes that would get the next generation to play."

As early as the mid-1990s up to 60 per cent of the income of the counties was made by payments from the board and that percentage was increasing. The counties may have wanted England playing fewer ODIs; they may have wanted to dictate the playing conditions under which limited-overs cricket was played. Their bargaining position in doing so was getting weaker by the moment. Change was needed, but it would take a while to happen.

1997–1998

The Hollioake years

T HE push for off-field change was just beginning in the wake of the shambolic 1996 World Cup and wouldn't have any real impact for a good few years yet, but there was a real move towards on-field changes. For one short period in the 1990s, England altered their approach to one-day cricket. It even brought them success in between the 1996 and 1999 World Cups. However, by the time the 1999 tournament in England came around this experiment had been all but abandoned and England picked a whole load of Test players.

There are few England cricket captains less English than Adam Hollioake. Born in Australia to an Australian father and a mother who was of Indonesian heritage, Hollioake first played cricket while he was living in Hong Kong, but he says his cricketing education began in England. His dad, John, was an engineer in the offshore oil business and as a result the family moved around a lot. By the time Hollioake was 12 his dad was working in Norway and the company were paying for him to go to a boarding school in England.

At the age of 12 Hollioake was already as big as most men and had a natural ability for sports. His boarding school was in Weybridge and at the age of 15 he was asked to play in the Surrey U19 side. He excelled, even though he was four years younger than his team-mates and opponents. After impressing at age-group level the call came to turn out for the Surrey Second XI. Yet again, success came easily, mostly as a bowler but also someone with a reputation for hitting the ball a long way. It was not long before Surrey offered him a pro contract at the age of 18.

When Hollioake tells the story he doesn't seem to think this was all that hard to do. It was all just a straightforward progression from schoolboy cricketer to professional with very few bumps along the way. Maybe there were, but it would be out of character for Hollioake to highlight those. You will not meet a more phlegmatic character.

International recognition came eventually, and for Hollioake England was the only real option, although he concedes he was going to be accused of betraying his roots no matter what he did.

"Whatever team I played for, no matter what decision I made, whether I chose to play for England, Australia or Indonesia or whoever it was, I was always going to be a traitor," Hollioake says. "If I'd gone back to Australia to play, people would've gone 'Hang on, you learned to play in England, all your cricket education was in England' so I would've been a traitor to England. I stayed in England, and everyone was like, 'He was born in Australia.' So whichever way I'd gone I was doomed. So I felt the right way to go was with the place that had actually taught me to play cricket and I'd come up through the age groups. I hadn't played any cricket in Australia, so that was the decision I went with."

It didn't help that Hollioake never stopped sounding Australian. Or acting Australian. Or going back to visit Australia. Or having family that lived in Australia. Or moving to Australia once he had retired.

Of all the ways that Hollioake's innate Australianness showed itself, the most obvious was on the field. Combative is probably too polite. Hollioake the cricketer is in stark contrast to Hollioake the man. Off the field he was quietly spoken and happy to share a beer with his opponents. On it he was horrible. He says he was a better sledger than he was a cricketer, and he was pretty good at cricket.

He speaks about mental disintegration as a science. For Hollioake, it was all about taking the player out of the moment. Cricketers are at their best when they have achieved a Zen-like calm where they are thinking of nothing but hitting the ball. So often when players talk about form they mention a "bubble" or being "in the moment". Hollioake felt his job as a fielder and a captain was to take them out of that space and into one where they are thinking about the past or the future.

He would remind them of a time when they failed. He would speak to them about how a failure today would mean they wouldn't be in the side the next time these two teams met. To hear him talk of it is to think it is art rather than artifice – although he will freely admit that it probably made not the slightest bit of difference.

In 1993 the 22-year-old Hollioake made a hundred on his first-class debut and was very quickly a regular member of the Surrey side in all formats, but it was in one-day cricket that he had the most success. His aggressive late-order batting and canny changes of pace when bowling made him a dangerous competitor.

Surrey went on to win the 1996 Sunday League, with Hollioake the leading wicket-taker in the tournament by a distance. That year was also when he took on the captaincy while Alec Stewart was away with England. It was a brave choice by the Surrey management, but it was to prove to be an inspired one. From 1996 to 2003, Hollioake's Surrey won three County Championships, two Sunday League titles, the Benson & Hedges Cup twice and claimed victory in the inaugural Twenty20 Cup. It was the longest period of sustained success since the great side of Bedser, Lock and Laker won seven Championships in a row in the 1950s.

With that amount of almost instantaneous success behind him, it is perhaps not surprising that an England team that were shaken by their World Cup failure in 1996 turned to Hollioake in the hope that he could replicate the success that he had at Surrey at international level. It wasn't quite a Brearleyesque selection based solely on his captaincy – he was worthy of his place as an all-rounder – but his leadership was undoubtedly something that England were keen to take advantage of.

※ ※ ※

Hollioake's first game was against Pakistan in the second ODI of the second series of the summer. England were already 1-0 up thanks to a 93-ball 65 from Mike Atherton in the first game. Hollioake replaced Graham Lloyd in the side to make his debut. England selection at the time is highlighted by the fact Lloyd had only just made his debut and was dropped the next game.

Coincidentally, Graham's father, David Lloyd, had taken over from Raymond Illingworth as England coach and it seemed that Lloyd senior was willing to give one-day cricket more focus than it had been given under the previous regime. Certainly all of the players that were coached by Lloyd were impressed by his enthusiasm. At times that enthusiasm would get the better of him, but it is always better to care too much rather than not enough. No one could ever say Lloyd didn't care.

Hollioake's selection that summer was not the only attempt to move towards one-day specialists. Nick Knight made his debut at the top of the order in that Pakistan series having had success as a one-day opener in county cricket and, earlier in the summer against India, England had selected Ali Brown as an opener.

While Knight went on to play 100 ODIs for England, Ali Brown only made it to 16 appearances. And that was in spite of scoring a measured hundred in his third match. In many ways Brown is a case study in England cricket selection in the 1990s. When asked about why he was dropped having averaged 51 in his first three games he said he just didn't know and told us we would have to ask David Graveney, the head of selectors at the time, why he was left out against Pakistan.

"I found that a very strange decision. I know my first ODI we played on a very spicy wicket at The Oval because it had rained for two days previous. In that series I think I averaged over 50 and was dropped," Brown says. "I couldn't quite understand that and I think that sculpted the way that I did in ODIs post that because I felt if I could get dropped for scoring a hundred then I didn't really feel there was the backing in that position that I could have had. I always felt I was a couple of games away from being dropped if I got out in a positive fashion and it was just deemed that it wasn't the right shot."

This seems odd because in the wake of the 1996 World Cup England appeared keen to identify a pinch hitter of their own. Having been obliterated by Sri Lanka in a World Cup quarter-final just a few months beforehand, they understood the value of having a player that could go hard from ball one. They had even tried Phil DeFreitas at the top of the order before that World Cup and Neil Smith during it.

The selection of Brown, far and away the most attacking opener in England with a proven record of success, was an acceptance that Sri Lanka had changed the game.

Many have said the introduction of T20 cricket was the moment when the sport changed, but the real antecedents of ODI double hundreds and scores in excess of 400 were at that World Cup in the tournament-winning batting of Sri Lanka's Sanath Jayasuriya and Romesh Kaluwitharana.

Even then, England still didn't get it right. "I just don't think we fully committed to the pinch hitter role right at that stage. They thought we should try... they certainly wanted to try," says Brown.

His treatment by the selectors bore this out. As was so often the case in those days players found out they were no longer in the side indirectly. In the age before central contracts England did not have the same relationship with players that exists today where the board has become their employer. It was all so much more haphazard. Brown found out that he wasn't selected for the series against Pakistan from Ceefax; those under the age of 25 reading this may need to use Google to find out what that was.

"It was rumoured and then next thing you know I'm not in the squad. I don't think there was a direct call to tell me I wasn't playing the game, I just wasn't in the next squad," Brown told us.

That 118 by Brown against India was rather out of character for the man that still holds the record for the highest score in a List A one-day game. It was cultured, thoughtful, well made and match-winning. The pinch-hitter played like a proper batsman and it still wasn't enough to keep him in the side. For all the talk of Brown as a one-day blaster it is worth remembering that he made 47 first-class hundreds and just under 17,000 first-class runs. He could really bat.

As for Hollioake's debut, it was a success. He claimed four Pakistan wickets and England won the match and the series. They had beaten both Pakistan and India in one-day series at home, using specialist one-day batsmen and all-rounders that could perform with both bat and ball. There was still a backbone of Test players, but it seemed that under David Lloyd's coaching regime there would be an attempt to focus on one-day cricket and select those best suited to winning games for England.

With Hollioake having been the leading wicket-taker in that series against Pakistan, claiming more victims than Wasim Akram, Waqar Younis and Saqlain Mushtaq, it made perfect sense for England of that time to leave him out of the tours that winter. The first half of the winter was against Zimbabwe, with the second leg in New Zealand.

Lloyd may have been keen to make changes, but it summed up the importance England placed on one-day cricket at the time that, even after the embarrassment of the 1996 World Cup, there were still no specialist one-day players taken on overseas tours. "Back in those days there wasn't separate one-day teams and Test sides, so that winter, even though I'd just taken two four-fors in the two one-day internationals I'd played, I didn't get picked to go on the one-dayers that winter because the Test team just stayed on and played," says Hollioake.

Mike Atherton was captain at the time and he told us this selection policy directly impacted on England's ability to succeed overseas. "We were a highly competitive team at home… and abroad we were less successful, but that was in the days when you picked a squad for Tests, and there wasn't enough money to have specialist ODI players coming out so you just stuck with the Test players."

That first half of the winter against Zimbabwe was a painful experience. The Test series had finished in a draw, although England felt they should have won it. They had been prevented from hitting the winning runs in the first Test by some extremely negative Zimbabwean bowling. The match ended in a draw with the scores level. The second Test was badly affected by rain. England had conceded a first-innings lead but were well placed to set up a defendable total when the final day was completely washed out.

David Lloyd was never a coach afraid of speaking his mind to the press, even at times when keeping his own counsel would have been the wiser course. He was angry about Zimbabwe's negative tactics in that first Test, prompting him to erupt with the now famous line: "We murdered 'em, we flipping murdered 'em."

His quotes hurt the Zimbabweans and when the ODI series arrived they were keen for revenge. They felt that England had acted with condescension towards them, and it wasn't the first time. Back at the 1992 World Cup an over-confident England had been blown away by that inspired spell from Eddo Brandes after Geoff Boycott had visited the Zimbabwe dressing room to gloat. Brandes was back for this series and the chicken farmer's wickets were just as telling as England lost the series 3-0.

The tacked-on nature of ODIs on England tours was perhaps never better highlighted. That summer England had committed themselves to an approach focused on picking specialist players; that winter the Test side were embarrassed 3-0 by a team that were not all full-time professional cricketers.

Things were a bit rosier in New Zealand. A Test series victory and an ODI series that was drawn 2-2 gave England a lot more to cheer, but, if further proof was needed that picking Test players and expecting them to succeed in ODIs was bound to fail, then the winter of 1996/97 provided it.

%% %% %%

In the summer of 1997 the Australians arrived for six Ashes Tests but, before the Test series, there were three ODIs. The first game against England's oldest foes at Leeds featured a partnership between Adam Hollioake and Graham Thorpe that took England home from real trouble at 40-4 chasing 175 for victory. Adam's somewhat brutish 66 not out was the perfect foil for Thorpe's nudging and nurdling. England were collapsing against Australia as they had done so often over the last decade. Hollioake's belligerence arrested the decline and secured the victory.

Hollioake produced yet another match-winning fifty in the second ODI. He was now averaging over 70 with the bat and 10 with the ball four matches into his career. There may have been better starts for England in ODI cricket, but not many. No one would say that Hollioake was the most talented cricketer, least of all the man himself. He is relentlessly modest and self-effacing. But what Hollioake lacked in talent he more than made up for in self-belief. He would do himself down but he never lost the faith that he could squeeze every drop of talent out of himself.

"Throughout his career he would say he was the least talented brother in his family," says Ali Brown. "And he was putting himself down in my opinion.

He was a very good player and a humble one as well. He was very clever. What you might perceive to be sledging, which is the Australians coming at you with a whole load of abuse, he could be quite humorous with his sledging. If there was a guide to psychology he would be the one to write it."

Brown wasn't having any of Hollioake's protestations of lacking talent. "Don't believe everything he tells you," he says.

That more talented brother was Ben, Adam's junior by six years. Ben made his ODI debut in the last game of that Australia one-day series in 1997 and played an innings that is still spoken of in gushing terms close to 20 years later.

Ben had made his List A debut the year before as an 18-year-old in the side that won the Sunday League, and made an almost immediate impact. In just his fifth game he claimed his best ever List A bowling figures. Taking on Derbyshire at The Oval, Hollioake took 5-10, and it could have been better. He began his last over with five wickets having conceded just six runs with professional number 11 Devon Malcolm on strike. Malcolm managed to hit Ben for four on his way to a career-best 42.

The younger Hollioake brother made the England side on potential rather than performance. He was 19 and playing in his just his 21st List A game. He had made just one half-century for his county and he was selected to bat at three for England. It really shouldn't have worked; it was the least English selection you could imagine. This was a side that had been in the World Cup Final the year before, a team that had the

Waugh brothers, Glenn McGrath and Shane Warne. It made what happened next all the more remarkable.

England were chasing 270 to win and began slowly. Mike Atherton was dismissed for just one run off 15 balls to leave his side 22-1. Ben strode out to the middle and got off the mark with a four drilled down the ground off the bowling of McGrath and then proceeded to flay a great Australian bowling attack for ten more fours and a six. With his upright batting stance and big backlift, the younger Hollioake raced to 63 from 48 balls before he played one shot too many and was caught at backward point by Steve Waugh.

The number of runs was almost irrelevant; it was the manner in which they were scored. At a time when a one-day strike-rate of 80 was considered excellent, Ben raced along at 131 runs per 100 balls. For so long England's one-day cricket had been meek and wont to surrender in the face of decent bowling. Ben showed that it was possible for an English batsman to play with the kind of freedom with which Sri Lanka had let loose at the World Cup the year before. It was only 63 runs, but it was ridiculously exciting and an English cricketing public starved of success got very carried away.

Ben only offered glimpses of that brilliance over the 19 further games he played for England, but we never found out how good he could have been. Just a few weeks after playing for England in an ODI series in India Ben lost control of his Porsche sports car close to his parents' home in Perth, Western Australia. It was a fatal accident. He had died at the age of just 24. It rocked those that knew him well; Ben was so alive and now he was gone. Alec Stewart described him as "the most naturally gifted cricketer that I have ever played alongside". But more than being a cricketer he was a brother, a son and a friend.

Adam and Ben were extremely close, despite the age gap. They played cricket together, they shared a flat, they even made their Test debuts in the same game. Adam says that cricket was never the same after he lost Ben – he would glance towards where Ben was supposed to be fielding and he wasn't there. He had lost part of him that he could never get back.

※ ※ ※

That 3-0 series win against Australia in 1997 cemented the Hollioake brothers' position as the future for England in one-day cricket in the eyes of the country's supporters. It seemed the selectors felt that way too, certainly where Adam was concerned. By the time England next took the field in an ODI Adam was the captain. It was just his sixth one-day game for England and he was leading the team.

Hollioake says he never wanted captaincy, at Surrey or for England; both times it was just thrust upon him. When they asked him to become full-time captain at Surrey in 1997 he says he thought they were talking to someone stood behind him. Hollioake was not so much a captain as a leader, says Graham Thorpe.

"People certainly followed [him], because of his personality, because of his character," Thorpe says. "He was very much always 'let's give these things a go, let's try and be a bit different how we go about things'. He was always trying to think differently. He tried to be a bit more flexible with his batting line ups."

Ali Brown is even more gushing in his praise of Hollioake the captain. "I have always described him as the best captain I have played under. The difference between him and other leaders is he was a proper leader," Brown says. "Whereas some captains will captain the side, Adam had a presence. And many times, and I am talking about with Surrey and England, in games that were close he had that overwhelming belief that we could win the game. Even if we were behind he would convince players, I mean you get some strong players and some players that are easily led. And he had the ability to lead all of the players with his belief and win games I don't think other captains would have done."

It wasn't just his colleagues at Surrey that had heard about Hollioake as a captain or were impressed with his approach to leading the side. Glamorgan's Robert Croft told us that Hollioake was an easy man to follow.

"He was very positive about everything he did. Just by the way he batted gave off that feeling of positivity," Croft says. "He had a lot of respect with some of the guys from Surrey, in the team at the time, Alec Stewart was in the team, Graham Thorpe was in the team, there were players who knew him very well. Word would get around what type of leader he was, so therefore it spread throughout the team pretty quickly. I think he was one of those guys that could command respect, which is always a nice trait to have."

Nick Knight had a very similar take on it. "[Hollioake's team] was a great pleasure to play in. There was a feeling of freedom, expression, all the words and catchphrases you get with cricket now. Go out and enjoy it, go out and show them how good you are. Almost that [absence of a] fear of failure, Adam was a great captain in that sense, engendering a feeling of self-belief of what you had and why you were in the team.

"And if you did run up the wicket and get stumped or get caught at cover trying to do what you do well, there was a genuine pat on the back saying 'no we will encourage that, we want to see more of that'. So there was a really good feeling within the camp I think. I certainly enjoyed playing at that time because of that. Any player will tell you when you have got that freedom and that sort of backing to play in that way, it is a really great place to be."

Ashley Giles was keen to point out how Hollioake was one of the first to look to innovate when playing one-day cricket. "Adam was a very modern leader. He was probably ahead of his team in terms of innovation and the way we played one-day cricket."

In fact the only person we spoke to from that time that wasn't full of praise for Hollioake was the taciturn Angus Fraser, who still managed to tell us: "He was very… positive."

The first series where Hollioake was in charge was in Sharjah in December 1997 on the back of a long season for the Test specialists. In a rare moment of foresight from those in charge of selection at the time, the decision was made to give the Test side some time off.

"I was already captaining well for Surrey, so they asked me to go out to Dubai and captain because Athers was taking some time off – all the boys had just had a hard Ashes series so [Darren] Gough and [Andy] Caddick and the likes of those guys didn't go to [the UAE]," Hollioake told us. "So I took a sort of second-string England side out there and they used it as a trial I guess – they were building for the World Cup in 1999. So we went out there – I don't think we were expected to win – I think the idea at the time was just to see how certain people did in the hope that maybe one or two might come through and we'd be able to slot them into the side."

It shocked Hollioake to be offered the chance to lead England, but he wasn't about to say no. "After five one-day internationals I was made captain which I felt was a bit quick, but when someone offers you the captaincy of England you aren't going to turn it down."

So at the end of 1997 Adam Hollioake departed for Sharjah with a team of one-day specialists, a couple of Test players and some second-string bowlers to face the West Indies, Pakistan and India. No one expected them to do well; it was a scouting expedition, not an attempt to conquer the world.

The India team was led by Sachin Tendulkar and featured Sourav Ganguly and Anil Kumble. Pakistan were captained by Wasim Akram and had Saqlain Mushtaq and Inzamam-ul-Haq. The West Indies had a team that was skippered by Courtney Walsh and boasted the batting talents of Brian Lara and Carl Hooper. England sent Adam Hollioake, Matthew Fleming, Mark Ealham and Dougie Brown.

There was also Alec Stewart, Nick Knight and Graham Thorpe, but this was a side built around the "bits and pieces" all-rounders that were so prominent in the county game. With a top three of Ali Brown, Stewart and Knight there was some serious firepower too, but the side also batted a long way down. They had Robert Croft batting at 10, and he would regularly open the batting for his county side, scoring hundreds in the process.

The first game was against Tendulkar's India and the experiment looked to have failed after the first innings. Stewart scored a century, Nick Knight made 42, Graeme Hick scored 32, and the "bits and pieces" players all made single-figure scores as England stumbled from 215-3 to 250 all out.

India made the surprising decision to move Tendulkar down the order to bat at five, but they were cruising to victory with Tendulkar and Ajay Jadeja putting on 108 runs for the fifth wicket. Then Matthew Fleming, on his ODI debut, changed the game with his medium-pace variations. He picked up the wicket of Jadeja and then had Tendulkar stumped for 91. India were left with no recognised batsmen and still needing 19 to win. Two more wickets for Fleming and one for Dean Headley left India dismissed eight runs short of the victory target. It was an unlikely win that came from an unlikely source.

In England's second match they took on the West Indies, a team that was still very much a cricketing force in the late nineties. Dougie Brown opened the bowling again, an example of how packed with all-rounders this England team was. Whereas Brown had struggled for control in the first match, against the West Indies he was an immediate success. He bowled Philo Wallace with his first ball and had Lara lbw with his third to leave the West Indies two wickets down without a run scored at the end of the first over.

After that dream start for England, Carl Hooper took control of the innings and produced a fine hundred that guided the West Indies to 197 off their 50 overs on a difficult pitch. England's long batting line-up helped massively in securing a second win in two games despite all of the top order bar Thorpe failing to make an impact. It was Ealham and Brown that saw England home with a hugely important partnership for the seventh wicket after Thorpe departed with 25 runs still needed.

More than winning games of cricket, this was an England team that was having fun. Hollioake would set the team a task of getting a random word into the post-match interviews. Mark Ealham was given the job of saying rhinoceros. He managed it. Playing for England wasn't always enjoyable back then; Hollioake ensured that his team were remembering that cricket was supposed to be a laugh. They all took up the game because they enjoyed it. In the high-pressure environment of professional sport, it is easy to forget that.

"That was probably the best atmosphere, the most relaxed atmosphere I ever played in," Brown told us. "That is the most enjoyable and relaxed I can remember an England series being."

It seemed to work. In the last of the group games England were playing Pakistan and looked set to lose. They set an under-par 216 to win and Pakistan were going nicely at 99-2, and again at 134-4. The all-rounders kept chipping away with wickets, Hollioake happy to keep mixing things up to make something happen. Hollioake did a fine job at bringing this disparate group together, and quickly.

"It was a side full of all-rounders and one-day specialists as opposed to the tried and tested sort of Test side with some occasional one-day players in it," Ali Brown told us. "We got on very well, we played very well. In all of those games I think they were quite tight until about halfway but we won them all and had a decent side."

The unsung hero in all of this was Robert Croft. While Mark Ealham had a better economy rate and Matthew Fleming took more wickets, Croft did a great job in the middle overs. England had struggled for a class one-day spinner for quite some time. Croft is Glamorgan's most-capped player of all time and in a period where there were so few spin options for England to consider he was the best by a distance, especially in white-ball cricket.

So England went to the final against the West Indies as the only unbeaten team and with a chance of winning a multi-team one-day tournament against three of the best teams in the world. That neither India nor Pakistan made the final was a massive surprise, and a real rarity at these Sharjah events.

In the final England lost the toss and West Indies chose to bat. They began brilliantly thanks to Shiv Chanderpaul and Stuart Williams, who was the form player for his team at the event. They cruised to 97-0 in the 22nd over before Williams smacked a ball from Croft straight to Ali Brown at mid-on. The dismissal came from nowhere, as so often seemed to be the case for England at this event.

The danger man for the West Indies was, of course, Brian Lara. He had made 88 against Pakistan in the group games and was the player that would have been spoken about the most in the team meeting before the match.

Lara had hardly arrived at the crease when a brilliant piece of thinking from Alec Stewart led to his dismissal. Ealham was bowling and Stewart was standing up to the stumps. Lara propped forward on the front foot playing a defensive shot, the ball passed the outside edge and into Stewart's glove. Stewart held the ball next to the stumps in his right hand for several seconds waiting to see if Lara would overbalance. The great left-hander took a tiny step outside his crease and Stewart tapped the bails off the stumps. After what seemed like an absolute age the third umpire gave him out. After a ropey start England were back in the game.

Even after the departure of Lara the game looked to be heading toward a West Indies win. On a wearing pitch that had seen a lot of cricket over the previous week batting first could well be crucial. Chanderpaul and Hooper were steadily taking the game away from England with a partnership that would go on to be worth 63.

One of the features of this England side was their excellence in the field. They were young, fit and very keen. Chanderpaul received a ball from Hollioake that he cut behind square on the offside. He was convinced that he had hit it well enough to earn himself at least a single and set off for a run. Matthew Fleming dived to his right and collected the ball with alacrity. By the time Hooper had sent Chanderpaul back it was too late and a direct hit from Fleming dismissed the unorthodox left-hander for 76. A crack had been prised back open for England.

Fleming was back in the action again for the next wicket, dismissing Carl Hooper lbw when he went back to a ball he should have come on to the front foot to play. He then repeated the trick to get Roland Holder out for a duck in that very same over. The Sharjah pitches were just perfectly suited to Fleming's bowling; the low bounce and turn meant his variations of pace gave his deliveries a real difference in the bounce they achieved. Fleming finished as joint top wicket-taker with Saqlain Mushtaq. He had more wickets than Wasim Akram, Courtney Walsh, Waqar Younis, Anil Kumble and Javagal Srinath.

Those Fleming wickets restricted the West Indies to just 235, a total that was competitive but not out of England's reach. Against all of the odds, with a team that was described by their captain as "second-string", England were 236 runs away from winning a multi-team one-day tournament overseas.

England started slowly and then lost Ali Brown for just one run. Knight and Stewart took them to 89-1 before Knight was run out. When Stewart went for 51 and England lost Graeme Hick two balls later, it appeared the impossible victory was just that. It looked even more improbable when England found themselves six wickets down with 61 still needed to win the trophy.

The man holding it all together for England was Graham Thorpe, who was always the key for Hollioake, the man who could do any number of jobs. He could play the anchor role or act as the aggressor. "Thorpe was crucial to the one-day side at the time, he was the guy who knitted it all together really," Hollioake told us.

"[Hollioake] would always generally have me floating really as a batsman instead of playing a specific role," Thorpe says. "If there were boundary hitters in our side as such, he was always prepared to throw them in at a certain time."

Thorpe made 66 not out in the chase in the Sharjah final, an innings that was exactly what the team needed at the time. While Thorpe was the man who set up the win it was that man Fleming who yet again finished the job. He made a blistering 33 runs from just 26 balls to win it for England. They had done it.

The scenes of the team celebrating together are so striking. A group of friends celebrating together in the wake of a remarkable victory. It felt like England had figured it out at last. They had found a way of using the resources that they had available to create a winning formula. Hollioake and Lloyd had created what England had been searching out for so long.

All they needed to do was replicate this success at the 1999 World Cup 18 months later.

※ ※ ※

The next limited-overs assignment for England was the one-day series at the end of the tour to the West Indies in March and April 1998 – and for the first time it was a group of limited-overs specialists that were sent to the Caribbean for this section of the tour; 10 of the 11 men that had triumphed in Sharjah played the first ODI in the West Indies. In the only change to the team, Ben Hollioake – rewarded for successes with the England A side – came into the side for Ali Brown.

It seems remarkable to those who follow cricket today to think that up until this relatively recent point in England's history there were no specialist one-day squads for overseas tours. England will now routinely name three different touring parties for the three different formats, but these days there is a lot more money in the ECB coffers thanks to Sky TV buying the rights to home matches. While there are downsides in terms of the visibility of the sport there are many positives in terms of the funding that is now available at every level of cricket in the country.

The Test half of the 1998 West Indies tour had been a bit of a disaster. Mike Atherton led England to a 3-1 defeat in the series where his own form was under a huge amount of scrutiny. Atherton decided he had done all he could with the captaincy. "A combination of our failure to win this series and my own form which has been well below my previous standards has led me to believe it is time for someone else to do the job," Atherton said at the time.

Speaking to us, Atherton said he didn't feel any pressure captaining both Test and ODI sides, but it was tiring. "I felt the weariness for sure, but not pressure. I enjoyed one-day cricket. I had a lot of success with Lancashire and a lot of success with England until the period we are talking about, when the requirements at the top of the order changed. I couldn't give you the stats but I won a lot of man-of-the-match awards up until 1996 for England relative to the number of matches I played.

"Then the requirements shifted, and I became less successful and the captaincy took its toll from 1997 onwards."

So with Atherton walking away from the leadership role the selectors decided to give the full-time ODI captaincy to Adam Hollioake, with the West Indies series his first assignment.

The first ODI was in Barbados and England won thanks to a brilliant Nick Knight hundred. Knight was fast becoming England's best batsman in one-day cricket. This 122 was his third one-day hundred in 17 matches and he had pushed his ODI average over 45. Combining with Alec Stewart he put on an opening stand of 165, a first-wicket record for England against the West Indies at the time. England reached 293 runs, a winning total that left Hollioake with a hundred per cent record as England captain after four matches. It was the dream start, but it was here that things began to unravel.

England were hit by two problems. The first was Graham Thorpe, the man Hollioake considered so vital to English success in one-day cricket, returning home from the tour with a back injury that was to plague him for the rest of his career. The second was losing the toss in game two.

"The second one-day international we lost a crucial toss – it was literally win the toss, win the game. And we almost won it; I think we lost off the last ball or something like that. I still think it was the best England performance I played in, in a one-dayer, to lose such a crucial toss and still almost win the game. It was unbelievable," Hollioake says.

Hollioake's memory is a little faulty here, but not much. England lost that game with a ball to spare when Ridley Jacobs hit the winning runs while batting with the number 11, Courtney Walsh. The pitch was very damp and would dry as the game went on; winning the toss was indeed vital. The West Indies had a very gung-ho approach to the target and were always a long way ahead of the rate but lost wickets at regular intervals. The West Indies top three all scored at better than a run a ball and were dismissed in the 20s. Regardless of how they went about it, the West Indies won and drew level in the five-match series.

"Then we went to St Vincent and lost two games there on pitches which suited them," Hollioake told us. "So all of a sudden we went from should've been 2-0 up in the series to being 3-1 down and by then we'd lost momentum and just wanted to go home at the end of the series. So we ended up losing that series 4-1 but it wasn't as disastrous as it looked on paper. It was just so near, yet so far."

England's biggest problem was that these pitches had truer bounce than the ones in the UAE. The class of Brian Lara and West Indies' top order made mincemeat of the England medium-pacers. Hollioake, Dougie Brown, Mark Ealham and Matthew Fleming all went at over five an over, significantly more expensive than they were in the desert in December.

This series had a massive impact on England's strategy going forward. Lara's 299 runs in five innings at an average of 59.8 was seen as proof that it was Test-match style bowlers that were needed for England to succeed going forward. The experiment was at an end after nine matches. It was time to return to the way things had always been done.

"Adam, people like Mark Ealham, Matthew Fleming played in that series in Sharjah and the West Indies. Ali Brown played in Sharjah, Nick Knight was there, so we had more of an approach into the one-day game," says Thorpe. "We still had a bit of a nucleus of Test players, and we did well and we won that Sharjah tournament. And then we went to the West Indies and Brian Lara smashed our bits and pieces bowlers all over the place. And then we went back and we changed again, we need more kind of Test-type cricketers again into the one-day side. Again, I feel like we just changed because of the whole series in the West Indies."

For Thorpe the change came too soon, and it certainly seems that way looking back. "I think they could have persevered. I always thought Adam Hollioake was a wonderful captain," he says. "Obviously, I played a lot with him at Surrey and I think he was trying to lead England in a very similar way as he did with Surrey. [He was] a very forthright captain. Lots of different ideas, you know. When I look at someone like Adam I almost compare him a little bit to how Dermot Reeve was as a one-day captain as well. The ideas and thoughts which they had. They were probably further down the line in their development as one-day players. But we always kind of end up nudging back towards you need more Test players in your one-day side."

So by the time England had returned for the ODI series against South Africa in England a month later the top order was almost exclusively made up of Test-match batsmen. Knight and Stewart kept their places at the top of the order, but the next three batsmen in were Chris Adams, Darren Maddy and Nasser Hussain. England had had a brief flirtation with doing things a different way, but a year out from the next World Cup they had torn up what they had begun and started over again.

It didn't bring them any more success. They lost the one-day series to South Africa and were beaten by the same opponents in the triangular series later in the summer. England defeated the reigning world champions, Sri Lanka, in the other match of that tri-series, but there was certainly no further movement towards England having a consistent and successful formula.

The lead-up to the 1999 World Cup could not have gone any worse. England had a chance to get some high-pressure game practice in the Wills International Cup in Bangladesh where eight sides would face off against each other in a straight knockout tournament.

"Again, we drew South Africa and they were the best side in the world at the time," Hollioake says. "We just needed to get on a run with a few victories but we had a real tough build-up to that World Cup. Australia in Australia, a home series against South Africa, and we just kept on losing and that basically led to the selectors making a lot of changes when really it might have been a better tactic to try and stick with a group of players and try and get some continuity through the team."

England played one game in that knockout tournament and lost. Neil Fairbrother was recalled for that match, having not played for England since the group stages of the 1996 World Cup, a further indication of the muddled thinking that had taken hold of selection. Fairbrother was a fine player, and brilliant in one-day cricket, but that he was suddenly seen as a solution for the 1999 World Cup when he hadn't been considered as an option in the three years in between was symptomatic of England's approach.

As it was, Fairbrother helped England to a respectable total after they stumbled to 95-5. In combination with Hollioake, Fairbrother put on 112 runs. Hollioake even made his highest ODI score, a knock of 83 not out that still wasn't enough to get England to a winning total. The South Africans made it home with ease, with more than three overs left unused.

Even before this game in Dhaka the decision had been made to change the captain. Hollioake was told at the conclusion of the games against South Africa and Sri Lanka that they were not going to retain him as captain. The last vestiges of the attempt at modernisation had been removed and the World Cup was just six months away.

"After the South Africa series they told me I wasn't going to be captain and I just made that one-off captaincy thing in Bangladesh because the Ashes were on in Australia," Hollioake told us. "David Graveney was the one who rang me and said: 'We're going with Stewie to try and get some continuity back to the one-day side and Test side.' Obviously, Stewie is a close friend of mine so I was happy for him, but obviously I was disappointed for myself. But I understood the way they wanted to go and I didn't have a problem with it."

Angus Fraser feels that the splitting of the captaincy was the beginning of the end for Atherton as a leader in both formats, and indirectly Atherton going as Test captain brought an end to Hollioake's time in charge.

"Athers was captain and obviously his place in the one-day side was questioned and Adam filled that. So [Hollioake] would have been very keen to make it his own, not in a sort of dismissive or in a challenging way to Mike Atherton, but I think it did undermine Athers a bit as the Test captain and I think it was something he was aware of. I suppose it put him under more pressure as the Test captain and he obviously resigned at the end and then both captaincies were brought together again for the new captain."

That winter, England lost the Ashes in Australia and then contested an interminably long triangular series with the Australians and Sri Lanka. After a three-team tournament that lasted 17 matches, England lost in the final to Australia. There was then a trip to Sharjah where England played one match against Pakistan, which they lost by 90 runs.

In the end, England's attempt to change the way they played in between the 1996 and 1999 World Cups was stillborn. In reality it only lasted a handful of matches. At the first sign that things were going badly the selectors panicked and reverted to type. Hollioake was given the chance to captain England in a total of 14 matches over 15 months. His success was sporadic, and never reached the heights of that first few hectic weeks in Sharjah in December 1997.

There was never a time throughout that period that England chose a core group of players and backed them over a sustained period. This team wasn't backed and neither was its captain. It was an ersatz attempt at one-day specialism. They stumbled upon a team that did well in the UAE and decided to have a punt on them in the West Indies. When the gamble failed it did not take the selectors long to cut their losses and move back to Test cricketers as the backbone of the limited-overs side.

For Nick Knight it was another example of England not seeing things through. "It is very easy to have a poor tournament in any sport or a poor set of results and suddenly change it. There has to be a period where you give that opportunity a proper go. And I felt during the time I played too often we would have a go at that and then say 'nah, we will scrap that' and try something else. And that was perhaps with the player personnel within the group and perhaps the way we wanted to play the game, we never wanted to be settled as a side often enough for long enough."

Adam played at the 1999 World Cup, but that was his last time in an England shirt. He continued to have success with Surrey, winning the County Championship that year and again in 2001 and 2002. A lot of his best cricket came after his last England game, but he was cast aside as a failed Frankenstein's monster. He wasn't the only player who played his last game for England at the 1999 World Cup, but he was the one whose career burned so bright and ended so quickly. He played 35 times for England. It should have been more.

1999 World Cup

Embarrassed at home

THE whole of 1999 was terrible for England. It began with yet another defeat to Australia in Australia. They were eliminated from a home World Cup before the knockout stages. They lost a Test series to New Zealand to leave them ranked as the worst team in the world in the format they held most dear. It was a fitting end to a woeful decade for English cricket that had seen them lose the Ashes five times, get selection wrong at almost every turn and fall from being World Cup finalists in 1992 to one of the worst sides in the world in ODIs.

Yet the darkest hour is right before the dawn, and while 1999 was English cricket's *annus horribilis* it gave those who saw that things needed to be different a chance to push their case. Pretty much every captain's report that Mike Atherton had submitted throughout his time in the role had requested central contracts for England players. His argument was that if England were to compete with the best in the world in international cricket they needed to be able to dictate when and where the cricketers that represented England played.

Atherton knew what needed to be done, but was unable to get it done. He was aware of it as far back as the 1996 World Cup, where he felt the South African and Australian sides were more professional and closer-knit squads.

Phil DeFreitas says Atherton tried to make some changes, but he had little actual power to do so. "I remember when I was the lead in bowler during the West Indies or New Zealand series. And I remember Michael Atherton saying to me 'when you go back to your county, don't play'. But you can't, you are contracted to your county. And he would say take it easy, rest. And he was all for trying to get the bowlers to have a rest between Test matches.

"During my international career there was never any rest, there was never any period when you don't play county cricket. If you look at my career, the wickets and runs I have at county level means I am playing all the time through my career. There has never been any time where I have rested between Tests or one-day internationals. You are hardly fresh, are you?"

Something needed to change, England were being left behind. Australia had introduced a form of central contract as far back as 1977, and it had proven hugely successful. It was obvious to almost everybody that it was the future. As time had gone by the amount of money that the English cricket authorities generated was less about the counties and more about England, but the counties still held the power.

The end of the 1999 season coincided with a raft of changes and poor performances on the field made that all the easier to push through. The agent for that change was Lord MacLaurin of Knebworth. He was elected as chairman of the newly created England and Wales Cricket Board which came into existence at the start of 1997. The ECB (the W for Wales is silent) combined the roles of the Test and County Cricket Board, the National Cricket Association and the Cricket Council. MacLaurin saw the need for modernisation and wanted it to happen, but it was far from easy.

"The counties were entrenched in their own little world and they didn't have any sort of reason for wanting England to be the best in the world at all. I think if you look at the World Championship table at the time we were ranked nine," Lord MacLaurin told us.

When he arrived in post he says the whole organisation was a bit of a mess. Reform was undoubtedly needed but those that would need to implement it were far from keen to do so.

"It was chaotic, to be quite honest with you. And the whole thing, from a business point of view, and that's where I came from, was just unbelievably bad," MacLaurin says. "And, you know, there was just no control. And we spent a lot of time getting control, and thankfully with the deal with Sky and Channel 4, that gave us financial control. So we were able then to hire people like the coach Duncan Fletcher, and get some sort of discipline into it.

"And some discipline with the players. So the players all wore England colours, so they all wore blue helmets. We had rows with them about that; I mean Alec Stewart said 'I'll never wear an England helmet.' I said, 'Well if you won't wear an England helmet, you're not going to play.' Jack Russell said, 'I'm never going to wear an England sunhat.' In the end he did. There were entrenched views which were utterly dark."

While those comments about dress code, or MacLaurin's insistence that players shaved, may seem like petty micromanagement there is no doubting that it had an impact. Vodafone took over sponsorship of the England team not long after the new rules about appearance came in, and MacLaurin credits those small changes for getting the deal off the ground.

It was impossible for things to continue the way they were if England wanted to compete. MacLaurin set about changing cricket's status as a broadcast sport so that the ECB could be free to sell their rights to Sky and Channel 4. The extra income that was generated from that deal meant there was both the desire to change from those in charge at the ECB and the money to make it happen. The first thing the money allowed for was the creation of 12 England contracts that would protect the workload of the top players so they could concentrate on England first and foremost.

But that wasn't the only change. The County Championship became two divisions and the ECB academy at Loughborough was instituted. It was all happening very quickly, and, while moves had been made to get this under way before 1999's horror show of a summer, the on-field performance only reinforced the necessity to do things differently.

"Fair play to the counties and the ECB," says former England captain Nasser Hussain. "After a while they started to realise a successful England team must be the main priority. Lord MacLaurin was very helpful towards that, he took people on, he absolutely helped us in many things, there was a bit of give and take in what he wanted from us and how he wanted us to behave and act as representatives of the board and what he could do for us."

MacLaurin's tenure only lasted one term, but during that time he had revolutionised the way England ran its cricket, both on and off the field. It was better off in terms of results and had a bigger bank balance. But he didn't feel he could continue when his five-year term was up.

"We were in pretty good shape then. I didn't stand again in 2002 because I went to all the county chairmen at the time and had either lunch or dinner with them and said 'I will stand again if you will want me to formalise the board'," MacLaurin says. "At that time it was all county chairmen and I wanted to have some non-executives coming in who weren't county chairmen. And I got, I think, two letters of support from the 18 county chairmen. So I said if that's the situation, I've taken it as far as I can go, I will resign. Or not stand."

Alec Stewart, who was captain for a portion of MacLaurin's spell in charge, made it clear that the chairman was the driving force behind the change.

Speaking to *The Cricketer* magazine, Stewart said: "It was MacLaurin who said the players are the shop windows of this business. He had a clear idea of how the business should go forward, even though the counties were reluctant to concede any of their power. Had he been allowed to do things as he wanted, the team would have become much better much sooner."

Those contracts that MacLaurin put in place have been revolutionary. In the 20 years since MacLaurin took over England have gone from a laughing stock to one of the most consistent Test sides in the world and have reached the number one spot in every format. While the angry and rabid orangutan of failure in global ODI tournaments still sits heavily on their chests, things have never been as good since these simple and not particularly radical changes took place.

"The emergence of central contracts was the biggest change for me," Alec Stewart says. "[Before that] the selectors at the time I think allowed the media to have too big a say, or an influence in the selection. There wasn't strong leadership at that time, and then Duncan [Fletcher] came in, and the Duncan and Nasser combination from the 99/00 tour to South Africa onwards, was when English cricket really started to move forward in the right direction."

Nick Knight never got a central contract from England, but it was clear to him when he came into the side after their introduction that they had made a massive difference. "People had been wanting central contracts for quite some time. And then obviously the resources became available and central contacts were in situ – I think there was a huge difference. The feeling [was that they had] become a team rather than a disparate group of players brought together from in-form county players to make up an eleven.

"It was the first time really that those that had the central contracts felt as if they were 'Team England', that they could build together and play together and develop more often rather than this group of players that happened to come together if they were in form. It was a really good era and it was a really good thing to do and I think it helped the players tremendously."

For all the understandable motives behind appointing David Lloyd as coach, with the hope that he could generate the kind of bonhomie that was so evident in Australian and South African sides that were full-time players for their country, it was a sticking plaster over a gaping wound. If the ECB wanted to have fully prepared and fully committed international cricketers that had England as their number one priority, it needed to employ them as such.

Lloyd departed after the 1999 World Cup, and it doesn't seem that MacLaurin was that upset about it when he did go. Lloyd, it would seem, had taken the side as far as he could.

"David Lloyd, you know I love him to pieces. Great, great man. He came to me and said; 'Look, I've had this offer from Sky, but I'd like to stay with the England side.' I said to him; 'Look, David, I think you'd be far better off taking the offer from Sky.' And he did, and he's been a superstar on Sky. He's just a wonderful, wonderful guy," MacLaurin says. "But there was a conversation we had, and I politely advised him to take the job at Sky. It's been a great success for him, and

I'm very happy for him. I can't speak highly enough of him."

MacLaurin may very well speak highly of Lloyd as a man, but had made it pretty clear that he agreed it was time to move on. Every player who worked with Lloyd was full of praise for Bumble. He was outgoing and fun, he genuinely cared for his players and wanted them to do well. Perhaps too much. While he may have been loved by the players, results were far from perfect.

The new coach was as vital as any of the other massive changes taking place at the time as far as Nasser Hussain was concerned. Duncan Fletcher was the vital cog that got the whole machine moving.

"The main thing was Duncan, he was very stubborn and wasn't for turning, other people would have backed down, but Duncan wasn't for moving – he had an idea of how he could get England progressing and wouldn't waver from that," Hussain told us.

Ashley Giles also pointed to the Fletcher/Hussain partnership as being vital to the success that England have had since. While Hussain was gone from the side before the 2005 Ashes triumph, Giles is keen to point out that he played his part.

"Nasser as a captain full stop has been, I don't know about undervalued, but certainly under-talked about all round with the changes in the England team," Giles says. "Nasser played a massive part in that. Nasser and Duncan Fletcher were crucial to all the success that has come since that time. The 2005 Ashes, that was a major part of that. What they put in place meant England were no longer a team where individuals looked after their own game and worried about their own selection. It was much more driven towards team goals. Nass was quite hard a driver, he was a disciplined man and he expected high standards but at the time that was what the team needed."

And for all the resistance, all of these changes worked. Without central contracts, two-division cricket and Hussain and Fletcher there would have been no Ashes win in 2005, there would have been no World Twenty20 win in 2010, there would have been no sprinkler dance in Sydney in 2011 as England beat Australia away from home. There would have been no victory in India and no rise to the top of the Test match rankings.

Even after all of that, England still didn't get one-day cricket right, but wins in Test cricket were more than enough for the ECB, the players and the fans to forget about white-ball woes.

%% %% %%

By the end of the summer of 1999 new contracts would radically change the face of English cricket, but the year began with a contract dispute about pay during the World Cup.

"There was a pay dispute before the World Cup started, which was pretty unpleasant, which lingered on and created a bit of a bad feel going into the tournament," Angus Fraser says.

The issue stemmed from the contracts having a divide between playing and non-playing squad members. Those that played all of the group fixtures would get £8,000, while those that did not play any would get £3,750.

Journalist Scyld Berry summed up the feelings of many towards this deal, writing in the *Telegraph* at the time. "Whether such a payment is insulting to the country's best one-day cricketers can be debated. What is indisputable is that the thinking behind such an offer is that of someone without any appreciation of the fact that cricket is a team game, in which a spirit of all-for-one and one-for-all should be created: rightly the players feel that they should all be paid the same."

John Etheridge of *The Sun* told us that all was not well within the camp, with a theory being floated that the captain was after a bigger slice of the pie. "Alec Stewart was captain and there was a theory amongst the players that he was trying to negotiate a better deal for himself because he was captain. And this cast a bit of a shadow over the games that England played in Sharjah as the warm-up to the World Cup."

Lord MacLaurin and David Graveney, the chairman of selectors at the time, met with the players at their base in Kent and defused the situation, but at the time they didn't have the option of just giving the England team more money, even if they wanted to. It was a far from ideal situation but for MacLaurin it was as much about the players pushing back to see what they could get for themselves as it was about real anger at the amount they were being paid.

"It was resolved in the end. They were probably the best-paid players in the whole of the World Cup. The whole situation at the time was that the ECB didn't have the rights or control over it, and eventually we

did get control over it. And things turned out right,"
MacLaurin says. "But there was sort of an attitude
among some players that they thought they ought
to get more money and they thought it was an
opportunity because the World Cup was being held in
England, in the UK. And it was all really quite sad that
the discipline wasn't there."

It may have been "resolved in the end" – but it did
have an impact on the squad, says Graham Thorpe.
"In home conditions we obviously felt we had more of
a chance, but the debacle leading into the World Cup
with our board and arguments over finance and money
didn't help. We were finally getting close to signing
central contracts but that was a mess. It was very
unfortunate to have that going on behind the scenes."

When England named the team for the World Cup
opener against Sri Lanka, the selectors threw up a real
surprise. It was a further move away from the one-day
specialists who had been the standard bearers of the
Hollioake experiment and back towards Test match
orthodoxy. Nick Knight had been near ever present in
England one-day sides since his debut in 1996. On the
eve of the World Cup he was dropped.

"I was gutted. Gutted, surprised, whatever words
you want to use," Knight says. "I thought we had spent
time building and planning for a World Cup in the
months and years prior to it. And the last thing I want
to do is sound bitter but England teams have done this
far too often in the past, not just in the 1999 World
Cup. Building, planning and then at the last minute
changing all the plans that have been put in place and
trying to find a short-term fix."

Knight had not been in great form leading into that World Cup – he had averaged 27 in 16 matches between January and May 1999 – but he was making starts rather than not scoring at all. The feeling was that the ball would swing during a World Cup in early-season English conditions, but it was not as if Knight, who had opened the batting for Warwickshire, would be unfamiliar with such a challenge.

He had been such a large part of England's team for so long, dropping him when they did made no sense. Throughout 1998 Knight had averaged over 50 in ODI cricket and his career average at the point where he was dropped was a very healthy 39. He had even made 84 against India in a warm-up match before the tournament.

He not only had a track record of success, he was also one of the very few attacking options that England had available to them at the top of the order. Even with the swinging ball in England they should have learned the lessons of 1996, the game had moved on. Survival wasn't enough, you needed to score quickly.

"The one thing I have to say is I wasn't in particularly good form, it wasn't particularly good timing on my part, I just lost my way a bit," Knight told us. "But having played in the team for a good few years up to that point you kind of back yourself to find your best form when it mattered most. You hope the selectors will see it that way as well but they didn't. It was a huge body blow and I can't see it any other way."

The man that replaced him at the top of the order was Nasser Hussain, who had played just 28 ODIs in the ten years since his debut. He had an ODI average of just 23 and a strike-rate of 60 runs per 100 balls at the point he was selected for the World Cup. He was a ponderous but effective Test batsman, but in limited-overs cricket he showed no urgency at all. Even when he was made captain of England in Tests and ODIs his place in the limited-overs side was a source of constant debate.

Even among the assorted nonsensical and badly-thought-out selection decisions in the 1990s, this was unquestionably one of the worst. Hussain finished the tournament as England's leading run-scorer with an average of 64.66. His strike-rate in the tournament, though, was 58 runs per 100 balls. The best batsmen at the tournament that year had a strike-rate of close to 80; Hussain's batting was measurably and undoubtedly too slow. Not that it was his fault. He performed the role that his team requested of him to perfection. The problem wasn't one of execution, it was one of tactics and planning. He was the right man for the job England asked of him; it was just entirely the wrong job. England had gone for a marathon runner when they needed a sprinter.

When England eventually missed out on a quarter-final spot thanks to net run-rate the decision to go with Hussain ahead of Knight looked even more questionable. It was yet another example of England's default position being to look to the Test team for inspiration when building the backbone of their one-day side.

In the ten ODIs before England began their World Cup campaign they lost eight and won just two, on the back of yet another terrible Ashes tour that had seen them lose badly once again. After abandoning the Hollioake experiment and returning to the core Test-match line-up with a few additions, England had actually regressed. They were looking to make things better by changing things up but it just made things worse by looking to be conservative and not keeping faith in limited-overs specialists.

For Robert Croft it all felt a bit confused. Too many things changed too late in the day for the players to feel settled.

"I think there was a little bit of disruption going into the tournament," Croft says. "Nick Knight wasn't selected, there was a few guys batting in strange positions or positions that we hadn't become accustomed to them batting in. So it was a little bit uneasy going into it. We had some sports psychology introduced during the tournament which I believe didn't really help us at the time because it should've been used more beforehand so it became more of the norm rather than a surprise. When you go into a big tournament as that you want to keep as much as normal as possible, we lost a bit of that feel to it."

It appeared England had become convinced that the tournament would be won or lost on the basis of swing bowling and picked a squad accordingly. It was a fair assessment with the tournament starting on 19 May and a white Duke ball being used for the event. Angus Fraser described the thinking of the England team.

"Because it was early season in England and it was likely specialist bowlers would make the most of helpful conditions and obviously specialist batsmen to cope with the new ball that's going to be doing a bit."

They just seemed to lose sight of the fact that, even with a swinging ball being a factor, one-day cricket is still about scoring as many runs as you can as quickly as you can.

※ ※ ※

While England's build-up was far from ideal the tournament itself was worse. The ECB decided not to go for just one big headline sponsor, but to instead seek out eight smaller ones that would get prime advertising space in return for their investment. The problem was they only found four of them. Scyld Berry wrote in the *Telegraph* that the ECB was some £8million short of its target for sponsorship income. Those four sponsors included NatWest and Vodafone, who were already paying big money into England cricket. A third, Pepsi, just wanted to beat Coca-Cola in Asia and as a result didn't really buy into the event itself, while the fourth, Emirates Airlines, paid much of their sponsorship in flights, some of which were far from direct for the players involved.

The ECB hired an Australian tournament director, Michael Browning, who John Etheridge described as "pretty confrontational". The pre-tournament hype was far from being hyper. Matthew Engel wrote in *Wisden* that Browning went for low-key but impressive. He failed.

"[Browning] specifically rejected the idea of one of those grandiloquent ceremonies that start Olympic Games, making old ladies gasp with admiration and hardened hacks groan. Instead, he went for the worst possible compromise, letting off a few cheap-looking fireworks and forcing several poor schoolgirls to stand around in the cold."

The launch event, held in central London a few weeks before the World Cup began, had some "celebrities" wheeled out for the assembled media, and the list was far from star-studded. There was TV chef Ainsley Harriott, opera singer Lesley Garrett and B-List model Caprice – all of them dressed in England kits. At one point Adam Hollioake, Alec Stewart, Stuart Law, Saqlain Mushtaq, George Salmond and Nixon McLean were dressed in their nation's kits for the tournament holding Caprice in the air in Leicester Square, the model still wearing her full England ODI kit.

This almost makes sense if you squint when you look at it, but then something else comes to your attention. Neither Stuart Law nor Nixon McLean was in their country's squad for the World Cup. The organisers had clearly found an Australian and a West Indian who were playing county cricket at the time and slung them a few quid to pose for publicity shots.

A few weeks later the ECB had finally found another company, Outspan oranges, to come on board as a "subsidiary sponsor". They arranged an event with TV presenter Anneka Rice in attendance. When Rice informed anyone that would listen that she found cricket deadly dull and wasn't the least bit interested in it there was some consternation.

The media were already inclined to be critical of Browning and his tournament, and then the ECB made a mess of sorting out accreditation for the press.

Keeping the newspapermen away from the rarefied air of the press box and the associated free lunch is no way to win friends and influence people.

"Local reporters with decades of experience were barred from press boxes by ignoramuses; it was rumoured, however, that a butcher from Chiswick was among those granted full accreditation," Engel wrote.

Even the "Carnival of Cricket" slogan came in for criticism with some arguing that it didn't really fit in with the quiet and dignified way the English watched the game, occasionally politely applauding good play. It had reached the point where Browning and the organising committee could have announced that everyone got a shiny new Rolex and it would be turned into a negative.

The format itself was an interesting departure from the tournaments that had gone before it, developed by Terry Blake, the ECB marketing director. It would be 12 teams as it was in 1996. They would be two groups of six, but rather than having quarter-finals the top three would go through to a "Super Six" instead. The teams would then play against the three teams that they hadn't played in their group and carry the points from the games they played against the others from their group that made it through.

It was to become a fixture of ICC events from this point forward. The big teams playing more fixtures means more lovely, lovely TV cash. And the format also added some jeopardy compared to 1996, when there were a ridiculous number of group matches when the quarter-finalists were all but decided before a ball was bowled – England's own progress to the last eight without beating a fellow Full Member being the most egregious example.

Even the new format wasn't immune from criticism, with many feeling it was too difficult to understand. The relatively evenly matched groups led to three-way ties in both. While this kept things interesting for as long as possible there was a sense of injustice that the badly misunderstood net run-rate was used as a deciding factor. Matthew Engel referred to it in *Wisden* as a "vile technicality". It would be something that England would fall foul of themselves.

Then there was the song. Dave Stewart of the Eurythmics got the job of writing and singing the musical accompaniment for the tournament. Etheridge told us that it wasn't written specifically for the World Cup, which would explain why there is no mention of, or even allusion towards, cricket. Rather *All Over the World* was, according to Etheridge, "just kind of a spare song he had tucked away in his bottom drawer somewhere".

The video that accompanied the song was even more bizarre. The producers clearly wanted to have a cricket theme and somewhere along the line someone seemed to have realised that both cricketers and inmates at a secure psychiatric unit wore white (apart from in one-day cricket such as, say, the World Cup, but never mind that). As a result, the music video for the song was a pastiche of Ken Kesey's *One Flew Over the Cuckoo's Nest* with the patients in Nurse Ratched's asylum going for a day out at the cricket with a prostitute.

In a brilliant finale to all of this, the song was released in record stores – yes, they still existed back then – the day after England had been eliminated from the World Cup. England, the host nation, were out of the World Cup before the official song was on sale. And when the song eventually did go on sale, it certainly didn't fly off the shelves. According to *Wisden* the two largest record stores in London recorded zero sales of *All Over the World* in the 24 hours after it was released. It failed to crack the top 100 of the UK singles chart. The Barmy Army's unofficial and grammatically unfortunate *Come on England!* was in with a bullet at number 45.

※ ※ ※

"We weren't quite up to it."

Alec Stewart's assessment of England's performance at the 1999 World Cup in the immediate aftermath of their exit was accurate if understated.

"It was dreadful," was the more forthright answer we got from Angus Fraser when we asked about the tournament.

And England were awful. In the three years since the 1996 World Cup, England had learned precisely nothing. Or at the very least swiftly forgotten anything they had accidentally picked up. Even the Hollioake experiment was over before it had started. They had not only reverted to type, they had become more English than ever. It was verging on self-parody.

The selection of Hussain was just one symptom of the bigger problem. When England were eliminated by that "vile technicality" of net run-rate they had no one but themselves to blame.

England actually started the 1999 World Cup with a win against the reigning champions, Sri Lanka. The first match of the tournament with the hosts playing the holders was dominated by bowlers, with the best performance coming from England's breakthrough bowler at the tournament, the left-arm seamer Alan Mullally.

Born in the UK, but brought up in Australia, the eccentric Mullally broke into the England side in the summer of 1996, and, while he had delivered some impressive performances in white-ball cricket up to that point, it was the 1999 World Cup where he peaked as an England player. His four wickets against Sri Lanka helped England restrict them to 204 all out. The pre-tournament obsession with swing was proved correct, and having won the toss England got the ball to hoop. Nine of the Sri Lanka wickets fell to catches behind the wicket.

Perhaps the best example of how much swing was expected, and how much was achieved, was how hard Ian Austin's bustling medium-pace proved to get away. Bowling eight overs straight with the new ball and returning to bowl another at the death, Austin returned figures of 2-26 from nine overs.

Come the second half of the match the sun had come out and conditions were far easier, but there was no urgency for England. Hussain opened the batting and made a 33-ball 14. Alec Stewart was his opening partner and he would go on to make a match-winning 88, but the innings was 146 balls long. England won by eight wickets but they took 46.5 overs to reach a small victory target. It was a win, and a win against the side that had battered them so brutally in the quarter-final of the last World Cup, but it was far less convincing than it could have been. It was also England's first World Cup win over a Full Member since the 1992 semi-final.

The game against Kenya was almost an exact replica with England winning the toss, bowling first and dismissing the Kenyans for 203. The only real resistance they got was a 100-run partnership between Steve Tikolo and Ravi Shah. Once Darren Gough collected the wicket of Shah it become a bit of a procession, albeit a slow one with the Kenyans really struggling to score against the English swing bowlers.

In England's innings things meandered again. Facing bowlers that were inexperienced and for the most part amateur cricketers, the England top three showed no urgency. Hussain made his first decent score as an opener at the tournament, finishing 88 not out, but it took him 127 balls to get those runs. England got to the total faster than they had against Sri Lanka but it still took them 39 overs, far longer than should have been necessary. England had two wins but were already facing a potential problem given the games still yet to play and with a poor net run-rate.

"We should've picked up on [the run-rate issue] to be honest," Adam Hollioake says. "It was obvious from the beginning that run-rate was going to come into it. So for us to not notice that and factor it into our tactics was, as far as I was concerned, it was amateur night. I actually brought it up in some team meetings and said 'What about this run-rate?' and I was told not to worry and to just concentrate on winning the game. I knew having played similar formats in the county game that the run-rate was going to be crucial."

England were happy with their wins, and winning is great, but they were tactically naïve in the extreme in not taking advantage of the opportunity against weaker sides like Kenya to boost their run-rate. They won the game by nine wickets; it wasn't as if they were ever in trouble. "We should have won that five or six overs quicker," Alec Stewart admits.

Angus Fraser pointed out that conditions in England did make it hard. These were early-season wickets with early-season movement.

"You turn up and you're given these completely different circumstances, you've suddenly got a damp, slow, seaming pitch rather than a pitch that resembles the white tablecloth that we're playing on now these days. There's obviously a desire to go out there and play a certain way but asking players to go out and play a game that is not natural to themselves is equally dangerous," Fraser told us.

Yes conditions were hard, and yes players needed to play in a way that was natural to them, but the folly of not pushing on against Kenya and Sri Lanka when they had the games won was exposed in the next game against a rampant South Africa.

England won the toss again and bowled first again and bowled well enough again. They restricted South Africa to just 225-7, but it should have been significantly less. Player of the tournament Lance Klusener came to the crease with South Africa 146-5 in the 37th over and he made a mockery of the idea of these being bowler-friendly conditions.

Klusener made 48 from 40 balls as he rescued his side. In the IPL age you can only imagine how much a player like him could have made with his powerful hitting and fast-medium bowling. As a 36-year-old he signed up for the short-lived rebel Indian Cricket League but even without that deal he would not have made top-dollar at the IPL that late in his career. He peaked ten years too soon.

His runs took the game beyond England, but they ended up losing by 122 runs as their run-rate issues became a full-blown crisis. It was the swing bowling of Jacques Kallis, Shaun Pollock and Steve Elworthy that did the early damage to England's chase. After that it was all about Allan Donald, who tore through England's middle order like a toddler through Christmas wrapping paper.

Donald's spell included a burst that took England from 39-2 to 60-6 and ended the game as a contest. In the end England crawled to 103 all out thanks to a painfully slow 21 from Neil Fairbrother.

It was one loss so things were not over for them. Victory against Zimbabwe and India would see them through, but they needed to bounce back and find a way to attack more with the bat. And they did, there was more urgency in the game against Zimbabwe. It wasn't the kind of attacking intent that we have come to expect in recent times, but it was quicker than the ponderous effort against Kenya. Not that Hussain went any quicker, he made a 93-ball 57 not out, but it wasn't his role to go quickly at the top of the order.

There was certainly a sense of urgency from Graham Thorpe who brought up his 50 off 56 balls.

England were chasing 168 after another outstanding spell of bowling from Mullally, claiming 2-16 off his ten overs, had seen Zimbabwe score at just 3.34 runs an over throughout their innings.

"I got runs in the Zimbabwe game – and I remember trying to get them quickly. I don't know how many balls I faced, but I remember being quite conscious of trying to get the runs quickly in the chase," says Thorpe.

The penny had dropped. The problem was it was already too late for England to have any sort of run-rate advantage going into their final game against India. The three matches they had won going into that India game had been won by margins of nine, eight and seven wickets. If they had won those games quickly as well as comprehensively they would have had a nice cushion ahead of the final group match against India that would have meant they could lose and still be in the qualifying positions in the group no matter what happened elsewhere.

A win in their final group game against India would have been enough to see England through no matter how quickly or slowly they went about it, and they would qualify with a loss as long as South Africa beat Zimbabwe. Even a win for Zimbabwe over South Africa and a small loss to India should have been enough. England were through to the Super Sixes barring a miracle.

Some newspapers were reporting that England had made it to the next round after their win over Zimbabwe. Nobody thought a set of circumstances that involved undefeated South Africa losing heavily enough to Zimbabwe to put England out of the event was a real possibility. In the end, that is exactly what happened.

This game against India may have been a one-day international but it took two days to complete when rain and thunderstorms arrived at Edgbaston on the Saturday afternoon. Meanwhile, down at Chelmsford, Zimbabwe were achieving the seemingly impossible and defeating South Africa. When England resumed their clash with India on the Sunday, they were suddenly under huge pressure to win, although they were well placed to do so.

India batted first having been inserted by Stewart and started well enough with Sourav Ganguly and Sadagoppan Ramesh putting on 49 for the first wicket before Mullally had Ramesh caught at second slip.

Ganguly looked in fantastic form and looked well set to go on and take the game beyond England before he was run out for 40 in the most unfortunate way. Rahul Dravid drove a ball from Mark Ealham back up the pitch and the bowler got his fingertips to it before it crashed into the stumps. Ganguly was out of his ground.

That wicket brought together Sachin Tendulkar and Dravid, who took the score to 139-2 before Tendulkar fell for 22 after an unusually frantic innings where he could well have been dismissed twice before he eventually fell trying to hit a six over deep midwicket.

India were well placed to make more runs against England than any team had managed at this World Cup even after Tendulkar fell. They were three wickets down for 139 in the 34th over, but from there they lost their way. Mark Ealham's wobbly medium pace proved almost impossible to get away as they only managed another 93 runs in the last 16 overs, eventually setting England 233 to win.

When Stewart had won the toss early on that Saturday morning the sun had been shining and the skies had been clear. When England went out to bat it had become overcast and the skies were darkening. They started badly thanks to the bowling of Debasis Mohanty who claimed the wicket of Stewart in the fourth over, caught at second slip by Mohammad Azharuddin. The first ball Graeme Hick faced was a wide. The next ball from Mohanty crashed into his stumps to dismiss him for a golden duck. England were 13-2 in a game they had to win to make further progress in their own World Cup.

A partnership between Hussain and Thorpe brought England back into it, with Hussain's stability an advantage in this high-pressure situation. They needed to recover from the blow of two wickets in quick succession so early on in the chase. The rain clouds were coming in and it was getting dark. Ganguly was bowling and he snuck one through Hussain to bowl him. England were now 72-3 and had lost their leading run-scorer just as they had begun to get things back on track.

Eight balls after the Hussain wicket, the rainclouds that had been looming did their absolute worst. There was no more cricket that day, and the game became the first in the tournament to go into the reserve day.

The Zimbabwe win bombshell had exploded by the time play resumed on the Sunday morning. Now the equation was a simple one. To guarantee a spot in the next phase of the tournament England needed 160 runs to win from 177 balls with seven wickets in hand. It wasn't a foregone conclusion that England would win from there, but they had a good chance. Then Thorpe got an absolute rotter of an lbw and it all went very wrong very quickly. Thorpe called it a "complete howler".

The fall of the Thorpe wicket presented another problem. The success the English top order had enjoyed in their victories meant the lower order had not got a chance to have a bat.

"The other thing that people didn't pick up on was we had all these batsmen at the top of the order who scored lots of runs and got us through games but if they'd got on with it and maybe they'd got out then some of the lower-order batsmen would've got a game," says Hollioake. "I batted for the first time in the final group game against India. I hadn't batted for about three weeks when I came into that game."

As Hollioake points out, the reluctance to lose wickets not only harmed England's run-rate by them going slower than they needed to, it also restricted the chances of others to get themselves into some nick.

When Thorpe fell, Neil Fairbrother tried to keep things moving by working the ball around while at the other end batsmen who had been short of practice tried to have a slog as the required rate started to climb. Andrew Flintoff, the big hope for the tournament going into the event, put together a painful innings that was neither one thing nor the other before he was dismissed lbw by Anil Kumble. He had made 15 runs in that innings, a duck in his only other knock, and had the worst average and economy rate of any of the bowlers. To make things even worse for the young man who was considered the heir to Botham, his bat was stolen from the dressing room in the aftermath of this defeat.

It became a procession towards to the end as wickets tumbled and England were defeated by 63 runs. England's World Cup was over and, for the first time in seven such tournaments, they had been eliminated in the first stage of the event.

※ ※ ※

For Hollioake, it wasn't as bad as people claimed. They weren't a bad team and had finished on the same points total as both India and Zimbabwe. "Even though that campaign is seen as a disastrous campaign, I think we were no different to most of the other sides. All had similar sorts of records, but they hadn't been caught out by the run-rate," he told us.

This probably says more about Hollioake's positive attitude towards life than it does about the actual cricket, but he does have a point. If results had gone differently elsewhere England would have made the Super Sixes, although it would have been unlikely for them to go beyond it.

Even the tactics weren't *that* bad. They were right that swing bowling was the key to the whole thing, and they were right that the chances were that batsmen with the best techniques would combat it well. They just took it a bit too far.

What it did do was wake England up to the need to change. Those central contracts, those two divisions in the County Championship, the appointing of Duncan Fletcher, they all led to England being successful in the years to come. And while that success manifested itself primarily in Test cricket, if it wasn't for the embarrassment of the 1999 World Cup the chances are it would have taken even longer for the much-needed alterations to take place.

Next time you cringe thinking about that England defeat to India on a reserve day in Birmingham try and be thankful.

"The big idea was that the World Cup might instil a love of cricket into the hearts of English youngsters, a generation unengaged by the idea of supporting a team which has contrived, for instance, to lose the Ashes six times running. That has probably had to be postponed until the next World Cup in England: 2019 on present projections," Engel said in *Wisden*.

It might not have been a success but it did inspire some young players. Ahead of the opening match of the 2015 World Cup the *Western Daily Press* newspaper based in Somerset printed a picture of a then eight-year-old Jos Buttler posing with the World Cup trophy during the 1999 tournament. Buttler's face is full of brilliant excitement. If the 1999 World Cup helped encourage England's most exciting one-day batsman ever to pursue the sport perhaps we have more than just the failure that induced change to be thankful for.

2003 World Cup

Cricket and politics make an ugly mix

IT is rare that a limited-overs match taking place outside of a global event resonates with the public long after it is over. Of all the many gripes people have about one-day cricket, the fact there are "meaningless ODIs" is the one levied most often. This for the most part is unfair. Test cricket is really just a series of friendlies. There is no larger prize on offer, no championship to build towards. In football there is a clear distinction between friendlies and the games that are played in order to gain qualification for a tournament or at the tournament itself. This is not the case with Test cricket; there is no goal beyond the matches themselves. Any context is created by the meaning that we and history give the games.

This is the case with bilateral ODIs too. They are a series of matches and no matter who wins or who loses the status quo remains the same. The difference is that the storied past of Tests imbues the endeavour with some greater meaning. ODIs are seen as what would be called "timepass" in India; they are nothing serious but that is only the case because we have decided to not take them seriously.

One game that remained in people's minds years later took place between the 1999 World Cup in England and the one that followed in southern Africa in 2003. It was a beautiful July day and England were playing India in the final match of a tri-nation series that had also involved Sri Lanka. The game itself was fantastic but it was as much remembered for two powerfully striking images.

The first is a visibly angry Nasser Hussain gesticulating wildly at the Lord's media centre upon reaching his maiden ODI century. The second was of India's captain Sourav Ganguly shirtless on the Lord's balcony celebrating victory several hours later. It was a rollercoaster affair where 651 runs were scored in 100 overs and England lost a game they should have won. It is a match Hussain told us still haunts him to this day.

%, %, %

England won the toss and elected to bat on a sunny day in North London. Much of the build-up to the game centred on the suitability of England's belligerent captain to lead this team. Hussain was the Test leader and in partnership with Duncan Fletcher was doing wonderful things in turning England into a force to be reckoned with in the longer form. They still hadn't beaten Australia, but they had defeated pretty much everyone else. At that time there was no real discussion about whether Hussain was the right man to captain England in one-day cricket, it was very obvious that he was. The real question was whether he deserved a place in the side as a batsman.

Hussain's batting in the 1999 World Cup was still strong in people's minds, and while he had been a lot more attacking since then he was far from a dasher. The final at Lord's was Hussain's 72nd ODI for England and he had never made a hundred. He averaged 30 with 13 fifties and a strike-rate of 65, one that was pedestrian even at the time. Some in the media, particularly Ian Botham, Bob Willis and Jonathan Agnew, were very critical of his selection, suggesting that he was not worthy of his place and England should look elsewhere – and if he was to be picked he shouldn't be batting at number three.

By that point Michael Vaughan was being talked of as a replacement, somewhat ironically considering similar questions would be asked about his worthiness of a place in the ODI team come the 2007 World Cup.

Looking back, Nick Knight says Hussain was aware of the questions over his place in the side. "I think he always felt under pressure and I think Nasser is the type of player that responded to that pressure. I think in a way he quite enjoyed the fact that people would question him because he was that type of player that wanted to prove everyone wrong."

Hussain agreed with that sentiment when we asked him about that match. He revelled in the prospect of proving the old lags in the press room wrong.

"I'm true to myself with who I was as a cricketer. Sometimes you don't read the reports and watch the highlights or have any contact with the media and sometimes you do and have to try and prove them wrong. It was in the latter period where I would try and read and watch and learn, and for months and years on end they were claiming that I wasn't a one-day number three.

"They were probably right about that. But I was someone who tried to back my own ability and I remember being 20 or 30 not out and thinking right, get a hundred, for once in your life, get a hundred and stick three fingers up to Botham, Willis and Agnew and when I got to a hundred, I thought, 'Shall I, shall I not?' But I thought, 'No, that's what's got me here.' I stuck my fingers up."

It caused quite a storm at the time, with people suggesting it was unbecoming of an England captain to behave that way. Hussain says he regrets nothing. "I don't look back with mixed feelings at all. That's not what I regret, I regret not saving 325. Mohammad Kaif and Yuvraj Singh smashing us at the end of that game, that's what I think about."

England did indeed fail to defend that total, and that despite making what was at the time their third highest total ever. Halfway through the Indian innings they had all but secured victory. The visitors were 146-5 and Sachin Tendulkar, Sourav Ganguly, Virender Sehwag and Rahul Dravid were all back in the pavilion.

India were not even halfway towards their target and had lost their remarkable top order.

Then England threw it away. They lost their lines and lost their way as they fed the favoured shots of Mohammad Kaif and Yuvraj Singh. At first it looked as if the partnership would just delay England's inevitable win, then you could see that England were worried. This side, for all of the progress that it had made since Fletcher took over, still had a problem with getting games won. Knight says he was aware of the difference between playing for England and playing for the all-conquering Warwickshire side of the 1990s.

"[That Warwickshire team] had that great feeling, that unusual feeling, that rare feeling where you felt someone in that team would get you over the line. Will it be Trevor Penney batting at seven, or Allan Donald with the new ball getting three quick wickets, whatever it was someone was going to have their day. It was a great feeling as there was a genuine belief that rather than just talking about it in team meetings ... that this team was going to beat anybody."

Comparing that to the England teams he played in he was aware that the feeling of invincibility Warwickshire had created over years of playing together and winning together wasn't there.

"You look around your dressing room and you see Graeme Hick, Alec Stewart, Marcus Trescothick, Darren Gough, all these very fine players who you have a lot of respect for and know what they can bring to the team and if they have a good day, great, you might win. That's fine, and playing personnel will get you so far but at the highest level against the best teams in the world, in the biggest tournament in the world what really matters is what goes on in the mind – do we genuinely feel we can win games of cricket when it gets tough because every game of cricket will get tough at some point," says Knight.

"In my own personal view, we hadn't won enough. During the periods leading up to the World Cup perhaps the team wasn't settled enough, didn't play together enough and we didn't win enough together. We didn't get through difficult phases as a team enough, and that is what really counts when you get to big tournaments. Overcoming those difficult moments, so yes we may well have had on paper a very fine England side, but what we didn't have was genuine self-belief that we could get through enough difficult moments to go on and win."

When the winning runs were struck off Andrew Flintoff, he fell to his knees. He couldn't believe what had happened. It is not very often a game moves from one side to another in 50-over cricket as much as it did that day. Five months earlier the scene was a very different one. Having lost to India in a gruelling Test series England went into the sixth and final ODI 3-2 down. They needed a win in that last game to walk away with a face-saving tie in the limited-overs games.

With three balls left in that game in India the hosts needed six runs to win with two wickets in hand, although, with India ahead in the series, five runs to tie the game would have been sufficient to secure a series win. First England ran out Hemang Badani and then the next ball Flintoff bowled Javagal Srinath to win the game. He set off in celebration, removing his shirt and waving it over his head in celebration. This angered the Indian team – their prickly captain Ganguly most of all.

It was with this Flintoff celebration in mind that Ganguly removed his shirt and waved it above his head on the balcony at Lord's as the winning runs were scored in 2002. He was caught up in the moment and trying to prove a point. Ganguly has said since that he regrets doing it, but it is an image people won't forget. "You make mistakes in life. I personally did not quite enjoy it. I don't enjoy when I see channels keep on repeating that footage on television. I have made so many hundreds, they should show that," Ganguly said in 2012.

What that game showed us was that this was a good England side, but not one that knew how to win. Come the 2003 World Cup an even starker reminder of this would appear, but before that there was a political fiasco to deal with.

%% %% %%

The relations between the United Kingdom and Zimbabwe were bad when Tony Blair's Labour government was elected in 1997. Between then and the start of the 2003 World Cup they became worse. The Robert Mugabe regime was at its worst at that time, at least in the minds of the British. Between 1992 and 1997 the British government gave Zimbabwe approximately £1billion in aid, a significant proportion of which was to be spent on compensation for white land owners who were selling off sections of their property to black farmers. Land reform had been an issue since the country gained independence in 1980 after a long and, at times, violent struggle.

By 1997 the British government had become increasingly alarmed at the authoritarian tactics used by Mugabe's Zanu PF party and was implementing sanctions against him and his government. The calls for his regime to be treated harshly became a clamour when the land reform programme turned violent following the elections in 2000. The UK government was becoming increasingly angry with events in Zimbabwe and wanted to cut off all ties.

This diplomatic standoff and cricket collided spectacularly in the lead-up to the 2003 event. Clare Short, the International Development Secretary, declared that England playing cricket in Zimbabwe would be "shocking and deplorable". She said Mugabe had stolen the recent elections in the country. The government was making it very clear it did not want England to go, but would stop short of forbidding them.

Prime Minister Tony Blair said the cricketing authorities should "reflect on the humanitarian and political crisis in Zimbabwe" but he made it clear the final decision was the ECB's to make. This ambiguity angered ECB officials. Chief executive Tim Lamb accused the government of double standards and said cricket was being "treated differently to the 300 other [British] businesses which continue to trade in Zimbabwe, which ministers aren't discouraging."

There were people in Zimbabwe who were very clear that England should not come. One member of the Zimbabwe national squad told the *Guardian* England should not come, but spoke only on condition of anonymity as he feared retribution.

"Ethical issues must be taken into consideration. It would be wrong to hold any World Cup matches here," the unnamed Zimbabwean squad member said. "With a multiracial crowd and teams playing here, are we not painting too rosy a picture of a country that is battling starvation, terrible poverty, corruption, human rights abuses? The matches will give credence to the organisation that is in charge."

The ECB wanted guidance from government, the players wanted guidance from the ECB, and the ICC was telling everyone there was no reason England could not travel to Zimbabwe. There was a threat made against the England team, although there were some questions over its veracity. A note was put under one squad member's hotel room door in Australia from an organisation calling itself "Sons and Daughters of Zimbabwe", threatening the team and their families. It looked like an amateurish effort at a threat, but it existed.

A decision should have been made, one way or another, as early as possible so the England team could concentrate on cricket, the Zimbabwe authorities could make preparations and fans, broadcasters and everyone else would know the situation. This did not happen. Instead England just wouldn't make a call until after the event had started.

And the decision was then left to a bunch of cricketers who didn't really understand what the hell it was all about.

Nasser Hussain says: "We were cricketers, and cricketers from various ends of the spectrum, young Jimmy Anderson and people like that just coming in from the Lancashire Second XI. And to sit in a room for a week to discuss the political ramifications of trying to go and play a game of cricket in Zimbabwe and the issues with Mugabe and the specific issues with Zimbabwe – some people didn't understand why it was different for us."

As captain of the team, Hussain took the brunt of the burden, but the whole squad was holed up in the Cullinan Hotel in Cape Town talking about politics. "I'd done a lot of research on the subject and had spoken to many different people about it," Hussain says. "I was pretty anti going to Zimbabwe for the moral reasons. In the end we ended up fudging it a little bit, going on security threats."

Nick Knight was keen to point out how much Hussain took on, but all of the team got caught up in the decision about whether to fly to Harare. "It was a very difficult time, particularly for Nasser who I thought again was outstanding in the way that he dealt with it on our behalf as a captain representing his team. I thought he was brilliant and you had complete trust and faith in the way he was managing it. There were endless meetings, and a degree of uncertainty, I think, about what the best thing to do was."

John Etheridge, who was covering the event for *The Sun*, had a similar view of Hussain's input. "Nasser was impressive. He really came into his own I think on that. He spoke very well and was a strong voice around the dressing room."

Hussain wanted to be given some idea of what the best move was, but no one gave him any real advice. They just kept saying it was up to the players.

"You were looking for more guidance from government, maybe the ECB, from the ICC, but we never really got it. So you ended up trying to get the opinion from a wide spectrum of people, different ideas and different views. And it wasn't easy. We were there to play cricket, we weren't there to discuss Mugabe and Zimbabwe political issues, so it wasn't a great time, it wasn't a great week," Hussain says.

"But it was what it was. When you take on the captaincy you are more than just a captain of a cricket team, you are also a spokesman. You're someone who is in a position of responsibility. And politics and sports, unfortunately, sometimes do mix and you have to realise as a captain that you are an ambassador for your country. Sometimes these issues do come up and you can't just bury your head in the sand. I was never just going to say, well this has nothing to do with cricket, we are just cricketers, we'll go and play cricket and not worry about the politics of it."

There was plenty of information available but very little guidance. Richard Bevan was there in his capacity of CEO of the Professional Cricketers' Association (PCA). The South African police gave the team talks, there were people outlining the pros and cons of travelling to Zimbabwe, but there was no one telling the England squad what they should do. If the UK government didn't want England to play then it should have made that call, instead of issuing strong statements that muddied the waters and then leaving it for a group of cricketers to make a complex political and diplomatic decision.

There also need to be some questions raised about the ICC's decision to agree to Zimbabwe hosting matches in the first place, just as there should be questions about the matches arranged in Sri Lanka in 1996. In order to hold a global tournament there needs to be stability and decent infrastructure. South Africa had more than enough stadia to host the event; there was no need to create this problem by giving games to a country in such turmoil.

In the end England didn't go; they said they weren't safe and wouldn't travel. Zimbabwe won the game as a walkover just as Sri Lanka had done when teams refused to come to their country in 1996. Knight told us he was pleased and comfortable with the decision that they made.

Not going may have been the morally and politically correct thing to do, but it would have an impact on England's chances of progressing in the event. The 2003 tournament was a 14-team event with two groups of seven. Rather than quarter-finals, the event had a Super Sixes stage just as there was in 1999, with the top three from each group progressing. For England to make the Super Sixes they would have to finish above Australia, India or Pakistan. Sacrificing potential points against the Zimbabweans in a game England were favourites to win was a massive handicap.

England had in effect lost their opening match of the World Cup having not bowled a ball. It was a game they would have expected to win. That was a decent Zimbabwe side, and it was not a foregone conclusion.

Had England travelled and won, however, they would have made it through to the Super Six stage.

"People mustn't forget that they were a damn good side," says Knight. "They had some world-class players, it took a lot of quality to beat them. We certainly didn't underestimate them and we did find it difficult at times against them. In their own backyard, with the side they had at the time, there were absolutely no guarantees."

Alec Stewart sees it differently. He says not going to Zimbabwe cost England a "probable win" and was the difference between England qualifying for the Super Sixes and not making it.

"Not going to Zimbabwe hurt us badly. And the distraction. There were meetings after meetings; the ECB should have made the decision. It shouldn't have been the players making the decision, it should have been driven by the ECB saying go or not go," Stewart told us.

"So you spent hours after hours, meetings after meetings, which didn't interfere with the cricket, but the last thing you want to do is be sat in meetings listening to the rights and wrongs, of what Zimbabwe was all about," Stewart says. "But there wasn't a definitive answer coming out of Lord's, which was frustrating. Nasser almost took it upon himself to be the political leader which in hindsight, he probably wishes he hadn't got as involved, but we got into a position where we didn't go, and that cost us dearly too."

While England were deciding not to go to Zimbabwe, Andy Flower and Henry Olonga were pointing out the issues in their country in their own way. In the opening fixture of the tournament, Zimbabwe took on Namibia. A statement was given to the press, signed by Flower and Olonga, saying they would wear black armbands to "mourn the death of democracy in Zimbabwe". It was to be a "silent and dignified gesture"; it was certainly a brave one. There was every chance there would be reprisals, although happening in the full glare of the world's press and TV made it less likely.

As it was, neither Flower nor Olonga played for Zimbabwe again after the tournament but both were given plenty of plaudits. Hussain even said he wishes his team could have done something similar.

"If anything, I'd have liked to have done what Olonga and Flower did, but I didn't really feel it was our place to come into another person's country and make some kind of political protest."

Hussain also says it was the right call not to travel. The only call.

"I think it was the only decision we could make really. It wasn't just my decision, it was a decision made by 14 or 15 different cricketers, and also the opinion at that time of the country. You think, 'why didn't we just go and play?', or, 'why didn't we just not play?', but at that time it was more complicated than that. Far more complicated. Once it became an issue and a story, you're in a losing position. You couldn't get the right result. It was a no-win situation."

England didn't fly to Zimbabwe and were already facing an uphill struggle to qualify before a ball had been bowled in their campaign. It was a decision that was understandable but the whole episode dominated their World Cup. It's hard to conceive a more draining and disastrous start to a tournament.

※ ※ ※

England's lead-up to this World Cup was dominated by the Ashes. Not even just the Ashes, an embarrassing Ashes loss. It was to become a theme for three World Cups in a row. Win or lose, England were arriving at the biggest tournament on the back of their biggest Test series and they were physically and emotionally drained.

They had some decent results in one-day cricket in the year leading up to the World Cup, but also some terrible ones. This was far from a poor side. It had Marcus Trescothick and Nick Knight at the top of the order, two men as good as any openers England have ever produced in one-day cricket. They had Andrew Flintoff and Paul Collingwood as all-round options and the bowling of Steve Harmison who at that time was amongst the quickest bowlers in the world. While there were doubts about Nasser Hussain's place in the team, before and after that hundred against India at Lord's, there was no doubt that he was a fine leader. This England side was as good as any since the 1992 World Cup finalists.

"We were [a strong side]," insists Hussain. "You speak to some of the players in that side and that was one of our better sides as far as one-day cricket goes. You've got to put it in context as to what happened leading into that World Cup, another Ashes drubbing, various players were injured, we were calling up Jimmy

Anderson at the last minute. World Cups at that stage always came on the back on heavy Ashes defeats and three months in Australia. It takes its toll on personnel and minds. And then obviously the whole Zimbabwe crisis kicks off and it takes a lot out of you."

As well as decent cricketers there was also a very impressive captain/coach partnership. Hussain and Duncan Fletcher's bond was very strong by this point and helped England take massive strides forward. Those central contracts that had been introduced in 2000 had allowed Fletcher to mould a team – something England had struggled to achieve in the past.

With Fletcher came a new focus on white-ball cricket, much more so than had ever existed before. In fact, Hussain told us that Fletcher was a lot more confident of making an impact in the one-day game.

"I know for a fact that when Duncan took over the job he was more worried about how he would cope with Test match cricket because he had never played Test match cricket. He was coming into the unknown, so Duncan was more worried about turning our Test match form around than our one-day form. Because he had obviously featured for Zimbabwe in one-day cricket and he knew quite a bit about one-day cricket," Hussain says. "In fact, at the end Duncan was a little bit disappointed that he didn't turn our white-ball cricket around a little bit more. He felt he could have done a lot more to turn us around. There was a lot more focus on white-ball cricket, but still not enough."

Fletcher was speaking about that increased ODI focus as early as 2001, after another disappointing winter for England in the format.

"Most other sides play five or more matches and are probably together for a lot longer than we have been this winter. I'm trying to address that with going to India and New Zealand next year for the one-dayers," he said.

Fletcher was keen to have a separate squad for the one-day games and was also resentful of the amount of ODIs other teams got to play in comparison to England.

"The more you play the game, the better you get at it. We played our last one-day internationals against Pakistan in November [2000] about the same time Sri Lanka played South Africa, but since then they have played a further 12 matches and we've not played any."

While Fletcher may well have wanted more focus on one-day cricket, the truth was that little had changed. The priority was still Test cricket, even leading up to a World Cup.

Ahead of the World Cup, England had spent four months in Australia. And it was not a successful trip. They lost the Test series 4-1, and looked set for a 5-0 whitewash before the batting of Mark Butcher and Michael Vaughan and the bowling of Andy Caddick secured a consolation win in the final Test. They then played ten ODIs against Australia and Sri Lanka. They won three games against Sri Lanka to see them through to the final of the tri-nation event but lost every match they played against Australia. By the time Nick Knight had joined up with the squad for the ODI leg of the Australia tour they were already a downhearted bunch.

"It is always a difficult situation," he says. "When you are one of the one-day players that is joining a Test match team just as a series has finished or in the middle of it as it was in that instance, it is difficult because the side were struggling at that time, especially in Ashes series. So your job is twofold. One is to get yourself into international cricket having been sat at home, and also trying if you can to bring some energy to some mentally tired souls. It always seemed to be that way. And you hope that some fresh faces and some fresh legs and new energy can invigorate the side again and we can kick on and really make an impact in the World Cup."

So mentally and physically drained cricketers, on the back of yet another kicking in Australia, then started their World Cup by sitting in meeting rooms talking about Zimbabwean politics. When England finally got to play a game in the World Cup against the Netherlands there must have been genuine relief.

That match against the Dutch presented no issues for England, with 20-year-old James Anderson picking up 4-25 in just his tenth ODI and Andy Caddick bowling ten overs for just 19 runs. When they followed that win with a relatively easy victory against Namibia, they had made the best possible start to the tournament considering the Zimbabwe fiasco. However, having lost out on points that they could have picked up in Harare, they were left needing to win two of the three games that they had left or rely on results elsewhere going their way if they were to get through to the Super Sixes.

As those three games were against Pakistan, India and Australia it was no easy task. The game against Pakistan came first and their opponents boasted an impressive bowling line-up. Wasim Akram, Waqar

Younis and Shoaib Akhtar were the quick men, Saqlain Mushtaq and Shahid Afridi the spinners, and there was also the useful fast-medium bowling of Abdul Razzaq. For England to do well they would need to bat to the limit of their capabilities.

When Marcus Trescothick fell to Wasim early, edging behind to the keeper, it was far from an ideal start. When Nick Knight then departed for a scratchy 15 off 28 balls, England were already in trouble. While there was little to get excited about in that Knight innings, he does have one claim to fame as a result of it.

Knight was facing the fourth over of the match and Shoaib was the bowler. He was already considered the fastest in the world, with only Brett Lee coming close in terms of pure pace. In 2003 both men were pushing the 100mph mark with their bowling but neither man had broken that barrier in a match. With the final ball of that fourth over Shoaib ticked past it. The ball to Knight was clocked at 100.23mph, and in reality it was a bit of an anti-climax as the batsman played it into the legside off the back foot with no real drama. Regardless, Shoaib was clearly delighted. He raised his hand to the crowd to acknowledge their applause. It was an achievement, but almost immediately there was scepticism about the accuracy and reliability of the reading.

"ICC has always said there is not enough uniformity in the various speed guns around the world for any one performance to be designated official," Rodney Hartman, the World Cup's director of communications, told *BBC Sport*.

Regardless, Shoaib is still very proud. When he appeared on Twitter over a decade later his handle was @Shoaib100mph.

Hussain departed not long after and, with England struggling at 59-3 after 13.3 overs, it did not look like they would set a competitive total. From there on Michael Vaughan took control, cutting the ball behind square off the seamers as they struggled to maintain their excellent line from the opening overs. He looked in complete control and when he fell to Shoaib it came as a surprise, but he had steadied the ship. The middle and lower order then pushed England up to 246-8, thanks primarily to Paul Collingwood, who top-scored with 66, and Andrew Flintoff, who made a useful 26 batting at seven. It was a decent total, but not one that appeared to be beyond the Pakistan top order that contained Saeed Anwar, Inzamam-ul-Haq, Younis Khan and Yousuf Youhana (before he changed his name to Mohammad Yousuf).

Any worries about England not having enough runs were allayed by the bowling of James Anderson and Andy Caddick. With an age gap of some 14 years there was a striking difference in the appearance of the two bowlers. Anderson was fresh faced with blond streaks in his dark hair, Caddick was all craggy features and greying at the temples. They combined brilliantly here but it was the younger man who made more impact in the wickets column.

Anderson claimed four wickets, and got all of them with balls that were pitched up and swinging. It was the first time that the cricket world had seen this from Anderson, and, while it took him a while to be consistent at this level, he would go on to become England's leading wicket-taker in both Tests and ODIs. He was raw and exciting in 2003 but few could have predicted that he would go on to be England's most successful bowler.

Against Pakistan the good work Anderson had started was finished off by Flintoff, who picked up two wickets, along with three victims for Craig White. Pakistan were bundled out for 134 in 31 overs with Hussain required to turn to only four bowlers. It was as good an England bowling performance as they had put together under his captaincy.

While England performed brilliantly there was a growing sentiment that batting under lights in this World Cup left teams at a real disadvantage. No one has ever really been able to properly explain why sometimes the ball swings and sometimes it doesn't. There are just pop-science theories that don't really have anything to back them up. Cloud cover, damp air, moist soil or any other variant of atmospheric conditions have been cited as swing-assisting factors, but the truth is it remains as big a mystery as the whereabouts of Lord Lucan or the length of Jade Dernbach's international career. Whatever the cause of it, the ball swung for England that day and it won them the game.

Whether the conditions were the reason for England's efforts with the ball or not, the win against Pakistan was enough to keep their hopes of progressing alive. England had made it three wins from three, and now needed only to defeat India or Australia to make it out of the group stage. India and Australia, though, were the two strongest teams in the group. They were the two teams that would go on to contest the final. The decision to not even contest the points on offer in Zimbabwe was still looking like keeping England out of the next phase.

The game against India was another day/night match and when Sourav Ganguly won the toss he had no hesitation in batting first. India got off to an absolute flier with Virender Sehwag and Sachin Tendulkar both brutal on England's opening bowlers. In the fixture against Pakistan both Caddick and Anderson had conceded less than two an over, but here they both conceded more than a run a ball. Tendulkar looked at his sublime best, with his most impressive shot coming off Caddick. A short-pitched ball outside off stump was seized upon and hit out of the ground over midwicket. With England having to bat under lights it looked as if India were set for a total in excess of 300.

It was Flintoff who restored some order, producing the sort of spell that would become his hallmark over the years to come. Bowling quick and getting the ball to rear up on the Indian batsmen, he dismissed both openers and conceded just 15 runs from his ten overs. It was thanks to him that England's eventual target was 250 rather than 300. They had a chance if they could find a way to counter any swing that the Indian seamers produced under the dark evening skies. The difference between Flintoff at this World Cup and the peripheral moping figure he cast in the 1999 World Cup was stark. This was the beginning of Andrew Flintoff's transformation into "Freddie".

The swing under the floodlights meant England were always up against it, but before they had a chance to see whether the ball was moving in the air they were in trouble. Knight clipped the ball into the covers and set off for a single that was at best ambitious. Mohammad Kaif swooped on the ball and threw down the stumps while diving forward. There had long been accusations of Indian teams being poor in the field but the one at the 2003 World Cup was the first that looked like a serious fielding unit.

In a torturous innings from Trescothick as he tried to counter the swinging ball, because of course it swung considerably, he made eight runs in 38 deliveries before Zaheer Khan claimed his wicket. England had reached 18-2 off seven overs, and from that point onwards it was the Ashish Nehra show. Nehra had been in and out of the India side in the four years since he made his Test debut with poor form and injuries both limiting his opportunities.

His performance against England was nothing short of a masterclass. He bowled ten overs unchanged in a spell that was full of pace, swing and control. At no point did any England player get on top of him and by the time he had finished, the game was over as a contest. He finished with 6-23. He bowled 47 dot balls and conceded only two boundaries as he returned the best ever figures by an Indian bowler at a World Cup. Of his six wickets, only Alec Stewart was dismissed in front of the wicket as the ball swung often and swung late.

Ganguly was quick to point out that not only had his bowler battled England, he had also battled injury. "He's had a swollen ankle for two days and it was sheer determination that made him play. He bowled a fantastic line. It's one of the best performances in a one-day international that I have seen since I started playing for India," Ganguly said after the match.

So England needed to win against Australia in their final group match to guarantee a chance of qualifying. If Pakistan beat Zimbabwe convincingly in their last group game there was a chance England could make it through by virtue of a superior net run-rate. However, if England wanted to keep their fate in their own hands they needed to beat Australia.

※ ※ ※

"I always look back at that game against Australia in Port Elizabeth," Hussain told us some 13 years later. "There are only two games I think about when I'm on the treadmill and think about how should I have done something different. The first is the NatWest series final against India in 2002 and the second is the game where we lost to Australia in the 2003 World Cup.

"That was a game that we were in a very good position and if you end up beating Australia then you take points through to the Super Six. It's not only a game we should have won, but a vital game that would have put us in a very good position."

It was yet another game this good England side should have won, looked set to win, and then managed to lose.

Having won the toss and decided to bat first, England got off to an excellent start thanks to an opening stand of 66 between Knight and Trescothick in just nine overs. They were looking good for setting a competitive total.

That was until Andy Bichel came on to bowl, collecting the wicket of Knight in his first over with a ball that swung away. Knight chased it and hit the ball straight to Damien Martyn in the slip cordon. For all of the superstars that were in this Australian side it was one of the least heralded who claimed the first wicket, and he wasn't done there.

It is important to remember just how good this Australia side was. Between their win at the 1999 World Cup and their eventual victory in the 2003 event they played 76 ODIs and lost just 19 of them. They had some of the best ODI players of all time. A top order of Adam Gilchrist, Matthew Hayden, Ricky Ponting, Damien Martyn, Darren Lehmann, Michael Bevan and Andrew Symonds was frighteningly impressive. Combine that with the pace of Brett Lee, the unerring accuracy of Glenn McGrath and the spin of Shane Warne, and you end up with as powerful a team as ever took the field in one-day cricket.

For this tournament, though, Australia were without Shane Warne. On the eve of Australia's first fixture, Warne received a call from the Australian Sports Drugs Agency to inform him that he had tested positive for a banned diuretic called Moduretic. It is commonly used to help people lose weight, and that was the reason Warne gave for taking it. It is banned because it can be used as a masking agent for other more nefarious drugs. Warne had already announced that the 2003 World Cup would be his last hurrah in one-day internationals. The positive test meant his

ODI career for Australia was over. He never played for his country in white-ball cricket again.

Warne's replacement was Brad Hogg who did a fine job at the World Cup, claiming 13 wickets at an average of 24 and he added to an already excellent team. It says a great deal about the quality of this Australian squad that they didn't miss Warne. The greatest leg-spin bowler of all time went home and they just shook it off.

In the Port Elizabeth match that England had to win, it wasn't one of those all-time greats who won the game for Australia. It was Andy Bichel. While a fine cricketer, he was not in the class of those around him. Eleven months after this performance against England he was out of the Australian side and would never get back in it.

Having claimed the wicket of Knight in his first over, Bichel was even more impressive in his second. With the first ball of the 12th over he induced Michael Vaughan to edge the ball behind. With the last ball of that over he picked up his third wicket when he bowled Hussain with a ball that the former England captain describes as "the ball of the century". It pitched on leg stump, seamed and swung away and clipped the top of off stump. There was nothing any batsman could have done about it. It was literally perfect.

England had gone from 66-0 after nine overs to 74-3 after 12. Things got worse when McGrath got Trescothick, and sunk further still when Bichel claimed his fourth wicket to leave England 87-5. They had lost five wickets for 22 runs as Bichel bowled a six-over spell of 4-12.

While Bichel bowled brilliantly, this was a tricky pitch. It had excellent pace and carry and the ball swung throughout. Alec Stewart and Andrew Flintoff did well to put together a partnership that allowed England to post a score in excess of 200. Stewart was batting at five and playing in what would be his last ODI. He was at that point England's most capped player in the format as well as his country's leading run-scorer. He had played in the 1992, 1996, 1999 and 2003 World Cups. His experience told as he put together a watchful innings of 46 from 92 balls. It wasn't particularly attractive, there was only one boundary, but it was mightily effective and he did a brilliant job of reining in the more outlandish instincts of his partner. Flintoff made 45 as the two men compiled a partnership of 90 that rescued the side from being bowled out inside their 50 overs.

Bichel still had more to say. He returned to the attack to dismiss both Flintoff and Stewart in quick succession as he finished with extraordinary figures of 7-20. England had posted 204-8, more than looked likely after Bichel's opening burst but nowhere near enough to feel comfortable defending against this stellar Australian batting line-up. If Australia had decided to bowl Bichel out, as the Indians had done with Nehra in the previous game, things could have been different.

While England had got off to a great start with the bat, the Australians did the exact opposite. Caddick was brilliant on this troublesome surface, dismissing the vaunted Australian top four in a spell of five overs where he conceded just 19 runs. At the end of the tenth over Australia were 48-4 and England were in complete control.

Darren Lehmann and Michael Bevan put together a steadying partnership of 63 that took Australia to 111-4, but England then produced another seemingly decisive burst of four wickets to leave Australia 135-8, still 74 runs short of victory and needing more than a run a ball. England had the game won. They were going to beat Australia and progress to the Super Sixes.

Then that man Bichel arrived at the crease and England somehow managed to lose. And they really, really shouldn't have lost.

"No question we should have won that game and it underpinned a lot of the problems that we had for a lot of the times that I played," says Knight. "That we didn't genuinely know enough about how to win games of cricket. And that was a game that we should have won, that we should have closed out, and we didn't always know how to do that I don't think. And that was a classic example of getting ourselves in a winning position and not winning the game and that caused us endless problems during the time that I played one-day cricket."

Bevan was the master of the ODI chase. There has never been a player better at judging exactly this kind of situation, but still England should never have lost that game from there. Bichel started going after the England bowlers, and why not, he had nothing to lose. And as he made his way to 34 off 36 balls England completely lost their way. Much is made of a team seizing up in tight spots, the clichéd 'choke' where a team lets a game go because they don't know how to finish it off, and from the outside looking in, that was exactly what it seemed to be.

As much as Hussain says he never felt the game was won even when the eighth wicket fell, it surely was.

"I remember having them 100 odd for eight and Ashley Giles bowling well," he says. "I probably should have said to him 'maybe come round to Andy Bichel'. I knew Bichel was a fantastic number 10 and obviously you had the greatest finisher in world cricket at the other end in Michael Bevan so we never thought we had won the game at any stage.

"I always felt that Jimmy Anderson, even at that stage as an unknown quantity, would handle pressure better than Andy Caddick at the end of that. Andy I didn't feel was the best death bowler, he bowled a length that might get smacked. So I went with my gut feeling and went with Jimmy. And Bichel smacked Jimmy straight into the scoreboard for six, his slower ball that had deceived everyone else for the last couple of months got picked and smacked for six and then Bevan took them over the line. Fair play to them, they played brilliantly, but we had our opportunities to win."

England lost the game with two balls to go but could still theoretically make it through to the Super Sixes. They needed Pakistan to beat Zimbabwe by a small enough margin that England remained ahead on net run-rate. It was the most likely result. Instead it rained in Bulawayo and the game was abandoned, one of only two No Results out of 54 games in that World Cup. It was desperately unlucky, but England had brought the chances of bad luck into play by not winning games they should have won and not travelling to Zimbabwe. They only had themselves to blame.

※ ※ ※

The ODI side of this era was a perfect example of a team becoming less than the sum of its parts. There were some really good players who could not find a way to win as a team, and that was in spite of a coach who had more of a white-ball focus and central contracts. The primary focus was still on Test cricket, as Duncan Fletcher was pointing out as far back as 2001.

The Ashes immediately before the World Cup didn't help, just as it wouldn't four years later, or four years after that, but England had still not created an environment where they could back themselves to win close games. It wasn't that Hussain and Fletcher weren't trying to create that spirit; both are as responsible as anyone for the great strides England made from 2000 onwards. They lost the Ashes at home in 2001 but in the ten years between 2002 and 2012 England lost just three Test series on home soil, and none of those losses were to Australia. In Test cricket, the Hussain/Fletcher partnership was the beginning of one of the longest periods of sustained success that the England side have ever had. They won the Ashes home and away, beat India home and away and became world number one in that format. That road began with Hussain and Fletcher.

The 2003 World Cup was the beginning of the end for Hussain. He never played another ODI and gave up the Test captaincy that summer. He carried on playing Tests for England until the start of the 2004 season when, after scoring a match-winning hundred against New Zealand at Lord's in the first Test of the summer, he immediately announced his retirement from all cricket. Even at the end of his career Hussain was making a statement.

The cricket that England played at the 2003 World Cup was patchy, the results for the most part poor, but Hussain emerged from it with a huge amount of credit. And he will never ever stop thinking about losing that game to Andy Bichel.

2007 World Cup

Caribbean go-slow

ENGLAND had a chance. Somehow they had a chance. They didn't particularly deserve it. They had beaten only Canada, Kenya, Ireland and Bangladesh to reach this point. They had lost to New Zealand, Australia and Sri Lanka.

But still they had a chance. Win one match, avoid absolute disaster in the next against the West Indies, and they're in the semi-finals of the World Cup. Beating a fine South Africa side was far from straightforward, but it was definitely a chance. Bangladesh had managed it ten days earlier.

And for all their problems, this England team had happy recent memories of grasping just such a barely-deserved opportunity. Only two months earlier, England had somehow contrived to win the Commonwealth Bank Series in Australia, losing five of their first six matches to the hosts and New Zealand before, incredibly, winning four in a row to complete an absolute mugging.

For all their travails on and off the field in the Caribbean up to now, here was another chance to snatch that which they did not deserve.

England lost the toss at Bridgetown and were inserted. Ian Bell played out a maiden from Shaun Pollock. Michael Vaughan played out a maiden from Charl Langeveldt. England's approach to the PowerPlay overs at the start of the innings had often been idiosyncratic; now it was almost sarcastic as Vaughan and Bell left ball after ball outside off stump. Occasionally, for a change of pace, there would be a solid push to one of the many fielders inside the circle – a field setting begun out of necessity due to the fielding restrictions, but quickly one surely of choice given the total lack of punches being thrown by England's batsmen.

They had blown it. Inside the first ten overs of the match, England had already blown it. Another World Cup campaign would end in disappointment and recrimination. Defeat to a South African side containing Smith, Gibbs, de Villiers, Kallis, Boucher and Pollock would have been disappointing, but understandable. But this was not just defeat, it was surrender. England not only failed to compete, they appeared resigned from the first ball to the fact they were entirely incapable of doing so.

After ten overs at the start of their innings, England had managed just 28-1. And they'd had to get a wriggle on to reach that point; for the first six overs England struggled to maintain a rate of even one run an over. It took 14 balls for the first runs to be scored as Vaughan and Bell took "watchful" to new heights of absurdity against the moving ball.

And this in a tournament where eventual winners Australia scored over 300 every time they batted first until a rain-reduced final where they mustered a mere 281 from 38 overs. England's plan wasn't just out of keeping with the one-day strategy of the successful sides; it barely qualified as the same sport.

While it would be fair to say that neither Vaughan nor Bell ever showed the same affinity for one-day cricket as Test cricket, neither could they be described as dour blockers. Both were stroke-makers of rare elegance and talent. Bell, while never truly mastering the format, would go on to become England's all-time leading run scorer in ODI cricket.

But on that day, they were paralysed. Whether it was fear, or confused thinking, or just a really terrible plan, they epitomised a team now devoid of hope. Even in the wake of a 5-0 Ashes defeat they had been able to foster enough devil-may-care spirit to perform their CB Series heist. That spirit was now long gone.

The plan, such as it was, had presumably been to lay a solid foundation and attack later. Inevitably, England's go-slow did the opposite, the walls tumbling down as the middle order tried to make up for lost time, chucking away their wickets trying in vain to repair the self-inflicted damage of the early overs. England were eventually all out for 154 in the 48th over. Andrew Hall bustled his way to scarcely-believable figures of 5-18 from his ten overs of industrious seam and swing bowling.

South Africa chased down their meagre target for the loss of one wicket in 19.2 overs, Smith furiously thrashing his way to 89 not out from just 58 balls as if on a successful, yet surely gratuitous, one-man mission to expose the flaws in his opponents' earlier approach. England were booed off the field and out of a World Cup they had barely appeared to be in.

There was still time for one last trick, a Kevin Pietersen-inspired chase of 300 to beat the West Indies in the final game of the Super Eight stage. Taken in isolation, it was perhaps the best game of a tournament blighted by one-sided games (six would be won by margins of over 200 runs, three of them by the champions Australia). Yet with the four semi-finalists already confirmed, and England and West Indies not among them, it mattered little in the grander scheme. It did, though, mean England finished fifth in the Super Eight table. This, therefore, was and remains technically their most successful World Cup campaign since 1992. What's the old saying about lies, damned lies, and flattering World Cup Super Eight finishing positions? Inevitably, England's nosebleed-inducing finish so high in the table owed much to the even greater failures of others.

% *%* *%*

The 2007 World Cup was a disaster, and not just for England.

Above everything else, the tournament was struck by genuine tragedy, when Pakistan's coach Bob Woolmer was found dead in his Jamaica hotel room the day after the team's shock defeat to Ireland. Woolmer was well-respected and had previously coached in South Africa and England. His death affected many of the sides still in the tournament, and cast a pall over proceedings.

A distasteful soap opera of whispers and speculation continued for months, with the Jamaican police hardly helping matters by insisting early on that he had died as a result of "manual strangulation" and opening a murder investigation. It would be almost three months after his death, and after countless unfounded rumours and hearsay about links to match-fixing or how he had been killed with poison or snake venom or weedkiller, before it was confirmed that Woolmer had died of natural causes. By then his death and the grubbiness that followed had long since overshadowed a joyless World Cup.

On the field, perhaps the most significant development beyond Australia's cold, remorseless excellence, and one whose ripples are still being felt, was Ireland and Bangladesh failing to play up (or perhaps rather play down) to their appointed roles as colourful and briefly exciting "minnows", to be patronised and patted on the head but then swiftly clear off and leave the biggest eight teams to contest the business end of the tournament. There was a whole stage of the tournament specifically designed to include the eight biggest cricketing nations, as the Super Six stage of the last two World Cups expanded in size. Expanding in size and being only for the biggest teams being, of course, very much a theme of recent World Cup history.

But Bangladesh toppled India, Ireland eliminated Pakistan, and the best-laid plans of organisers, teams and supporters were scuppered.

Clearly, an error had been made. The World Cup format was dangerously vulnerable to precisely the sort of unpredictability and unexpected result that is literally the thing that lifts sport above other pursuits but which cricket does its best to engineer out of its big events. Ireland's reward for their insurrection and cheek was to set off a chain of events making it far harder for them or anyone else to ever do anything so thrillingly unlikely or financially damaging again.

Because above all else – fairness, excitement, tension, drama – the World Cup needs India and Pakistan. Specifically, it needs India v Pakistan. Not just as a sporting contest, but as a money-maker. Cricket makes its money from TV deals, and the biggest show in TV town is India v Pakistan. In 2007, India v Pakistan became Bangladesh v Ireland.

Months of planning in Barbados had gone to waste, fevered anticipation came to nought. Thousands of Indians and Pakistanis from the expatriate communities of the United States and Canada were expected to descend on the island for the game. The idea that either India or Pakistan might not make it through had apparently not been considered. Bangladesh v Ireland was not quite the same draw. Over 5,000 had been expected to attend; fewer than 800 made the trip. Hotels were left with empty rooms and cancellations, while local residents expecting to lease out rooms in their houses were also out of luck. According to *Wisden*, even Brian Lara was affected. His recently-acquired 18-acre plantation house had been leased to sponsors for functions that were all cancelled after India's early exit.

The format of the 2007 World Cup would never be repeated. Not because it was as unwieldy and overlong as South Africa 2003, but because it carried with it the genuine risk that a big team, even – heaven forbid – India, could be eliminated after just three matches.

The total fixtures in 2007 had been trimmed slightly to 51. Far from ideal, but as TV-friendly World Cup schedules go it actually had plenty going for it.

Four groups of four meant a record 16 teams were involved despite the reduction in total games. Everyone got three games to try and extend their stay at the tournament – a perfectly fair amount and one that raises no eyebrows at football's global gathering.

In theory, the seeding would result in the big teams beating the small teams so that in the expanded Super Eight the ICC would have all their big fish – the ten Full Members minus Bangladesh and Zimbabwe – in the main body of the tournament for a league round-robin reminiscent of the 1992 event. Any points from the group stage game against a fellow qualifier would be carried through to the next stage, meaning the game between the big two in each group still mattered.

If only all the associates and minor Full Members had behaved like Bermuda – thrashed in all their games while providing a highlight-reel moment when a fat man took a slow-motion diving catch – then all would have been well. The ICC and TV companies would have had the tournament they wanted, and we would not in all likelihood have a ten-team World Cup now.

The ICC had taken a risk by creating the possibility – however remote – that one of the big teams could be eliminated so early in the event. They have made sure never to repeat that mistake. The sport and tournament are poorer for it, in every sense other than financial. Not that *Wisden* editor Matthew Engel agreed. Writing in the 2007 Almanack he attacked the move to expand the game:

"The ballooning of the World Cup derives from one fact alone: the delusion of expansion. From well-intentioned beginnings, this has now become an outright menace. The error is right up there at the start of the ICC's mission statement. It will lead, it says, 'by promoting the game as a global sport'. It should change its mission statement."

It is rare that the great cricketing publication has got a sentiment so wrong.

The format, though, was just about the best part of a World Cup won at a canter by an embarrassingly dominant Australia, who won all 11 of their games across seven weeks when they were rarely placed under any meaningful pressure.

The organisation, meanwhile, was a shambles. The shiny new venues were barely finished on time, were often inaccessible and appeared to have been specifically designed to strip away all the joy and atmosphere synonymous with Caribbean cricket by ensuring nobody who might create any of that joy and atmosphere could get into the grounds. Frequently the camera would pan away from a game in progress and show the hardy spectators who had made the trip schlepping across the dirt from some faraway car park.

Had the World Cup committee tried to organise a piss-up in a brewery, they would have started by throwing out all that booze that was clogging up the place. Especially if that booze was not manufactured by an official piss-up sponsor.

But the organisers could not be blamed for all the tournament's problems. While they shouldn't have assumed the big teams would all qualify, they could reasonably have expected India and Pakistan to perform better. And it was hardly the organisers' fault that no team was able to live with Australia, who repeated their 2003 trick of winning every game. But in that tournament, Australia had at least been made to work for it a couple of times, notably against England and New Zealand.

Here, nobody laid a glove on Ricky Ponting's all-conquering Aussie machine. Four of the tournament's top ten batsmen, and four of its top seven wicket-takers, were Australian.

The only significant opposition Australia met came in the final, in part from opponents Sri Lanka but more significantly from atypical Barbados weather and the officials' failure to follow the rules correctly.

A wildly optimistic recalculation after three hours were lost to morning rain meant only 24 overs were initially cut from the game. The rescheduled finishing time for the 38-overs-a-side match was 5.45pm, when sunset was 6.12pm. At a ground with no floodlights. Adam Gilchrist made a scintillating 149 off just 104 balls as Australia racked up 281-4.

It was in Sri Lanka's innings that things really went wrong. They had reached 149-3 off 24.5 overs when further rain removed two more overs from the game and reduced their target to 269 off 36.

It was already clear these overs would not be completed. When play resumed, Sri Lanka had only one choice, and that was to try and get up to the Duckworth-Lewis par score for each over. But they were always behind.

With Sri Lanka having completed 20 overs of their innings, the match was official. If play was abandoned, the result would stand. Yet the umpires and match referee Jeff Crowe, all hugely experienced ICC officials, remained inexplicably insistent that all 36 overs of Sri Lanka's innings had to be bowled before the result was confirmed.

When the bad light closed in and halted play after 33 overs of Sri Lanka's game attempt to overhaul the daunting Australian total, the big screen declared Ponting's men the winners by 38 runs. When told by Aleem Dar that the players would have to return the next day to bowl the remaining three overs, Ponting assumed it was a joke.

It was not. Eventually, the three overs were sent down in the dark by spinners as both teams agreed to just get the game finished to the umpires' mistaken satisfaction.

The closing ceremony, which cost the Barbados taxpayer $750,000, was lost to the darkness.

When ICC boss Malcolm Speed appeared the following day to apologise for the farcical conclusion, a heavily-branded advertising hoarding fell over, hitting him on the shoulder. "A fitting end to the tournament from hell," was the Australian's deadpan response.

Of all the World Cups, 2007 probably boasts the closest synergy between England's efforts and the overall event. Badly organised, poorly planned and littered with embarrassing mistakes until the very end. The 2007 World Cup was a seven-week England batting PowerPlay.

※ ※ ※

England's preparation for the 2007 disaster began, as these things always do, in the wake of the previous World Cup's failings.

Nasser Hussain stood down as one-day captain to be replaced by Michael Vaughan. While Vaughan had yet to really establish himself in the one-day team, he was an obvious choice. He had already been identified as Hussain's likely successor and there were few doubts about his long-term one-day credentials after a winter spent smashing one of the all-time great bowling attacks all around Australia and rising to the top of the Test batting rankings despite England's customary Ashes defeat.

Things started well. Duncan Fletcher wanted England to play more one-day cricket, and in 2003 that meant an addition to the schedule. There would be a standalone three-match NatWest Challenge ODI series against Pakistan, followed immediately by the bigger, three-way NatWest Series against that summer's touring Test sides, Zimbabwe and South Africa. England won both.

England and Vaughan were perhaps fortunate to be playing sides emerging from their own post-World

Cup recriminations and embarking on rebuilding work. Both Pakistan and South Africa had suffered early exits at the 2003 World Cup, while Zimbabwe were significantly weakened by the retirements of Henry Olonga and particularly Andy Flower. Pakistan jettisoned eight players between the World Cup and the tour of England, while South Africa were also starting afresh under a young, new captain in Graeme Smith.

Pakistan's tour was a brief affair, all over in a fortnight. A handful of warm-up games were followed by three ODIs. England won 2-1 thanks chiefly to the batting of Marcus Trescothick and the bowling of their new poster boy James Anderson.

The NatWest Series that followed was arguably more impressive still. England and South Africa made the final as expected. Less expected was the ease with which England would win it, Anderson and Darren Gough leading the destruction as South Africa were routed for just 107. England knocked the runs off in a little more than 20 overs as the match barely reached half distance.

Vaughan's contributions with the bat remained short of his Test returns, but his captaincy was an instant hit. Vaughan won his first two campaigns as ODI skipper "while barely raising his voice once", noted *Wisden*, which even at this early stage was noticing "helpful implications in the long run-up to the 2007 World Cup" for this exciting new-look team.

This carefree, youthful exuberance would have significant implications later in the summer. When Nasser Hussain returned to lead the Test side against South Africa, he sensed a change had occurred in his absence during the two one-day series. This was Vaughan's team now.

Although England held on to draw the first Test on the back foot at Edgbaston, Hussain revealed he had made the decision to stand down as early as day one. As Graeme Smith and Herschelle Gibbs pummelled the England bowling, Hussain felt he "wasn't quite the captain England needed or wanted".

"I feel it's coming to a change of era in the England cricket team and I feel that Michael Vaughan has shown over the past few months he's a very capable leader and that's what I've been waiting for, for someone to hold their hand up," an emotional Hussain said after announcing his decision.

The next summer, at a time when Vaughan's Test team were sweeping all before them on the foothills of their ascent to glory in the 2005 Ashes, much of the early optimism around the one-day team had dissipated. England won every Test that summer against West Indies and New Zealand, but failed to reach the final of the Tri-Nation NatWest Series involving the pair. India were beaten 2-1 in a NatWest Challenge series, though.

One-day cricket wasn't quite finished there for 2004, the summer ending with the Champions Trophy on home soil.

The tournament was held in September, literally and figuratively an afterthought to the English summer. It was poorly organised, sparsely attended and largely unnoticed by the wider sporting world. It was, as Matthew Engel put it in his *Wisden* editor's notes, "a terrible idea from the start, a turkey of a tournament".

But it was, undoubtedly, a chance for Michael Vaughan's young side to make some noise against the best the world had to offer. And for so long, it looked like England's long wait for a global ODI title was finally over.

They had comfortably the leading run-scorer in the short tournament – Marcus Trescothick – as well as the two leading wicket-takers in Andrew Flintoff and Steve Harmison.

England made short work of Zimbabwe and Sri Lanka to top Pool D in the 12-team, four-group event and reach the semi-final.

There they would have perhaps their finest limited-overs moment under Vaughan's leadership. On 21 September 2004, England won a one-day international against Australia for the first time since 17 January 1999, a sequence of 14 matches. Since England had last beaten them, Australia had won two World Cups. But all bad things must come to an end, and England ended the hoodoo in style.

By this time, Vaughan's continued and conspicuous failure to translate his Test success into one-day runs was starting to attract some unwanted attention. His record really was astonishingly modest; heading into the semi-final against Australia, Vaughan had passed 50 only eight times in 54 ODIs and boasted an average of just 23.64. He had made just 17 and five batting at number three in the victories over Zimbabwe and Sri Lanka. England had just shorn themselves of one ODI captain who had doubts over whether he merited a place in the side, and they appeared to have replaced him with another.

The semi-final was more than just a victory for his team; it was a personal triumph for Vaughan. On a slow pitch and bitterly cold day – only 8,700 people turned up to watch at Edgbaston – he bowled his full allocation of ten overs. This was unusual for him, but canny. There was little reward for quick bowlers, and Vaughan bagged the crucial middle-order wickets of Damien Martyn and Darren Lehmann at a cost of just 40 runs.

Still, though, England needed to score 260 runs and shake off five years' worth of baggage in order to win. Vaughan made 86 before England's breakout star of the summer Andrew Strauss applied the finishing touches with an unbeaten 52 off 40 balls to win the match with more than three overs to spare.

Pakistan's batting crumbled in the second semi-final, leaving England needing only to beat West Indies to claim the title. It may have been a slapdash and unloved tournament, but as a "mini World Cup" it still carried some legitimacy. For a start, it featured two more nations than will contest the 2019 and 2023 World Cups.

On a tired, bowler-friendly Oval pitch, England scrambled to 217 all out on the back of Trescothick's eighth ODI century. It looked enough when Harmison and Flintoff set about the West Indies top order. When Shivnarine Chanderpaul's resistance was ended on 47 by Paul Collingwood, West Indies were 147-8 and the game appeared done. England wouldn't make a mess of it this time.

But the asking rate was still only around 4.5 an over. Courtney Browne and Ian Bradshaw had time to play themselves in, and they did so. Vaughan was left with a decision to make. He went to his strike bowlers, Flintoff and Harmison, in faltering light. But Browne and Bradshaw first survived and eventually flourished.

Vaughan found he had no more bullets to fire. With his main bowlers bowled out, he continued to back seam over spin – Ashley Giles didn't bowl a ball – and the Barbados pair gave a forgettable tournament an unforgettable conclusion. As the light closed in, Bradshaw struck the winning boundary off Alex Wharf to spark wild celebrations.

A decade later, Vaughan – discussing one-day cricket on *Test Match Special* – succinctly if rather harshly summed up England's tournament: "We got to a Champions Trophy [final] in 2004 and we were rubbish. We just happened to get to a final in English conditions."

England still await that first global ODI title. As for Vaughan's side, before 2004 was out a team including Kevin Pietersen for the first time would travel to Zimbabwe and thrash them 4-0 in an ODI series the board had agreed to in order to ensure Zimbabwe's controversial 2003 tour of England went ahead. England would then not win another ODI series home or away until their smash-and-grab raid in the Commonwealth Bank Series on the eve of the 2007 World Cup.

%% %% %%

That CB Series on the back of a harrowing annihilation in the Ashes would represent the end of England's latest four-year cycle of preparing for the next World Cup. Four years of careful preparation and meticulous planning to ensure they arrived at the World Cup in the best possible condition to try and win the trophy. Four years spent perfecting game plans, defining players' specific roles within the team, making sure everyone knew exactly what was required of them.

Which is why four England players made their ODI debuts in the CB Series. One of those four, Mal Loye, played seven games at the top of the order in the series and was never seen in England colours again.

While hardly given the best opportunity of success, Loye had struggled against the extra pace and accuracy of international bowlers. His selection appeared something of a desperate, last-minute move of the sort that has become England's trademark as World Cups approach.

Loye had enjoyed great success as an innovative and unorthodox opening batsman in county cricket. He was the leading run-scorer in the 2006 Cheltenham & Gloucester Trophy with 543 at an average of almost 68, and was one of only three players to score more than 200 runs at better than a run a ball in Division One of that season's Pro40.

Loye's main claim to fame, though, was his signature move of sweeping fast bowlers. His international career may have been brief and largely unsuccessful, but he still managed the unlikely feat of getting down on one knee and sweeping Brett Lee for six at the Gabba.

But a journeyman county player sweeping Brett Lee for six at the Gabba was only the second most unexpected thing to happen in the CB Series. The most unexpected thing that happened was that England won it. It remains one of the more inexplicable events in recent cricketing history given what both England and Australia had done in the months before it, and what they would do in the months that followed.

On the back of England's Ashes thrashing, things started as expected. England were dispatched by eight wickets in the opening game. Kevin Pietersen made 82, but was hit by a Glenn McGrath bouncer and suffered a broken rib that put him out of the rest of the series.

Wicketkeeper Paul Nixon was one of those to debut in the CB Series, and he recalls finding a tired and battered squad on his arrival in Australia. "A lot of them were very down, and disheartened and extremely frustrated. It's a tough place to be for a sportsman when you're being hammered by opposition that are consistently better than you. The players were tired. You don't realise it at the time, but I think when you look back you realise that you were a bit subdued. It's that conveyor belt – here we go again," Nixon says.

England did finally register their first international win of the tour against New Zealand in the next game, but that was to be their only win in the first six matches of the competition. England were bowled out for 155 and 110 by Australia either side of a 120 all out against the Kiwis.

After those first six matches for each side, the only good news for England was that New Zealand had also lost all three of their games against Australia. The upshot was that if England could somehow win their last two group games, they would be sure to advance to the final as long as New Zealand lost again to Australia.

And, almost miraculously, that is exactly what happened. An Ed Joyce hundred and three wickets for Liam Plunkett helped England to their first win over Australia of the tour, and a handsome 92-run win at that.

Michael Vaughan, by now back in the side after the knee injury that kept him out of the Ashes defeat, was dismissed first ball in what amounted to a semi-final against New Zealand, but a century from Paul Collingwood proved decisive in a 14-run win and, from nowhere, England found themselves in the final.

They had won only three of their eight group games. Australia had won seven of theirs. Yet it was England who prevailed twice more to take the best-of-three final with a game to spare. Collingwood was again the star, making another century in the first win and a crucial 70 in the second when rain interruptions also played into England's hands.

Vaughan had sat out the two finals as he continued to manage his return from injury, meaning Flintoff was once again at the helm to gain a modicum of revenge for the Ashes hammering. "The guys in the dressing room are cock-a-hoop," he said after the astonishing turnaround. "It's been a tough tour and we've stayed together throughout."

England, somehow, had stumbled into the World Cup on a winning note. Australia, meanwhile, subsequently lost the Chappell-Hadlee Series in New Zealand 3-0 to enter the World Cup on the back of six defeats in seven games.

The significance, or otherwise, of those results would be revealed in the Caribbean, and Andrew

Strauss remembers a squad still low on confidence heading into the World Cup despite their belated success in Australia.

"We had some pretty humiliating moments in that one-day series. The Australia Day game at Adelaide where it was finished before the floodlights went on was a particular low moment. We somehow miraculously came back to win that series but it was one of those very hollow victories where you thought we managed to win it but we aren't playing great. Australia were almost practising for the World Cup, and we just didn't know where we were."

The long CB Series – England and Australia played ten games each including the two finals – also added to the weariness of an England squad that had endured so much during that traumatic Ashes winter.

"We arrived at the World Cup knackered having been away from home for six months," says Strauss, "with no real clarity on our game plan. It just felt that we were hoping that we might win some games but there was no sort of expectation that we were going to do particularly well."

Kevin Pietersen describes the 2007 World Cup as "sort of a holiday" for a group of players "mentally hammered" after three months in Australia. "We'd had our arses whipped for three months and confidence was at an all-time low. So we didn't expect much and I suppose we didn't deliver as much as we should have. But playing in a World Cup after an Ashes would never help the England team."

It was against this backdrop that the World Cup campaign would begin with another damaging defeat.

England's first game was also their most important of the first group stage, against New Zealand.

England's latest shuffle at the top of the order had left Ed Joyce and Vaughan in position when the music stopped, with Ian Bell at three. Where other teams looked to attack the PowerPlay, England looked for a solid start. They could not even manage that. Joyce fell for nought, Bell for a ponderous five, and Vaughan for 26 off 52 balls. Pietersen ground out a half-century, and it needed an unbroken eighth-wicket partnership of 71 between Nixon and Liam Plunkett to get beyond 200.

Although New Zealand lost three early wickets in reply, they eased to a six-wicket victory thanks to half-centuries from Scott Styris and Jacob Oram.

It was a poor performance and disappointing result for England, but not terminal. The group draw had been kind, with only Canada and Kenya – who had fallen dramatically from their 2003 peak – standing between them and the Super Eight. No Ireland or Bangladesh blocking England's path.

But even if England did progress, they would now carry no points through to the next stage having lost to Stephen Fleming's side.

The meekness of the display makes the disappointment in a squad that had seemingly at last thrown off the shackles in Australia a month earlier understandable.

What happened that night would cause far more damage than the New Zealand defeat, and come to define England's tournament.

Fredalo.

The details by now are well known. Flintoff had actually had a decent game against New Zealand. His eight overs had cost just 17 runs, and he'd held a fine catch at slip to dismiss Ross Taylor. In a fair world, it would be better remembered than Dwayne Leverock's effort for Bermuda. Yet it was a painful defeat, and a significant one.

Flintoff and five other England players went out after the New Zealand game. "One or two drinks turned into too many," says Nixon, one of Flintoff's companions that night. "You've got to celebrate success as a sporting team, but we'd got beat by New Zealand, Freddie probably wasn't in a great place mentally at the time being under the pump against the Aussies and his way out was having a few beers. Sadly it just got too many."

Flintoff, so the story goes, having stayed out late drinking with team-mates, attempted a seafaring expedition aboard a pedalo. He fell overboard and needed to be rescued before he did himself a mischief. He later insisted that he didn't actually fall off the pedalo, but had rather failed in an attempt to board it. Details.

How the story came to the public domain is slightly less clear. The *News of the World* broke the story from London. The official version is that England fans who saw the Fredalo incident contacted the paper, who then notified their reporter covering the tournament in the Caribbean, David Norrie.

Let us just say that it's certainly possible that a group of England fans emerging from a beach bar at three in the morning saw Flintoff's antics, thought the best thing to do was contact the *News of the World* from St Lucia, and then found the right phone number for the office in London and got through to the correct people.

There could be no defence of Flintoff's actions. England's next game may only have been against Canada – "a game we would win 99 times out of 100", according to Nixon – but it was still a must-win encounter after the New Zealand defeat and it was just two days away.

Flintoff had let himself and his team-mates down. And it was not the first time in that difficult winter. In his autobiography, *Behind the Shades*, coach Duncan Fletcher lifted the lid on an earlier indiscretion in Sydney that had almost cost Flintoff the captaincy.

"You just hope the players will not let you down. Sadly Flintoff did," wrote Fletcher. "We went to Sydney for a vital match against Australia and a fielding practice was arranged for 10am. Flintoff turned up still under the influence of alcohol. Flintoff was in such a state that he could not throw properly. He had to pass the ball to the bloke next to him to do so. And when it came to trying to catch the ball I honestly thought I was going to hurt him, so uncoordinated was he. I was fuming and stopped the practice early. Remember: this was the England captain in this state."

Only the desire to avoid further bad publicity during a nightmarish tour spared Flintoff instant punishment.

"My instinct was telling me I simply had to drop him as captain," Fletcher said. "But then again I was thinking about how much pressure I was under anyway, having already been targeted by the media. Imagine what they would do now if I demoted Flintoff, the national hero."

Flintoff escaped that time, but there could be no such allowances made now with the Fredalo story already out there. The decision was taken by Fletcher and Vaughan that Flintoff would be stripped of the vice-captaincy and suspended for the Canada match.

The other members of Flintoff's big night out – James Anderson, Liam Plunkett, Jon Lewis, Ian Bell and Nixon – were fined.

The management, in truth, had little choice. How could they do anything less? But the squad never really recovered. Care must be taken to avoid hagiography here – England had already turned in a painfully timid and fearful performance against New Zealand before the Fredalo incident. But it affected the mood in a squad where any confidence that might have built up by the end of the CB Series remained fragile.

Later that summer, Michael Vaughan pinpointed the Fredalo incident as key to England's poor World Cup campaign.

He told the *Guardian*: "We arrived at the World Cup in a positive frame of mind. We had great preparation in St Vincent but unfortunately incidents happened which affected the team. You have to be honest. The Fredalo incident did affect the team. It did affect morale. Those incidents are bound to affect team spirit.

"Suddenly you've got players who have no freedom left. I like to see players enjoy themselves but no one would dare go out after that incident – and you can't create any spirit then.

"That incident changed the whole atmosphere in the camp. We went into the New Zealand game with a really good attitude but we didn't play well and after Fredalo we just started taking it all too seriously. That might sound silly but everyone was too tense and desperate. There was no escape – and even on the field you have to be pretty free, especially in one-day cricket."

Vaughan later denied using the word Fredalo, prompting the *Guardian* to publish the audio of his quotes to confirm that he had used the term. But that was not the important word in that interview. The important words here are ones like spirit, freedom, attitude, tense and desperate.

Vaughan was not the only one to speak of Fredalo in such terms. The following year, Ian Bell – who made 211 runs in the tournament at an average of 26 and a strike-rate of barely 60 – may have deployed a 'Scottish Play' style avoidance of the word itself but said: "I'll never forget the way the St Lucia experience weighed me down and the massive impact it had on my cricket in those World Cup games. It took away the sense of freedom you need."

Thankfully for England, Canada and Kenya offered little resistance. While there was little really to be achieved in those games beyond avoiding utter humiliation, there was encouragement at least in a pair of half-centuries for Ed Joyce and runs for key men Collingwood and Pietersen, the latter showing no apparent lingering ill-effects from the broken rib that had cut short his tour of Australia. The victories were workmanlike rather than emphatic.

England carefully made their way to 272 batting first against Canada. Always a winning score against those opponents, but hardly laying down a marker. Against Kenya they took 33 overs knocking off 178, with only Collingwood's cameo of 18 not out made at better than a run a ball.

The bare minimum had been achieved. England had avoided the fate of India and Pakistan and made it through to the Super Eight stage even if Flintoff's seafaring had captured the imagination more than any of his or his team-mates' on-field efforts.

England's first Super Eight fixture was against Ireland, and allowed the team to record a third straight win since Fredalo. But again, the associate nation was hardly put to the sword by Vaughan's men.

Joyce and Vaughan both fell cheaply. In a neat statistical quirk, Joyce – playing against the country of his birth – was dismissed for one by Ireland's budding young quick Boyd Rankin. Six years later, Joyce would once more be dismissed for a single by Rankin in a one-day international. But by 2013, it was Joyce in the green of Ireland and Rankin in the blue and red of England.

Back to 2007, and another ponderous Bell innings was eventually put out of its misery on 31 from 74 balls as the O'Brien brothers, keeper Niall and all-rounder Kevin, combined.

It was left once again to first Pietersen and then Collingwood to inject some momentum into the innings. England finished on 266-7. Again it was to prove a safe winning score, Ireland eventually falling a never-threatening 48 runs short despite a fine half-century from Niall O'Brien.

England had three successive victories, but none of them entirely convincing and all of them against associates. England's top three was still made up of similar players: Joyce, Vaughan, Bell. It was all a bit samey, and a bit safe. And safe was becoming pretty dangerous as one-day cricket developed.

Nixon, despite his involvement in the Fredalo affair, had been a bright spot. Although another last-minute selection before the World Cup, he was experienced enough to cope with being thrust into international cricket and the glare of a global tournament.

In an England squad featuring plenty of Test players trying to be one-day players, Nixon was unusual. He 'got' one-day cricket. Leicestershire, one of the smaller counties on the English circuit had been a surprise hit in Twenty20 cricket, winning two of the four titles at that point. "I didn't know much about international cricket because I hadn't played it until then," Nixon says. "But I knew what worked well in Twenty20 cricket, I knew what tactics worked well, I knew what time management worked well, I knew ways of keeping the runs down. And there was a lot of things that could transfer to ODIs."

And Nixon knew something was not quite right in England's top three. Even now, Pietersen insists there was nothing England could have done differently with their batting. "I don't think we got it wrong. I think we played with the players that we had and you can't expect guys to go out and slog, you can't expect Strauss or whoever to go open the batting and smash a hundred off 80 balls when he's not that kind of player."

Nixon saw it differently. Nixon thought, why not change the type of player?

"If Kevin opens the batting, or bats in the top three… If he bats out a maiden in the first over, the next six balls he'll get three or four, the next six he'll get five or six, the next six, he'll get seven or eight, the next six he'll go up and up. It was about getting our best players up front, but on the slower pitches, we needed more hitters up front.

"There was only probably Barbados and St Lucia that were belting pitches, the rest of them you have to play the situation. And slow pitches, it's easy to score up front. I think we had to play an extra batsman, and go harder earlier on."

Up next was Sri Lanka. In a rarity – for the tournament as a whole, not just for England – it turned out to be something of a cracker.

With Anderson, Flintoff and Collingwood miserly and Sajid Mahmood taking four wickets, Sri Lanka were restricted to just 235, losing their final wicket to the last ball of their innings.

England's openers failed again. Bell and Pietersen steadied the ship with a watchful partnership of 90. But 101-2 became 133-6 as England's middle order capitulated. Bell, Pietersen, Flintoff, Collingwood. The experienced core of the batting, gone in a flash.

It was left to a pair of rookies at different ends of their career to salvage something for England. Nixon and Ravi Bopara almost pulled it off. They added 87 in 15.2 overs to bring the target within reach.

Nixon, who by his own admission had attempted to run before he could walk in the CB Series, was now using all his one-day nous to get England close, including one audacious reverse-sweep for six. "I made sure I got in. I gave myself a bit of a chance. I didn't just try and hit boundaries.

"I learned my lessons, play like I played for Leicestershire and Kent. My job was in the middle order as a striker to come in, get in, and hit boundaries and be a finisher."

When he fell England needed 16 more from seven balls. Bopara swiftly reduced that to 12 from six with a rasping square drive to end the over and Lasith Malinga's spell.

Bopara and Mahmood scrambled nine more from the first five balls of Dilhara Fernando's over. One ball left. Three to win. Bopara on strike. The delivery was on a good length, and Bopara swung his bat at it. The ball ran away to the third man boundary. "It's gone for four! Bopara!" exclaimed Ranjit Fernando on commentary. Indeed it had. But sadly for Ranjit, Bopara and England, via the off stump rather than the outside edge. Bopara was out for 52. Sri Lanka won by two runs.

Bopara was named man of the match, but it was Vaughan's post-match comments that caught the eye. "We recovered to 101-2 and that's a position you'd buy every game," he said. "If you can be 101-2 with 25 overs left you sometimes should be getting over 233. Today it wasn't to be."

England were still laying foundations while the rest were blasting away. And England were still failing to build anything meaningful on those painstakingly constructed foundations.

The game had been one of the best of the tournament, but an England win would really have shaken things up. There was already a feeling that a dominant Australia side, dragging Sri Lanka, New Zealand and South Africa behind them, were destined for the last four. England's chances of crashing the party had receded.

And they had Australia to deal with next. England finally made a change at the top of the order, but they were merely shuffling the deckchairs. Bell moved up to open, with Strauss in at number three.

The overall approach was much the same. While Strauss would, to his enormous credit, successfully adapt himself into a fine one-day player by the end of his career, he was not there yet. England had replaced one technically-correct and talented stroke-maker with another. They had added no muscle in their top order.

Nevertheless, things looked promising while Bell was compiling his most assured 77 runs of the campaign alongside Pietersen's century after Vaughan and Strauss had been blown away by the pace of Shaun Tait.

Then another collapse wrecked their hopes of stunning a team that was by now the overwhelming favourite for a third consecutive title.

164-2 in the 30th over – a much more viable platform than Vaughan's wished-for but rickety 101-2 off 25 – became 246 all out in the 50th.

Australia eased home by seven wickets with almost three overs to spare on the back of Ricky Ponting's 86. They never looked in serious trouble.

England were still just about in there fighting, though, and victory over Bangladesh set up that virtual quarter-final against South Africa. Win that, and they would pinch a semi-final spot as long as they avoided getting badly beaten in the final game against West Indies.

But they never gave themselves a chance.

Most frustratingly, the penny finally dropped for England in their final game of the tournament. The capitulation against the Proteas had confirmed the semi-final line-up, reducing the clash with West Indies to a play-off for fifth place. When the West Indies made 300 all out in 49.5 overs, the hopes of England's blockers and plodders looked remote.

But something clicked that day. Pietersen ended a decent personal tournament on a high note with a 91-ball century as England won a thrilling if inconsequential match by one wicket with one ball remaining, Paul Nixon and his 20-year-old Leicestershire team-mate Stuart Broad steering the team home after Pietersen departed with 32 still needed from 22 balls.

The real revelation, though, was Vaughan. Finally, here was the one-day batsman he was surely always born to be. The tension of the tournament, the on-field struggles and off-field controversies melted away. For the first time since Fredalo, perhaps for the first time in one-day internationals since the Champions Trophy of 2004, Vaughan was playing with freedom.

In a tournament where Australia had scored at 6.5 an over and the other three semi-finalists around one run per over less, England had scored their runs at 4.73. Australia hit 67 sixes in the Caribbean, and even West Indies managed 42. England cleared the ropes just 22 times.

Yet now, Vaughan took on the bowling with relish. Good-length balls were not carefully watched through to the keeper or pushed to fielders, but smacked to and over the fence. He reached 50 from 33 balls with five fours and two sixes, eventually slowing slightly before falling for 79 off 68.

Vaughan had finally cracked the one-day international code. He never played another.

Twenty20

The inventors playing catch-up

I T is Saturday, 1 November, 2008. The camera pans to a balcony. There sits the avuncular Texan, Sir Allen Stanford. He has a woman perched on his knee with two other ladies sitting beside him. There is smiling, but it all seems a bit awkward. Then it emerges that the women are the wives and girlfriends of the England cricket team who are in Antigua to play in a one-off game for $20million against the "Stanford Superstars". The British press, already unimpressed with the gaudy show that the Stanford event has become, jumps on this embarrassing scene. It is yet another example of the ECB having sold the soul of English cricket to this flamboyant American.

While the bouncing of Mrs Matt Prior on Stanford's knee was the only moment anyone seems to remember from the Stanford 20/20 for 20 event, there was a lot more going on. Stanford possessing an Access All Areas pass that allowed him entry to the dressing rooms was highlighted as an example of him making the event all about him. England grumbled that he was swanning around like he owned the place. England's problem was that he did. The English cricket press did not like this guy; his smarmy shtick was anathema to them. And even those not of a traditional mindset felt there was something not quite right. It all seemed a bit too good to be true.

The England team didn't seem to want to be there and massively underperformed. The Stanford side they were there to take on were very keen to get one over on opponents who appeared to be looking down their noses at the event. The Superstars dismantled England by ten wickets with 44 balls to spare in the big-money game. It was embarrassing for the English on and off the field, and you wondered how they had found themselves in this position.

The answer, as is so often the case with cricket in the 21st century, comes from India. The Board of Control for Cricket in India (BCCI) had created the money-making behemoth that was the Indian Premier League, masterminded by the divisive but brilliant Lalit Modi. England wanted no part of it. As it became increasingly apparent that the cash-rich and superstar-packed IPL would be a massive success, England realised they were losing ground. The BCCI, Cricket Australia and Cricket South Africa had created a T20 Champions League that had secured a $900million TV rights deal. England were allowed to send a side along, but they got no share of the profits. The T20 cash cow was being milked by someone else and the ECB couldn't let that continue.

Having decided not to deal with Modi and the IPL, the ECB needed to find a replacement and Stanford was the prime candidate. The Texan had already been running a T20 tournament in the West Indies since 2006. The second edition of the Stanford T20 was part of the official West Indies Cricket Board (WICB) calendar. He was very much part of the cricketing establishment by the time the ECB was looking for an alternative T20 revenue stream.

Stanford announced his arrival in the minds of English cricket fans in typically showbiz fashion. He landed a helicopter on the nursery ground at Lord's with a Perspex box stuffed full of $20million in cash. It later emerged that most of the money wasn't real, which would later prove a fitting allegory for the whole affair.

The ECB chairman, Giles Clarke, was there shaking Stanford's hand. It was both a clash of cultures and also a meeting of minds. The two men seemed to find working together very easy. Stanford and Clarke both wanted to further their own agendas, and they saw in each other the opportunity to do that.

The plan was for the England cricket team to travel to West Indies for a single match, with $1million for each member of the starting eleven at stake as prize money. The ECB, Stanford and WICB would share the profits that were generated. The original deal was for five such encounters on an annual basis. There were to be return fixtures during the English season when the West Indies would come and play T20 fixtures, although it was never confirmed if this would be the Superstars that belonged to Stanford or a West Indies side.

The Texan wanted to expand his Twenty20 reach and had already made the offer to the South African and Indian boards, both of whom had turned him down. They had the Champions League to look forward to. England, on the other hand, were desperate to find something that would allow them to keep pace. Almost everyone at the ECB, Giles Clarke included, had wanted to create an "English Premier League" but the counties would not go for that. The ECB wanting to modernise the game and the counties resisting it has been the running theme of English cricket since the ECB was created in 1997.

For all of Stanford's very obvious failings he was among the first to see the commercial potential for Twenty20 cricket and how that could be packaged with Caribbean culture as a hugely attractive proposition to broadcasters and sponsors. Before the IPL had combined cricket and showbusiness so successfully Stanford had already found a similar mix that was working.

Stanford was interviewed from his prison cell by the BBC's Dan Roan in early 2016 and, while his protestations of innocence in the face of overwhelming evidence against him generated headlines, the really interesting things he said were about his cricket tournament and his vision for it. He admitted that he was looking to exploit cricket for revenue generation, but that was because he saw how big T20 could be.

"I was trying to grow the Stanford brand globally," Stanford told Roan. "What nobody understood is that I anticipated this new generation of players that we were going to uncover. When we had our first cricket tournament, we broadcast that and I gave the TV rights away globally. We had over a billion people watch our matches and that was the island-versus-island competition."

In 2008, Stanford was quoted as saying he wanted to help bankroll an English version of the IPL as soon as the Indian league had commenced. He saw the potential of a "franchise" league in England earlier than almost anyone.

"The ECB, for my estimation, need to be the driver," Stanford said in April 2008. "The organisation here is better, the management is better, the structure is better. It's inevitable that the ECB will create a Twenty20 league, it's inevitable that it will involve the private sector and it's inevitable that the game will evolve."

It is yet to happen, but the ECB has been pushing for it ever since and the franchise model has been a huge success wherever it has been tried. Stanford "got it".

The Stanford Super Series tournament would see the winners of the English domestic T20 Cup taking on their West Indian counterpart for the grandly titled Trans-Atlantic Twenty20 Champions Cup and then his "Superstars" were to play England in the big-money affair.

In 2008, Trinidad & Tobago beat Middlesex Crusaders and the Superstars thrashed England. And that would be the first and last Stanford Super Series.

His arrest and subsequent imprisonment for 110 years for one of the biggest frauds in human history put an end to it.

%/ %/ %/

Even as that first tournament was taking place there were many asking serious questions of Stanford, his motivations and what he was getting out of the deal with the ECB. In fact, Andrew Miller was raising concerns as soon as that helicopter touched down at cricket HQ.

Writing for *ESPNcricinfo*, Miller said: "There is something undoubtedly awkward about all this, although it would be wrong to be out-and-out cynical. Money is something that English cricket desperately needs, both to promote the game domestically and to compete at boardroom level internationally, and let's not forget that, back in 2003, the entire English media (and I include myself) was wrong in its initial impression of the Twenty20 Cup. But in keeping with the Texan connection, there is more than just a hint of cowboy about the way in which the ECB has leapt into bed with the first and highest bidder."

By the time the event was taking place the view was even darker. Stephen Brenkley summed up the views of most when he wrote about the tournament before a ball had been bowled.

"Of all the short-form matches currently being organised the conclusion is easily reached that Stanford Superstars vs England is the most offensive. It has no context as a proper sporting competition; it is neither country versus country, club versus club or invitation XI versus invitation XI. It is a rococo hybrid. It has money but nothing else going for it."

It is easy to be down on cricket that is just a money-making venture, and it is vital to remember that no matter how romantic we want to be about the sport it has always been a way to generate income for someone, but the Stanford event was a gaudy mess. In attempting to avoid the grasp of the BCCI and Lalit Modi, the ECB had in fact helped create something that had less context and more unfettered commercialism than the IPL could ever have managed.

The context under which this event was created is important. English cricket was worried it would lose its best players, that it was being left behind. The arrival of the IPL led to an increase in England's central contracts as the authorities sought to ensure they hung on to their star names.

It may seem odd to us now, but there was a very real and very legitimate worry that England would be left out in the cold with its most important asset, its players, plying their trade elsewhere. Stanford was seen as a way to counter that.

The way the Stanford Super Series was run was of huge concern to the players and it did not take long for their misgivings to become public. Amongst those that made their worries known was Sean Morris, the then chief executive of the Professional Cricketers' Association (PCA).

"I've spoken to a number of the players and there are real and significant concerns about this whole thing. We had reservations from the beginning and everything we were worried about appears to be happening," he said.

Graeme Swann told *The Cricketer* that both captain and coach had made it very clear that they were not there for the money, they were there to play cricket.

"It was drummed in to us by Peter Moores and Kevin Pietersen that this game was not about the money. We were not allowed to say in the press that it was about the money. This was about a big match, a high-pressure game that would stand us in good stead moving forward. What a load of tosh! Of course it was about the money!"

The money was up for intense debate inside and outside the dressing room, as Swann explained in that interview.

"The way it was organised, all eleven players were going to get a million each, and the four players who didn't play shared a million," Swann said. "[Andrew] Flintoff decided it wasn't on, so called a meeting and informed us all that we would be voluntarily giving 100 grand of our winnings to a pot that would mean the four squad players getting a lot more money. Great, but I just think a lot of people assumed the money was in the bag: 'We'll walk this.' We'd lost it from the day before the game if you ask me."

The players never really went out of their way to meet Stanford, and Swann said the only time he came across him was when he "waltzed into our dressing room".

Swann told *The Cricketer* it was clear that Stanford's arrival inside that inner sanctum was a cause of discomfort. "Such was the way that the ECB kowtowed to him that you were told if he turns up, you have to let him in. I saw Peter Moores in the corner, biting his lip, thinking, 'What the fuck's going on? Get that clown out of here.'"

England lost the game and it was clear that they didn't really have any idea of how it should be played. There was an overwhelming sense of embarrassment from everyone involved. The only reason people continued watching was because of what Joseph Conrad described in *Heart of Darkness*.

"The fascination of the abomination – you know. Imagine the growing regrets, the longing to escape, the powerless disgust, the surrender, the hate."

Jonathan Agnew described the feeling of most fans when he spoke of the immediate aftermath of that defeat. "Because the game finished early I did a phone-in on Radio Five Live. It was the only time I remember England cricket supporters phoning up pleased that England had lost. It was a relentless barrage of calls, everyone glad."

When it emerged just months after the farcical events in Antigua that Stanford was in fact the perpetrator of one of the biggest frauds in history, no one seemed that surprised. He was accused and convicted of running a Ponzi scheme that left investors with a collective loss of around $7billion. It was reported that some of the West Indies players who had won a share of the $20million bounty had given that money to Stanford to invest. When his financial web of deceit collapsed, they were among the victims. Shivnarine Chanderpaul, Ramnaresh Sarwan, Kieron Pollard, Sylvester Joseph and Dave Mohammed all gave their massive prize to the Texan and all of them lost the lot.

Long before the details of Stanford's criminal activities emerged there were calls for heads to roll at the ECB. Rod Bransgrove, the chairman of Hampshire County Cricket Club, was suggesting Giles Clarke should lose his job as the man in charge of the ECB even before the details of Stanford's fraud had been exposed.

"I asked the ECB to do a lot more checking on Stanford and this competition. We made it very clear that we should not enter into this agreement without proper checks but he [Clarke] had already done the deal. The board should resign collectively," Bransgrove said in October 2008 before the $20million match had even taken place.

The press corps smelled a rat and the stench was pervasive. Stanford was taken to prison in June 2009, but it seems there were concerns about his business practices long before that. The *Guardian* reported in 2012 that US diplomats had warned government officials not to be photographed with Stanford three years prior to his arrest. The US government, therefore, was concerned enough about Stanford to issue warnings two years before he did his deal with the ECB. Despite that, the English cricketing authorities were happy to jump into bed with a man who looked shady, acted shady and was shady.

Of all the poor decisions English cricket administrators have been involved in there is none that should be more shaming than this whole sorry episode.

Twenty20 was created in England for the 2003 county season. Twenty-over cricket had long been the staple of midweek amateur leagues, but this was the first time it had been attempted as a professional enterprise. The change in the government's stance on cigarette sponsorship of sport had left the ECB in need of a replacement for the one-day Benson & Hedges Cup, and also looking for a way to bring crowds into the mostly empty grounds in the shires. There were no plans for a World Cup based on the format, no one expected there to be million-dollar contracts for playing 20-over cricket for six weeks. It was a marketing idea, and no one involved in it knew what it would become.

Stuart Robertson was the head of ECB marketing at the time and had been tasked with finding a way to generate interest in the county game. Attendances had been falling for five years in a row and there was a real concern that the trend could not be reversed. A massive piece of customer research was carried out with Channel 4 that surveyed 4,500 households. By Robertson's reckoning there was a completely untapped potential cricket market in the UK of 19 million people. It was these people they were aiming to attract.

"The very clear objective of Twenty20 was as a means to an end, not an end in itself," Robertson told journalist Tim Wigmore. "It wasn't designed to be a standalone competition or format. It really had to be the entry point to cricket. We didn't want it to look and feel different to longer forms of the game that we wanted people to progress to. It was really important that it stayed 11-a-side and looked like cricket. Because if someone went to a T20 game, got really excited by that and came back to a longer format game that looked completely different, there'd be no chance of that migration up through the game. It was really key it looked like cricket."

The market research made it clear that those that weren't already cricket fans found the sport inaccessible. "Women thought of it as a man's sport, young people that it was for old people, ethnic minorities thought it was not for them," Robertson said.

It wasn't an easy sell for the counties, many of whom remained resistant to change, which was nothing new. As has already been mentioned throughout this story, the counties have all too often been a handbrake on progress rather than pushing for things to change.

Wigmore wrote of the worries about getting agreement from the counties ahead of the meeting for *ESPNcricinfo*: "Despite the strength of Robertson's research, this did not look likely, despite the support of ECB executives John Read, Terry Blake, Tim Lamb and Lord MacLaurin. As the ECB's desperation mounted on April 21, the morning of the vote, MacLaurin decided to 'flatter the fuck' out of the county chairmen, as Read later recalled. Minutes before the vote Bill Midgley, the 60-year-old Durham chairman, who had opposed T20, likened the situation to that 40 years ago, when there was staunch opposition to the creation of one-day cricket. Enough chairmen were convinced: the vote of the counties and MCC was won 11-7, with one abstention."

T20 was created with the intention of increasing attendances and in its first year it succeeded, with

Lord's, the home of cricket and the largest cricket stadium in the UK, selling out the "London Derby" of Middlesex versus Surrey. That Surrey team was led by Adam Hollioake and they were to go on and win the inaugural event. Hollioake says he was amazed when he was told that he would be taking part in the kind of hit-and-giggle cricket that clubbies played on damp weekday nights throughout the summer.

"I don't even think we saw it as fun, we just saw it as a joke. When someone told me we were going to be playing Twenty20 cricket I just thought the ECB's lost their mind. This is ridiculous, we play 20-20 cricket on a weekday evening for our club sides, 16 eight-ball overs we played, against pub sides. They've finally lost their mind," says Hollioake. "Because it was at a time when 40-over cricket was in, and the rest of the world was playing 50-over cricket and I was saying 'This is crazy, why would we go and play 20-over cricket when one-day internationals are 50 overs? This is just ridiculous.'"

Hollioake is happy to admit he got it "completely wrong" and it didn't take long for Surrey to start thinking of different tactics that could see them compete at this new form of the professional game.

Perhaps the most surprising thing about Twenty20 cricket is not that it has become phenomenally successful – anyone who saw the first few matches in 2003 could see the massive potential – it was the speed with which that success manifested itself. The format spread to every cricket-playing country and Robertson said on reflection that shouldn't really have been a surprise.

"With hindsight why wouldn't it have worked overseas? If globally people were feeling the same pressures that we were – they were becoming cash rich and time poor, and people wanted an instant return on the investment of their leisure pound. Why wouldn't that apply as much in South Africa or Australia or anywhere else?"

English cricket may have been the first to create T20 leagues, but it did not take long for the rest of the world to first catch and then overtake them. The IPL was the first league to really rip up tradition and start again. India has 27 teams competing in its Ranji Trophy first-class tournament with that number set to increase to 28, but for the IPL there were just eight teams. It was a streamlined event that would last a matter of weeks. Every game would be televised and private investors would be sought out to be team owners. It created its own blueprint.

The same cannot be said for cricket in England. While it has innovated when it comes to the format of the cricket that is being played, it remains intransigently wedded to the existing first-class structure. Twenty20 was created not out of some desire to innovate; it was created out of necessity.

There had been a 17 per cent drop off in attendances at county fixtures in the five years leading up to 2001 when Robertson was charged with finding a solution. The average attendance at a floodlit one-day county game was between 3,500 and 4,000 spectators. The target for Twenty20 in that first year was an average attendance of 5,000. They managed 5,300. Twenty20 cricket in England has been a success, but it has been a qualified one. If there are indeed 19 million potential new cricket fans then over a decade later English cricket has not even scraped the surface.

Elsewhere, Twenty20 has been used to increase attendance and create a new audience. In England the sentimental attachment to the county structure has prevented that. While the IPL has been selling out stadiums, it is not all that fair to compare that to the county game; cricket is still the number one sport and national obsession in India.

The real comparison comes when you look at what Cricket Australia has done with its T20 league, the Big Bash. There the authorities have designed everything to attract new fans, and they have done it brilliantly.

Will MacPherson wrote at the end of the 2015/16 season on the numbers of new fans that have been drawn in by the Australian T20 spectacle.

"[The Big Bash] jumped into the top 10 best-attended sports leagues in the world, with an average crowd of 28,906 over the group games and semi-finals, including a record 80,883 for the Melbourne derby at the MCG on 2 January. Perhaps most impressively, the Big Bash's target audience – those who have never watched a cricket match before – is not just being tapped, but hammered. The first edition saw 10% of fans attend their first BBL game, the second 13% and the third 22%. Last season 26% of fans were at their first BBL game, and 17% their first cricket match."

Compare that with the English T20 Blast during the 2015 season. There was a record number of people that attended matches – the ECB announced that 704,205 people went to watch a Blast match – but that was over

122 games. That gives an average attendance of around 5,700 people. A little while later this total attendance figure was increased when it became clear that county members were not in the original numbers. The new figure was 827,654. It was like the ECB had found a five pound note in a pair of jeans they had just washed.

England and Australia are not the same. In the UK the population is much larger but not as concentrated around a few large cities. In England the grounds where cricket is played are much smaller. Even if every ticket was sold it would be impossible to achieve the same average attendance as the Big Bash. But to suggest that an average attendance of 6,000 is what cricket in England should be aiming for is embarrassing.

The voices calling for change have often been those of the players themselves, not least England's current ODI captain, Eoin Morgan. Speaking at a sponsor's event in late 2014 Morgan chose his words carefully, but made it clear change was needed.

"If you look at where our domestic T20 competition is at and our international campaign is, we're falling behind massively and the reason is right there in front of us," Morgan said. "Guys aren't exposing themselves enough to the better standard of opposition and it is right in front of our eyes."

One who has long proselytised the idea of a franchise-style T20 tournament is Kevin Pietersen, to the extent that it has caused him no end of arguments with his former ECB employers.

"I've been fairly vocal about [franchise T20]. They [the ECB] have to, they've got to start because they would definitely gain a lot from having a lot more players who are ready to play, who understand the game and who have experience of playing with other players to call on," Pietersen told us.

While county cricket has many loyal and loving supporters, ultimately it exists to do two things. The first is to create players for England's international teams. The second is to generate interest in the game. While the county game has done a decent, if a somewhat sporadic, job at producing international cricketers it hasn't maintained the interest of the public. And the English game's refusal to change even in the face of this is to its detriment.

※ ※ ※

In February 2005 there was the first international Twenty20 match between Australia and New Zealand, although the game itself was not taken particularly seriously. The New Zealanders wore a retro beige kit and the players had nicknames rather than surnames on their shirts. It felt more like a testimonial than an international sporting contest.

The next T20 international match was taken far more seriously, by England at least, who saw it as a chance to land some early blows on the touring Australians. A Michael Vaughan-led England posted 179-8 with Andrew Strauss batting at seven. They bowled out the visitors for 79 for a 100-run victory that started the momentum for that most golden of English summers. Even with England's attitude towards beating their fiercest rivals, T20 was still much more about entertainment than serious cricket. The real change in attitude towards T20 came when the inaugural World Twenty20 took place in South Africa in late 2007. The idea was conceived in the wake of the absolutely disastrous ODI World Cup that had taken place earlier that year in the Caribbean. A meandering tournament that began with India going out early and finished with the final being played in near darkness was perhaps the least well run ICC event.

Malcolm Speed, the ICC chief executive at the time, saw this new format as an antidote to the overly long World Cup that had taken place six months earlier; with this streamlined two-week event there was a chance to showcase modern cricket. Speed wrote in his autobiography that the ICC had to do something or risk being left behind.

"There were entrepreneurs, broadcasters, sponsors and multinational businesses that would seek to claim the right to run the international version of T20 if the ICC did not stake its claim and actually hold the first event," he said.

There was a great deal of resistance. The Pakistan Cricket Board chairman, Shahryar Khan, was opposed on grounds of tradition but the real issue was the attitude of the BCCI. Niranjan Shah, the BCCI honorary secretary, was reported to have been scathing at an ICC board meeting in March 2006. "T20? Why not ten-ten or five-five or one-one? India will never play T20."

When the 2007 World Twenty20 took place, India not only played but won the whole thing. The Indian Premier League, that was already due to be launched in 2008, suddenly had a lot more impetus.

It was that first ICC event, the subsequent capturing of the Indian public's imagination with the IPL, and the huge sums of money involved that turned T20 from a sideshow to the main attraction. It also seemed to alter the attitude of the BCCI. India had only agreed to take part in the first World T20 if they didn't have to do any warm-up matches and sent a largely second-string team to the event itself.

By the time that second-string India side returned home as world champions the potential of this new format was obvious. The 2006/07 regional T20 in India wasn't televised; by the time the IPL started in 2008 T20 was a national obsession.

English cricket was ideally placed to be the front runner in taking advantage of the huge worldwide interest in this new version of cricket. They had been playing the format longer than anyone else and had the chance to lead the way both on and off the field. Of the 22 men that played in that first T20 international between Australia and New Zealand, 13 were making their debut in the format and eight had played their first match in England. Here was the chance for England to be ahead of the curve and lead the world.

Instead they ignored the IPL, failed to follow the lead of other countries in creating streamlined "franchise" leagues and did a deal with the crooked Allen Stanford. But England had begun underperforming in the format on the global stage even before the disastrous decision to choose Stanford.

That 2007 World T20 was a 12-team event. There would be four groups of three teams, with the top two from each mini group making it through to a Super

Eight phase that was in fact two groups of four. As simple and straightforward as ever.

England came through that opening round with a convincing victory against Zimbabwe, but lost all four of the other fixtures that they played. The one well-remembered match was against India when Yuvraj Singh hit Stuart Broad for six sixes in an over in Durban.

India played with real freedom throughout that tournament, led by MS Dhoni early in his captaincy career, yet had only played one game of international T20 before the 2007 event. For all of England's experience in the format they were found out. They couldn't find a way to compete in an ICC event and few were surprised. Where other countries seemed to have an instinctive feel for the new format, England were found wanting.

It was a similar situation come the 2009 event, but by then the world had moved on again – the years since that first T20 game in England have been full of monumental shifts that have been abrupt and at times violent.

This time the tournament was hosted by England and they began it by losing to the Netherlands in the opening match. England made 162-5, and that should have been plenty against a side that had a fraction of the funding, player base or experience. As it was, England cocked up their defence of the target as all the bowlers other than James Anderson and Ryan Sidebottom struggled to keep the Dutch partnership of Ryan ten Doeschate and Tom de Grooth under control.

It all came down to the last ball. The Dutch needed two runs to win. Stuart Broad was the bowler. Edgar

Schiferli was the batsman. Broad bowled a length ball that Schiferli attempted to pull into the legside. The batsman only succeeded in hitting the ball back towards Broad who dove on it and attempted to throw down the stumps. With all three stumps to aim at and enough time to steady himself, Broad managed to miss completely allowing the Dutch pair to complete their first run, add an overthrow, and win the game. Broad looked more broken than at any point during the over in the previous tournament when Yuvraj was carting him for 36. The delight of the Dutch as they ran on to the pitch at a packed Lord's was the image of the tournament, closely followed by Broad's dejected face.

It was another white-ball event, and another embarrassing performance from England. They managed a convincing win against Pakistan, the eventual winners, which was enough to get them through to the Super Eights, but there they could only manage one more win from their three remaining fixtures.

Then England won the next World T20 and no one, least of all England, really saw it coming.

※ ※ ※

In the lead-up to the 2010 event England were still playing T20 very rarely. Between the end of the 2009 event and the start of the next one in 2010 they played a total of five matches, winning two and losing two with one no result. The World T20 began in May, and England's match practice before that was a pair of games against Pakistan in Dubai. For those matches in the UAE, the opening partnership was Jonathan Trott and Joe Denly.

By the time the World T20 got under way there was a brand new opening partnership; Michael Lumb and Craig Kieswetter made their T20 international debuts in the opening match of the tournament and neither Trott nor Denly played T20 for England again.

That new partnership was discovered almost by accident. England took on the England Lions second team in a warm-up match for the series against Pakistan. The second-string team won, with Lumb and Kieswetter setting up that victory with an opening stand of 97. England had stumbled upon an attacking opening pair and decided to gamble on them at the World T20.

As has always been the way with England on the eve of a global event they reshuffled the pack at the last possible minute. The difference this time was that it worked out. Just like the star of *The Simpsons* accidentally saving the town from nuclear disaster, England had "pulled a Homer" and succeeded despite idiocy. It is what they have always hoped would happen when the tinkering starts just before an event; it had to work out sooner or later.

Kieswetter finished second on England's run-scoring list, Lumb was fourth. Their 68-run partnership in the semi-final against Sri Lanka transformed the kind of chase that had so often troubled England in high-pressure games in the past into a comfortable stroll.

After the stumbled-upon opening partnership came Kevin Pietersen. Despite missing one of the matches when he flew home to be at the birth of his first child he finished as England's leading scorer and man of the tournament.

He admits that when England arrived they didn't expect to emerge victorious.

"We didn't go in there with any expectations, we didn't think that we were going to win. We went there just as an England team turning up at a World Cup and some of our players and key players [did well]," says Pietersen. "I had a great World Cup but Kieswetter, Eoin Morgan, Graeme Swann, Ryan Sidebottom with the ball had an unbelievable World Cup. [Sidebottom] got very crucial wickets at crucial stages and took early wickets and put pressure on the opposition. Yeah I whacked it a little bit but so did some of the other batters."

The England side at that World Twenty20 were led and led well by Paul Collingwood, who after a trying stint as one-day captain in 2008 had returned to take charge of the T20 side for the 2009 event on home soil. It was a time of lots of captaincy changes for England but Collingwood brought some stability in this format. This was one of the few times where the captain of an England limited-overs side was undoubtedly worthy of his place as a player, but he also had the advantage of flying slightly under the radar. He was not the captain that was wheeled out for the press conferences; he was not a household name.

In fact when newly elected Prime Minister David Cameron was congratulating him on leading his team to victory at this tournament he called him "Colin Wood".

Perhaps that absence of expectations helped England to play in a carefree way, but they had some bad luck followed by some good fortune in the early stages of the event.

The bad luck came in their first match against the West Indies. England batted with brilliant freedom to reach a very impressive 191-5. There were some excellent contributions from almost all of the top order with England being particularly brutal on Ravi Rampaul's bustling medium pace. They were well placed to get a win on the board when rain arrived. The Duckworth-Lewis-Stern (DLS) method intervened and when the game resumed the West Indies were set 60 runs in six overs. It was a simple target and they reached it easily. As ever with DLS it struggles when it generates very short chases; this is when its 'resources remaining' approach is at its weakest.

England were upset and with some justification. Collingwood spoke about that frustration after the match. "There's a major problem with Duckworth-Lewis in this form of the game. I've got no problem with it in one-dayers, and I know it's made me very frustrated tonight because I've come off the losing captain, but it's certainly got to be revised in this form. Ninety-five per cent of the time when you get 191 runs on the board you are going to win the game. Unfortunately, Duckworth-Lewis seems to have other ideas and brings the equation completely the other way and makes it very difficult."

The good luck came in England's next game when the rain intervened again, this time with England in danger of losing to Ireland and being eliminated at the first possible opportunity with two defeats against their name. With England having massively underperformed with the bat, scraping together only 120-8, Ireland were looking certain winners even after Paul Stirling lost his wicket early on. Then the rain arrived to force a No Result, and England progressed to the Super Eights on the basis of having lost to the West Indies less heavily than the Irish. It was not a great start, but that opening match against the West Indies made you think England had the batting to at least challenge in the next stage.

As it was England did not lose another game during the tournament, winning five in a row and walking away with the trophy. How they achieved it was actually pretty straightforward. While the batting of Pietersen was a highlight, the victory was primarily down to the bowling of Graeme Swann, Michael Yardy and Ryan Sidebottom.

England were one of the first sides to realise that the left-arm seamer was a run-saving and wicket-taking option in T20, and one of the first sides to work out the slower-ball bouncer using this angle was particularly effective. Sidebottom was brilliant both with the new ball and at the death, and his ten wickets at an average of 16 were vital to England's win. Sidebottom combined with Stuart Broad to be both penetrating and miserly in the PowerPlay overs.

From overs 7-14 England gave the ball to Swann and Yardy, who prevented sides from accelerating. Swann's ability to get the ball to turn was the perfect foil for Yardy's left-arm darts. Wickets up front and strangling the run-rate in the middle meant that teams had to risk even more at the end. It was this tactic that meant that England conceded less than 150 in every single match and were unbeaten during the Super Eights and knockout stages.

By the time England had reached a final against Australia they were brimming with confidence, and even in the build-up to the match things felt different. This was not like previous times England had faced Australia with a white ball and coloured clothing. This wasn't the world-beating Australia team that had won three World Cups in a row; it was an inexperienced side that did not quite have that much-fabled aura and indomitable mongrel spirit.

England won the toss and chose to field. Sidebottom was brilliant in the opening overs yet again. He had Shane Watson caught at slip by Swann, via a deflection off Kieswetter's gloves. In the next over Michael Clarke pushed the ball into the covers and took off for a tight run. The run went from tight to non-existent when Michael Lumb swooped on the ball and ran out David Warner with a diving throw. Australia had lost both openers for seven runs.

The score was 8-3 as Sidebottom picked up his second wicket when Brad Haddin was given caught down the legside. Haddin hadn't hit the ball and was desperately unlucky to be given out, but England did not care. They had gone a long way towards winning their first ICC global event with the first 13 balls of the match.

A recovery of sorts took place when Clarke combined with David Hussey to get Australia to 45 before the fourth wicket fell. The younger Hussey was the man responsible for Australia getting to a reasonable total. His 59 runs from 54 balls anchored the innings and got his side up to 147, although his brother Michael and Cameron White played their part.

England needed 148 to win, but they lost Lumb early when he pushed the ball in the air to mid-on off the bowling of Shaun Tait. This did not slow them down at all. Pietersen and Kieswetter put together a partnership of 111 runs in 11.2 overs that took England to the brink of victory. It was all so straightforward. Both men lost their wickets within an over of each other but Eoin Morgan and Paul Collingwood finished the job.

England would go on to beat the Aussies in Australia that winter in the Ashes. All vestiges of invincibility had fallen away from the old enemy, and that World T20 win helped make that happen.

※ ※ ※

Come the next World T20 two years later in Sri Lanka, the huge strides forward that had been made in 2010 had been reversed. England had fallen out with Kevin Pietersen, again. This time it was as a result of text messages sent to South African opposition and amidst allegations of Twitter parody accounts being run from inside the dressing room. It all meant he was not considered for selection.

In fact Pietersen's eventual falling out with England had some of its antecedents in the aftermath of the 2010 World T20 win. He was left out of the one-day squads for the games against Pakistan at the end of 2010 English summer and he wasn't happy about it. He sent a tweet, but it was probably meant to be a private message.

"Yep. Done for rest of summer!! Man of the World Cup T20 and dropped from the T20 side too.. Its a fuck up!! Surrey have signed me for l ..." The missing word seemed to have been "loan" as he was to move on from Hampshire and the deal was at first temporary before becoming permanent.

National selector Geoff Miller was far from impressed. He told the *Guardian*: "I don't like that kind of language and I don't use that language at all. I don't follow Twitter and I'm not a great believer in that kind of thing. I don't think it is necessary. I'm still the national selector and what I do is select sides with my co-selectors that we think is right for England. My priority is the England side and it is not about individuals."

In truth the decision to give Pietersen a break was justified. He had looked an increasingly forlorn figure throughout that summer, looking short of form and confidence. By late 2012 the relationship between Pietersen and his employers looked to be fractured beyond repair. England were without their best T20 batsman and the man of the tournament in their only ICC event victory when they next played in a World T20.

England were led by Stuart Broad in the 2012 event and he did not have the same success that Collingwood had in the role. He was tactically naïve and seemingly unwilling to bowl himself at the beginning or at the end of the innings. His side beat Afghanistan easily enough in the opening round but it was the game against India where we saw how far England had tumbled in the two years since becoming world champions.

India batted first and made 170-4, a score that was bigger than it should have been. The fault for that lay primarily with Jade Dernbach, who conceded 45 runs in his four overs in a spell that went for six boundaries and three wides. The only bowler that walked away with any real credit was Steven Finn who conceded the fewest runs and took two wickets. Broad looked listless when he bowled himself in the middle overs. He would have been a better bet at the start of the innings than either Tim Bresnan or Dernbach but he bowled just one over in the PowerPlay and brought himself off despite only conceding a run a ball.

England once again made the Super Eights and then only managed one more win against New Zealand before another early exit. It had only taken two years for the English to revert to type and worse was to come at the 2014 World T20.

The format had changed so that the "big" teams did not need to qualify for the main event so England were in the Super 10 straight away. Once again they only managed one victory, a brilliant effort against Sri Lanka where Alex Hales become the first English centurion in T20 internationals as they chased down 190. That was the one moment of brightness but England ended with real darkness.

Having been set 134 to win against the Netherlands they managed to lose to the men in orange for the second time at a World T20. It was horrible viewing as a muddled England succumbed to 88 all out. What the coach Ashley Giles describes as a "typical end-of-the-tournament poor performance from an England team" cost him his job, but he was far from the problem. The real problem was how far behind the English had fallen compared to the rest of the world. The year-round nature of England's schedule meant that there were few opportunities for them to learn how to play in T20 leagues that had become a finishing school for cricketers from the rest of the world.

That is changing. Andrew Strauss has made it clear that the attitude towards England players taking part in other leagues has evolved, but it was still two years in the future before the policy changed. By the time the 2016 tournament got under way the England side were unrecognisable from the jaded bunch that lost to the Netherlands in 2014. It may be a few years before England reap the rewards of allowing their players to take part in the IPL and tournaments like it, but they have already got some remarkable returns from allowing their players to let loose their attacking instincts.

Things have changed, but for too long England viewed T20 through narrowed, suspicious eyes.

2011 World Cup

Entertaining failures

T HINGS were going pretty well for Andrew Strauss' side when the pink-haired Kevin O'Brien strode to the crease. In a World Cup already blighted by some drab games, dreary old England had been recast in the unlikely role of entertainers. In their first two games they'd scored – and also conceded – well over 600 runs. Now they'd run up another 300-plus total against Ireland. Somehow this team led by the very sensible Andys Flower and Strauss had turned up at the World Cup as if being led by Ossie Ardiles and Kevin Keegan. They'd chased down almost 300 to beat the Netherlands and then shared 676 runs with India in a giddy Bangalore tie where Strauss had played the greatest ever one-day innings by an

Englishman in a match that surely could not be beaten for entertainment.

Now, though, once again back at the M Chinnaswamy Stadium things were looking far more straightforward. England had amassed 327-8 from their 50 overs against Ireland on the back of a quick half-century at the top of the order from Kevin Pietersen and then a 178-run partnership between Jonathan Trott and Ian Bell. The innings had fallen away rather at the end, with the last ten overs yielding only 70 runs as wickets began to tumble. No matter. As the man with the pink hair takes guard, the score reads 106-4 after 22.2 overs. The equation: 222 runs to win from 166 balls with six wickets in hand. Two overs later a Graeme Swann delivery slides past Gary Wilson's attempted sweep. A thud on the pads, a roared appeal and Billy Bowden's crooked finger make it 111-5. It's very early days and South Africa have only played one game, but England are going top of the Group B table with five points from their first three matches.

The man with pink hair has different plans for this day. "We said to ourselves it can go one of two ways now, we can sort of prod around from here and get a respectable 250-7 or something, lose the game by 60-70 runs, but walk off with our heads held high, or we can just go for everything, let our hair down and have some fun."

Bleaching your ginger hair and then dying it pink is not the decision of a man about to settle for 250-7. It is the decision of a man who is going to let his pink hair down and have some fun.

He slog-sweeps Graeme Swann into the stands beyond midwicket. Then he does it again. In the batting PowerPlay, a James Anderson bouncer is hooked behind square leg for six as O'Brien reaches 50 from 31 balls.

In all, the PowerPlay brings 62 runs from five overs. A 102-metre six over wide long-on completes an Anderson over that costs 17 runs. The frenzy of the pink-haired attack on the defenceless English bowlers is so brutal that at one point commentator Mark Nicholas remarks that England spinner Michael Yardy has been "murdered through mid-off – literally". At the end of the PowerPlay, the total runs required has dipped below 100 with 14 overs and still five wickets in hand.

The PowerPlay may now be over but the approach has not changed. It is still raining sixes at the Chinnaswamy. O'Brien sends another ball high into the sky. This time, though, the trajectory is wrong. It has too much elevation, too little distance. England's captain sprints back and underneath the ball, looking over his shoulder as it descends from an inky Bangalore sky. He grabs it, juggles it, and, finally, drops it. Strauss' head sinks into the Chinnaswamy dust. The match too is slipping from his grasp. Five balls later, Kevin O'Brien, his pink hair poking out from beneath a green Ireland cap, scampers two runs to complete the fastest ever World Cup century. He has faced just 50 balls, slashing 16 balls off the previous record held by Matthew Hayden. O'Brien has made the impossible not just possible, but now intoxicatingly probable. Attempting a second run that is never truly on, O'Brien is out for

113 from 63 balls with his Ireland side 11 runs short of a famous victory, but his team-mates ensure his efforts will not be in vain. There will be no heroic failure here. The winning boundary is clipped through midwicket by John Mooney from the first ball of the final over.

Ireland beat England by three wickets.

※ ※ ※

After the 2007 World Cup, the first half of the now-familiar four-year start-preparing-for-the-next-one-and-just-you-wait-because-*this*-time-we'll-be-ready cycle was spent with England continuing their circuitous and troubled route to finally noticing the captain who had been in front of their eyes all along.

Like that woman from that film realising she had been in love with her best friend all along in a five-out-of-ten late-1990s rom-com, England were busy going through unsuccessful flings with unsuitable men before finally rushing to the airport to confess their undying love for Andrew Strauss.

Before the 2007 World Cup was even over, one great bromance of English cricket was already at an end. It would be a couple of months later that the end of Michael Vaughan's one-day leadership was confirmed, but Duncan Fletcher had already decided it was time to move on. He had made the decision before England's exit was confirmed by that South Africa defeat, and the announcement was made two days before the consolation victory over the West Indies.

His contribution to English cricket was vast. The work he started alongside Nasser Hussain and completed with Vaughan saw the England cricket team transformed from a national joke to national treasures. Ashes winners. MBEs.

Fletcher first made England competitive, and then made them winners. But that had all been in Test cricket. That success had not quite been replicated in the one-day game.

Peter Moores was promoted from the England academy to take Fletcher's place as head coach. He was well-respected for both the work he'd done with England's youngsters as well as coaching Sussex to their first County Championship title in 2003.

Moores' first game in charge was a Test match against West Indies at Lord's. Andrew Flintoff had re-injured his ankle and would not play for England again until August, while Michael Vaughan's long-awaited return to Test cricket after an 18-month absence would be delayed a further week by a broken finger. So Strauss stood in for the stand-in captain in a rain-affected draw in a game best remembered for a swashbuckling hundred on debut for Matt Prior.

That's how it had been for Strauss. He was a stand-in for a stand-in, having first captained the side in the absence of both Flintoff and Vaughan in India a year earlier, and again in all formats for most of the 2006 summer. The summer was a success, but it was the returning Flintoff – who had not played since June due to an ankle injury – who was back in charge for the Ashes.

"We had two outstanding candidates in the absence of Michael Vaughan," said chairman of selectors David Graveney at the time. "It was a decision which did take a long time and a number of meetings. Andrew Strauss, typically of him, was very quick to point out, 'Be assured, you have my 110 per cent support for Freddie.'"

Typical of him. The nice guy. The best friend.

In the second Test of the 2007 summer against the West Indies, Vaughan returned with an emotional century on his home ground, Headingley, and it would be almost two years before Strauss would lead the side again.

Another leadership change was on the way, though. During the West Indies Test series, Vaughan reached a decision. He would relinquish the one-day captaincy to focus on the Test team, with the long-term goal of regaining the Ashes in 2009. His knee problems were well-documented, and his one-day record poor. It was four years until the next World Cup and he could not be sure he would still be around. Although Vaughan didn't formally retire from ODI cricket, it was understood by all what relinquishing the captaincy would mean.

"Since our disappointing performances in the World Cup, I have been giving careful consideration as to what is the best way forward for the England one-day team and my own role within the side," said Vaughan in an ECB statement. "I reached this decision some time ago, but I did not want to announce it until after the end of this Test series to avoid it becoming a distraction to the team."

The one-day captaincy's unofficial standing within the England set-up was rather given away later in the statement, with Vaughan saying his decision would "allow another player to gain additional experience of captaincy in the one-day international arena."

Although Strauss had led the team the previous summer, the two men in the frame now were Paul Collingwood and Kevin Pietersen. Collingwood was chosen, and endured an unhappy time in the role. There was controversy when he refused to withdraw a run-out appeal against New Zealand's Grant Elliott after the batsman had collided accidentally with England bowler Ryan Sidebottom.

Collingwood was under no obligation to withdraw the appeal, but the New Zealanders were incensed and the England captain gave a shame-faced post-match apology in a doomed bid to soothe the spirit of cricket which had been so grievously wounded by an unfortunate yet legitimate dismissal.

Collingwood led England to the World Twenty20 in South Africa, but stood down the following summer on the same day that Vaughan relinquished the Test captaincy to pave the way for Kevin Pietersen to take over as captain in all formats.

It seemed Collingwood's dalliance with captaincy was over, saying not long after: "I had a year in the job doing the one-dayers, and you feel as if you've had your go. I would take a lot of persuading to do the job again."

Pietersen, however, declared himself "thrilled and excited" to have the chance to captain his country. National selector Geoff Miller stressed the importance of "a player who could lead the team in all three forms of cricket". Once that criterion was in place, Pietersen was top of a shortlist of one.

Strauss had not played a one-day international since the World Cup, while you had to go back further still to June 2006 for his last appearance in the T20 side.

And Pietersen was undoubtedly a bold and exciting choice. He was the team's best player, and thought more deeply about the game than many gave him credit for. He could have been a great England captain, and made a classically Pietersen start with a century and a victory in the final Test of the 2008 summer against South Africa, the country of his birth, at The Oval. The series may have already been lost, but Captain Pietersen had made an instant impression. Just as he had when first picked for the one-day side. Just as he had when first picked for the Test side. And just as he had when first playing against Nasser Hussain's England for Natal all those years ago as a cocksure young off-spinner who gave the ball a bit of a whack.

It would not, perhaps could not, last. Pietersen was England captain during interesting times. After defeat to South Africa, Pietersen led the side to the West Indies for the Allen Stanford Show, whose gaudy grubbiness was thrown into yet sharper focus by the tour of India that followed. England lost 5-0 in a one-day series reduced to irrelevance when it was curtailed by the Mumbai terrorist attacks. Pietersen led the team back to India a fortnight later for two Test matches. England lost the series 1-0 after a masterclass fourth-innings run-chase from Virender Sehwag and Sachin Tendulkar in Chennai.

While the fact Pietersen was the captain who led his team back to a country in pain helped cement his hero status in India, it had been a brutally tough introduction to captaincy both on and off the field.

When Michael Vaughan was overlooked for the tour of the Caribbean in early 2009, Pietersen snapped.

He was unwilling to continue working under Moores. He succeeded in ousting Moores from the head coach's role, but it cost him his captaincy.

In essence it appeared that while Pietersen's misgivings over Moores were shared, being seen to accede to his demands would set a dangerous precedent. Pietersen would have to go as well.

At a hastily-arranged press conference on Wednesday 7 January, ECB managing director Hugh Morris confirmed: "The ECB late this afternoon have accepted with regret the resignation of Kevin Pietersen as England captain."

Pietersen insisted he had not resigned, but instead stated that "in light of recent communications with the ECB, and the unfortunate media stories and speculation that have subsequently appeared, I now consider that it would be extremely difficult for me to continue in my current position with the England cricket team."

Whether he jumped or whether he was pushed or whether he had simply been misunderstood mattered little; England were now without a head coach or a captain, and there was a Test series a fortnight away.

Here comes the airport scene. Andrew Strauss, who had not long won his own battle to first return to and then stay in the Test side after a dramatic loss of form, was finally handed the England captaincy. Assistant coach Andy Flower stepped up to the role of interim team director and thus was formed an alliance that would prove every bit as significant as those between first Nasser Hussain and then Michael Vaughan with Duncan Fletcher.

Things would not start well for the Flower and Strauss axis, though. England collapsed to 51 all out to lose the opening Test and, although Strauss made huge runs in the rest of the series, some conservative declarations left England unable to force a victory to even square the series, let alone push on for a win.

As captain, Strauss returned to the ODI side after what was by now almost a two-year break, and made a century in the second match of a series England edged 3-2.

The nascent Flower–Strauss axis had shown enough for Flower to be handed the team director role on a permanent basis. The 2009 summer went outrageously well, with swift revenge exacted on the West Indies and then, miraculously, the Ashes somehow regained despite Strauss being the only England batsman to score any runs.

The one-day series that followed was lost 6-1 but, as in the Tests, Strauss was the leading series run-scorer in a list otherwise dominated by Australians.

From there, England headed straight to South Africa for the ICC Champions Trophy. Expectations were not high, but victories over Sri Lanka and the hosts saw England reach the semi-finals.

Another thrashing at the hands of Australia lay in store, but Strauss' side had exceeded expectations and remain the only England side to reach the last four of a global 50-over tournament away from home since 1992.

Eighteen months out from the World Cup and with Strauss having done plenty to justify his place not only as captain of the ODI side but just as importantly as a batsman, it should have been a launch pad for that side.

Four of the XI beaten by Australia at Centurion would not be among the 19 players England called upon at the World Cup. Two of the top three that day, Joe Denly and Owais Shah, were already playing their last one-day internationals.

Shah's disappearance from the scene was particularly surprising. He was an established part of the one-day side and in the previous 12 months had scored 782 ODI runs for England – almost 200 more than anyone else. Of the seven England batsmen with over 300 runs in that time, only Pietersen scored his runs quicker than Shah. Against South Africa in the Champions Trophy group stage, Shah's 98 at better than a run a ball had been a crucial part in a vital and impressive victory.

From the outside, there seemed no reason why his place in the one-day side should have been under scrutiny, but Shah believes he was paying the price for failures in Test cricket.

"It was more Peter Moores than anyone who I really enjoyed playing under," says Shah. "Strauss and Flower took over and they were more geared towards Test cricket, I think it's as simple as that. The way the team went – Jonathan Trott took over at number three – they wanted to mimic Test cricket and not worry too much about one-day cricket. Not to say they didn't want to win in one-day cricket, but Test cricket was held in a higher regard I think than one-day cricket. That's why I found myself out of the team. I got a couple of Test matches in the West Indies, after which I was not picked. And within six months of being dropped from the Test team I was also not picked in the one-day team. It was, I felt, because I didn't do well in those two Test matches in the West Indies they were like 'Hmm, don't really want him in the one-day team either.'"

For Strauss, the 6-1 one-day series defeat immediately after the Ashes had been a pivotal moment. "That was a real moment for us to reset and go, 'Hold on – what are we doing in one-day cricket, what's our strategy, what's our plan?' And on the back of that we had quite a lot of success."

The Champions Trophy had come too soon for any meaningful change, but by the time England were back in South Africa two months later for a bilateral series, those changes had started to take place. Shah and Bopara were the biggest casualties, with Ashes hero Jonathan Trott named in the squad. His only previous ODI had come three months earlier in a slender Duckworth-Lewis victory over Ireland, and he made nought.

Before the tour began, Trott had been forced to deny accusations he had celebrated with South Africa during the 2008 series in England. Michael Vaughan, in his autobiography *Time to Declare*, wrote: "It was a sad day for English cricket that on my last day against South Africa I saw Jonathan Trott celebrating with South Africa, when the week before he had been our 12th man at Headingley. I was going into the press conference and I saw him patting them on the back. It hit home what English cricket has become like."

In response, Trott said: "I've known Paul Harris since I was 16 and we played together at Warwickshire.

I just said something like, 'Cheers, well done on your victory.'" For his part, Strauss declared himself "100 per cent happy with Jonathan Trott's commitment."

Kevin Pietersen was also back in the squad after the Achilles injury that had cut short his summer, while there was even a place in the squad for Alastair Cook after a pair of back-to-back late-season Pro40 centuries for Essex. Sajid Mahmood returned, while Liam Plunkett returned to the squad after a two-year gap as injury cover.

England won 2-1 in a series bookended by washouts. That England remained a work in progress was highlighted by the results: a pair of thumping seven-wicket wins either side of a 112-run defeat.

Yet to focus on the heavy defeat rather than the impressive wins would be wrong, and on the back of the Champions Trophy there were encouraging signs. Trott made a pair of half-centuries, while James Anderson and Stuart Broad took eight and six wickets.

It set England up for an excellent 2010. They played four series in the year and won them all, alongside a one-off victory in Scotland.

They beat Bangladesh home and away, and edged a pair of tight five-match series against Australia and Pakistan.

England roared into a 3-0 lead over Australia, prompting Graeme Swann to hail Andy Flower as the chief architect of the team's "joyous approach" to one-day cricket.

"The satisfying thing for us is that we sat down 18 months ago and said we want to be number one in all formats and asked how are we going to do it?" Swann said on *ESPNcricinfo*. "We have plotted our way to this point and everything has gone well. We have won the Ashes, won the World T20 and won this series after just three games, which you might expect against some teams but possibly not Australia, which is testament to the way we are playing.

"The great thing Andy Flower has done is to instil a confidence in everyone to back their natural ability and perform on the big stage like they do in the county games."

Australia being Australia, they won the last two games of the series in London on the back of bowling blitzes from first Ryan Harris at The Oval and then Shaun Tait at Lord's.

England's optimism, though, was clear. As for Strauss, he had surely proved his credentials as a modern one-day batsman by making 154 against Bangladesh in an innings that included five sixes and then stroking 126 to help England overhaul Pakistan's 294-8 at Headingley. In 2010, Strauss averaged 57 in ODIs at a strike-rate of 95.

By the end of the Pakistan series, the pieces seemed to be falling into place for the England one-day team. Wicketkeeper-batsman Steven Davies was opening alongside Strauss with Trott the side's Mr Dependable at number three. Paul Collingwood, Kevin Pietersen and Eoin Morgan provided power and smarts in the middle order. Michael Yardy's success bowling in tandem with Graeme Swann in the World T20-winning side had been transferred across to the longer format, giving England two genuine spin threats behind a pace attack led by Stuart Broad and James Anderson.

"We won quite a few series in a row starting with that South Africa tour and we kind of felt that we were on a bit of a roll there," says Strauss.

There was a problem on the horizon, though. It had scuppered World Cup campaigns before and would have to be negotiated again. Before the World Cup, England would have to go to Australia for the Ashes.

Demoralising and debilitating Ashes defeats had been contributing factors to the World Cup failures in 2003 and 2007. If you don't want to know the result of the 2010/11 Ashes series, look away now. This time, things would be very, very different. Yet the more things change, they more they stay the same. England roared to a 3-1 victory, winning the Ashes in Australia for the first time since 1986/87. Alastair Cook scored 766 runs – 766! Graeme Swann did a dance. England won three Test matches by an innings. They had not just beaten Australia, but demolished and broken them.

And the Ashes still managed to screw up England's World Cup planning. Australia won the one-day series that followed the Ashes 6-1, and suddenly euphoria was replaced by doubt.

Strauss says: "We hit the one-dayers in Australia, and we should have rested more of our players for that series. We decided not to because it was the last series before the World Cup and actually we just sort of sleepwalked our way through that one-day series. Australia are always a strong one-day team at home and we had our confidence knocked at exactly the wrong moment."

It took just one game for England to start second-guessing themselves and discarding the plans that had been forged during 18 successful months of one-day cricket. Steve Davies made 42 off 35 balls in the first ODI, but was promptly replaced by the Test keeper Matt Prior. The Ashes win had been a monumental achievement, and Strauss acknowledges that the environment England had cultivated during that series had left a powerful mark.

"We had identified Steve Davies as the opener, the attacking opener to go alongside myself, and then on the back of Matt Prior playing brilliantly in the Ashes and the presence that Matt had in the team environment at the last moment we decided that he should replace Steve Davies. Which I think, looking back, was poor thinking on our part. The team was relatively settled, we had won quite a few matches, and that just sent shockwaves through the team which is unhealthy in any team environment."

Decisions about the one-day team being made based on Test match credentials. We've been here before and we will be here again.

Prior was dismissed for three-ball ducks in his first two innings of the series. He would make a 58-ball 67 in the next game, England's only win of the series as they successfully defended 299-8, but two more low scores would follow.

The clarity and purpose with which England had closed out their 2010 one-day cricket had gone. When Eoin Morgan suffered a broken finger that would rule him out of England's initial 15-man World Cup squad, Prior moved back down into the middle order and Davies returned to the side to open the batting with Strauss. To further confuse matters, Davies – having seemingly been ousted by Prior and returning only due to an injury elsewhere – took the gloves. Who was England's first-choice wicketkeeper? Who was Andrew Strauss' opening partner? A month earlier, England had known for certain that the answer to both questions was Steven Davies. Now there was no clear answer to either.

The answer to the first question proved to be Matt Prior. The answer to the second therefore became tricky. England settled in the end on an out-of-form Kevin Pietersen, who had never opened the batting in any of his 110 one-day internationals up to that point.

"Matt was meant to open the batting and he didn't come off in Australia and then it was like, where do we go?" says Strauss. "And KP in sub-continental conditions – that might be a good option for us to take, to hit the opposition hard. KP wasn't in great form but maybe that was a way of kind of challenging him and getting the best out of him. But you just never want to be in a situation where you don't know the shape of your team come the first game of the World Cup.

"It was a big mistake on our part. It was another example of best laid plans going out the window, and poor thinking on my part and Andy Flower's part in my mind."

Graham Gooch, then England batting coach, backed the decision at the time and still does, saying: "I was in favour of him opening. Because it's quite a simple rationale in one-day cricket: you give your best players all the opportunity, you give them the whole 50 overs to impact the game to the maximum. Plenty of precedent for that – Sachin Tendulkar, Mark Waugh with Australia – and it is a tried-and-tested method and I still believe in that. It depends on the player obviously, but wouldn't you give your best player the chance of opening in one-day cricket? You get through the new ball, the field spreads out and you give them the most opportunity."

Tried-and-tested with Tendulkar and Waugh, but not until now with 110-cap Kevin Pietersen. To make matters worse, Pietersen was also carrying an injury that would eventually cut his World Cup short. Even in victory, the Ashes had taken its toll on bodies and minds. "I was in no good shape going into that tournament," says Pietersen. "I was injured, I had a double hernia." Should he have played in the World Cup at all? "I tried, because that's what I do, I try and play until I can't play anymore. I did that with my Achilles and I did that with my double hernia. So, I'm not a pussy, I don't just jump out of scenarios because I've got a little bit of pain. I've got a very high pain threshold and I'll try and commit for as long as I can until I can't do it anymore and then I'll stop."

Pietersen stopped after four games at the World Cup. The experiment was not a total failure, but neither was it a huge success, with Pietersen making a slow 39 against the Netherlands, a quick 31 against India and a half-century against Ireland before scoring just two against South Africa.

Injuries were to be another problem undoubtedly exacerbated by playing the World Cup on the back of an Ashes tour. England's revolving 15-man World Cup squad ended up featuring 19 different players, with Eoin Morgan managing to get injured and replaced by Ravi Bopara only to then recover in time to return to the squad as Pietersen's replacement. This also says much for just how interminable the Cricket World Cup is. It really does go on. For completeness, the other enforced changes to England's squad due to illness and injury during the tournament were Chris Tremlett for Stuart Broad, Jade Dernbach for Ajmal Shahzad, and Adil Rashid for Michael Yardy. Neither Dernbach nor Rashid played a game.

※ ※ ※

In 2007, England had been by far the dreariest of the major nations. They had scored their runs more slowly and less excitingly than any of the teams that finished ahead of them. They had somehow managed to suck yet more life out of a joyless tournament.

In 2011, England managed to be exciting and entertaining. Often this was unintentional, but there was no denying it had happened.

In the wake of the early exits for India and Pakistan, the World Cup format had changed once again. Never again would an important country for the financial success of the tournament be allowed to leave after playing just three matches. Now everyone would play at least six. It seems an awful lot, and it seemed to take an eternity to get through them.

The format was fundamentally the same as that used in 1996, but with two groups of seven rather than two groups of six before the knockout stages.

It's not a terrible format. Certainly nobody could complain about not getting a fair chance after six games, but there was a significant risk that the tournament would succumb to predictability. Risk for those watching and hoping to be entertained, that is; for those who had created the format this was less a risk and more a hope. The sheer number of games reduced the potential for excitement dramatically. Whereas Ireland and Bangladesh had shown – and how – in 2007's format the carnage that could be wrought by one giant-killing shocker, any such result in a seven-team group would need to be backed up elsewhere before it had the serious potential to affect which four teams would qualify from each group. The overwhelming likelihood was that Australia, England, India, New Zealand, Pakistan, South Africa, Sri Lanka and West Indies would contest the quarter-finals.

So you're left with a six-week tournament that spends its first month and its first 42 games just deciding the bracket for the seven matches that will actually settle matters.

"You're arriving at eight predictable quarter-finalists and spending a month getting there," says *Wisden* editor Lawrence Booth. "I'd just take out the quarter-finals personally. Keep 14 teams, two groups of seven and only the top four – the top two in each group – go through. Which means every game would count. Even in games against the so-called minnows, run-rate would be an issue. You lose four quarter-finals, but you'd be making every group game as meaningful as a quarter-final in effect. And you keep the associates involved too."

That's one solution. The other is to have a team produce a string of inexplicable performances that strike hard and true at the heart of the very concept of predictability so that even when you do end up with the expected quarter-finalists, that in itself has become unpredictable and unexpected.

There's a word in cricket for the team that does that sort of thing. For the team that triumphs when disaster appears inevitable and trips over its own feet with the finish line in sight. That word is Pakistan. In 2011, England were the Pakistan.

In their review of the tournament, *Wisden* noted as much:

"Thanks to England and Ireland, the group stage (or at least Group B), which had seemed doomed to be a procession of one-sided strolls, became gripping. England were the new Pakistan, winning matches from the dead against vaunted opponents, and sinking to defeat from dominant positions against weaker ones. They were involved in the tournament's only tie, its most spectacular upset, two low-scoring thrillers, and, against West Indies, a virtual knockout before the knockouts."

While the quarter-final line-up ended up being exactly as everyone expected it, England had done their bit. "England's capers ensured drama and intrigue. As long as they were around, they were the life and soul of the party."

England, normally the party guest who corners you in the kitchen to talk about the mileage he's getting from his new Ford Mondeo, were instead doing shots and telling great stories that often threatened to turn into incoherent rambles but always delivered a killer punchline in the end. Sure, they were sick on their shoes a couple of times, but they'd kept everyone hugely entertained throughout and at least had the decency to sober up and leave the party at a reasonable hour.

Maybe England were actually great at the 2011 World Cup.

Andrew Strauss' side served notice that they could be the team to inject some life into the interminable group stage right from the start. In their first game, England were up against the Netherlands. England had famously lost to the Dutch in the 2009 World Twenty20 (and would go on to do so again five years later) but as opening games of a World Cup go, it's a penalty kick. But then England, World Cups and penalty kicks don't always have a happy ending.

This game did, just about. Things started sensibly enough. The Netherlands innings was going along steadily enough, but they'd lost a couple of quick mid-innings wickets to sit at 149-4 in the 33rd over on a flat pitch in Nagpur.

Crucially, they still had Ryan ten Doeschate at the crease. Ten Doeschate, objectively the greatest ODI batsman of them all thanks to his stunning average of 67 (sorry, Sachin fans), played splendidly as he helped himself to 119 before skipper Peter Borren joined the fun to help the Dutch plunder 104 runs from the last ten overs of their innings and reach 292-6. It was their highest total against a Test-playing nation.

It was by no means an impossible score to chase in benign batting conditions, but it was undoubtedly a ticklish one for an England side that had seen its confidence knocked at the back-end of the Australia tour and who had form for making a hot mess of World Cups.

Sadly, though, England were only just getting into their comedy stride and went on to win the game quite comfortably. Kevin Pietersen, opening for the first time, attempted to inject some interest into proceedings by taking 61 balls over his 39, but Andrew Strauss and Jonathan Trott played fluently to leave England needing 72 off the last ten overs. Paul Collingwood and Ravi Bopara got them home by six wickets without much fuss.

England had served notice of their potential, though, and weren't about to take their foot off the gas. Chasing down 293 to beat the Netherlands would prove by far the most mundane of England's six group games.

Next it was on to Bangalore to face tournament hosts and favourites India in a quite extraordinary match that both sides managed to lose and win countless times. In the final reckoning, neither of them managed to do either.

Perhaps the biggest compliment to the sheer dizzying madness of England's cricket that day is that they managed to reduce Sachin Tendulkar scoring his 98th international hundred, in India, in a World Cup, to a footnote. An elegant, expertly paced footnote, but a footnote nonetheless.

England's performance could perhaps be boiled down to two record-breakers, but that's too simplistic. Even so, James Anderson's 1-91 – England's worst World Cup analysis and matching his figures from the Sydney ODI earlier in the year – and Andrew Strauss' 158 – England's greatest World Cup innings – were both remarkable statistical notes. There have been five 150s made by England batsmen in one-day internationals, and Strauss has scored three of them.

It seems wrong to skate over India's innings, but this match really was all about England's chase. For a while there was a glimpse of what this thrown-together Strauss–Pietersen opening partnership could look like, and it looked good. With the situation demanding a quick start – the target was a mammoth 339 – England had been propelled to 68 inside the first ten overs before Pietersen fell to a freakish return catch by Munaf Patel. Pietersen leathered the ball back at the bowler who stuck his hands out as much in an attempt to preserve himself as to dismiss Pietersen. The ball bounced up off Munaf's palm as the big fast bowler tumbled to the ground only to see the ball coming right back to him. Sitting on the ground, he grabbed hold of the ball and some respite for the hosts.

Trott departed relatively swiftly and that was fair enough. This was no place for his serene and sensible accumulation. Strauss and Bell then set about winning the game for England. They were doing so at an absolute canter. Strauss carved and heaved his way to a 99-ball century and accelerated from there, depositing Yuvraj Singh's left-arm spin into the stands for a huge six. Bell was into the 60s at a run a ball and an unthinkable 339 from 50 overs was down to 59 off eight overs with eight wickets and a PowerPlay in hand. England had it in the bag.

Five PowerPlay overs later, India had it in the bag. Bell, by now struggling with cramp, top-edged to mid-off, and Zaheer trapped Strauss lbw with the very next ball. England lost four wickets for 25 runs in the PowerPlay, and 59 from eight overs had somehow become 29 off 12 balls with only three wickets in hand. Swann, Tim Bresnan and – most memorably – Ajmal Shahzad all managed to clear the ropes in a frenzied finish to the game. A scampered bye to the keeper left England needing four from two balls. Swann burgled two from the next before checking with the umpires what would happen if the scores were level. Swann squirted Munaf's final delivery to mid-off for a single and England had tied a game they had already lost, won and then lost again.

As Swann and Shahzad scampered the match-tying run, the cameras cut to the England dressing room. Strauss and Pietersen were applauding and smiling, toasting the unlikely point gained. Behind them, in the shadows, stands a scowling Andy Flower brooding over the point thrown away.

Next came Ireland, and Kevin O'Brien's joyously destructive masterpiece as Bangalore was treated to another England thriller. As well as breaking the record for the fastest World Cup century, O'Brien propelled Ireland to their highest ODI score and the biggest ever World Cup run chase.

"It was an amazing innings," remembers Strauss. "He chanced his arm and everything he did came off. He completely transformed the game from one where we were cruising to one where suddenly we were under pressure. Then it becomes that train wreck where you see it happening and you are just hoping that he does something wrong. You wouldn't want to take anything away from him in any way, it was a brilliant knock on the biggest stage of all, and quite correctly he should be remembered for one of cricket's greatest moments."

O'Brien insists Ireland were confident of chasing down England's score. "We'd seen the wicket, which was very good and of course the ground is very small, and it's also at altitude, so it was always in the back of our mind. We felt we had a good chance of knocking off the runs, especially after seeing England and India tie a few days beforehand on the same ground."

England by now had played three high-scoring thrillers and were in serious danger of going out in the group stage. Imagine how embarrassing it would be to get eliminated in the first round when the format has been specifically designed to help you get through. It didn't bear thinking about.

England's cricket had been riotously entertaining, but only half the time had that been intentional. They needed to change the pace. In a tournament that had seen stacks of runs – although mainly, in all the other dull non-England matches, only for one side in each match – it was time to bring out perhaps one-day cricket's greatest treat and rarest delicacy. The low-scoring thriller.

There really is something special about the genuine low-scoring thriller. Sighted rarely – more rarely than the high-scoring thriller despite people always using the once-or-twice-a-tournament appearance of a good old low-scoring thriller as evidence that you don't need all those runs to have a good time – it delights because every individual moment becomes so much more important. The missed chance, the run-out-from-nowhere, the edged four past the keeper's despairing dive, the "fuck this" tailender who swishes and swipes 20; all become so much more significant as runs, the game's base currency, become exponentially more valuable.

Of course, what normally happens when the team batting first gets a low score is that the team batting second just wins easily. Often there will be a minor wobble to get the low-scoring-thriller-spotter's Spidey-sense tingling before nerves are steadied by a solid fourth-wicket stand of 72 from 97 balls that slowly but inexorably sucks the tension from the atmosphere and everyone drifts back to whatever they were doing before. But that's how it should be. Rarity is the ultimate secret of the low-scoring thriller's cachet. If low-scoring thrillers happened every other game they would soon lose their frisson.

England's next opponents would be a South Africa side in the middle of a textbook South Africa campaign, one in which they would absolutely cruise through the group stages before immediately losing to a weaker team once the knockout games came around.

They were doing it perfectly having dispatched West Indies by seven wickets in their first game and the Netherlands by 231 in their second, but even the Proteas were powerless to resist being drawn into England's chaos. They were like a twister tearing up a trailer park in a big budget Hollywood blockbuster.

Having scored 296-4, 338-8 and 327-8, England crumbled to 171 all out on a dusty track in Chennai. It was surely the last thing that South Africa expected and therefore great tactics. Strauss and Pietersen both fell in the first over to left-arm spinner Robin Peterson, and only a watchful 99-run stand between half-centurions Trott and Bopara prevented England's innings being a total write-off. Maybe that would've thrown the South Africans even further off kilter, who knows.

In any case, England's bold gambit looked to have failed when South Africa retained their composure sufficiently to reach 63 without loss. Swann, though, got one to spin and flick Graeme Smith's glove on its way through to Prior and the Proteas captain was given out on DRS review before Stuart Broad removed Hashim Amla and Jacques Kallis in the space of six balls. This is the point where South Africa's insistence on constantly talking about choking in a bid to stop people talking about choking starts to affect them.

James Anderson, reversing the old ball before the mandatory change after 34 overs, removed AB de Villiers with one that shaved the off stump so gently a moment passed before first Matt Prior and then everyone else realised the bails were on the floor. Faf du Plessis was brilliantly run out by Ian Bell from short leg, and South Africa became gripped by fear and descended into strokeless paralysis as wickets tumbled. Dale Steyn attempted to hit his way out of trouble and dragged his team within sight of the target before Bresnan and Broad returned to knock over the last three wickets.

All ten South Africa wickets fell for just 102 runs to leave them on 165 and six runs short of England's total. Broad's match-winning 4-15 was his last involvement in the tournament as he succumbed to a side strain, while Pietersen too would fly home for surgery on his hernias.

England were back on track, and now had a 100 per cent winning record in the tournament when they scored less than 300 runs and a zero per cent winning record when they scored more than 300.

That data surely explains a ponderous batting performance from England next time out, when they eked out 225 in Chittagong against tournament co-hosts Bangladesh. Only Eoin Morgan, rejoining the squad in Pietersen's place and going straight into the team, found any fluency in a 60-ball half-century.

Matt Prior was now back opening the innings as he had done so unsuccessfully in Australia, and his dismissal summed up an increasingly weary England's lack of remaining fuel. Having survived a stumping attempt, Prior wandered from his crease and was stumped for real this time as Bangladesh keeper Mushfiqur Rahim gleefully plucked a stump from the ground. "They looked exhausted," says Lawrence Booth. "Matt Prior just looked zoned out. That summed up that team."

Despite their clear and understandable fatigue, England looked all set to reprise their antics from the South Africa game when Bangladesh slipped from 155-3 to 169-8. The collapse was triggered by sharp fielding from Ajmal Shahzad to run out Imrul Kayes for 60, and he then dismissed Mushfiqur and Naeem Islam in quick succession.

The game had one final twist, though, an unbroken ninth-wicket stand of 58 between Mahmudullah and Shafiul Islam steering Bangladesh to their target as heavy dew spiked England's guns. Swann, unable to grip the ball, saw his last over go for 16 runs and lost ten per cent of his match fee for the nature of his complaints to umpire Daryl Harper. The players were forced to remain in their dressing rooms until 2am while police regained control of the astonished and delighted Bangladesh fans outside the ground and the teams' hotel.

Plenty of time for England to reflect on another game lost from a winning position and a quarter-final place back in jeopardy.

"We had three nights at home in six months and there were some tired bodies around that World Cup," says Strauss. "And I think what we saw during that campaign was the games that we could get ourselves up for we actually did fine, but the ones that were 'ergh, we're just playing Bangladesh or we're playing Ireland' we just weren't at the races. That cost us dearly. Not that we were good enough to win it, but still."

England's last group game was against West Indies, with Strauss' men knowing that defeat would send them home humiliatingly early and even victory wouldn't absolutely confirm their place in the last eight. All England could do was win the game, and then hope either Bangladesh or the West Indies failed to win their own final games.

There were more injury problems for England. Shahzad was the latest to pull up lame, while an exhausted Anderson also missed the West Indies game, along with Paul Collingwood. Luke Wright, James Tredwell and Chris Tremlett all made their first World Cup appearances in this must-win game.

England were back in Chennai, but not on the same pitch where they had stolen South Africa's sweets 11 days earlier. This next-door neighbour was much better for batting, and Trott scored six fours in his first nine balls to suggest another big total was on the cards. England's innings faltered against spin, though, with Devendra Bishoo taking 3-34 on debut. Wright's 57-ball 44 batting at number seven got England up to something-to-bowl-at territory, but at 243 all out no further than that.

Gayle immediately put England under pressure with 16 runs off overs from both Bresnan and Tremlett. Tredwell trapped Gayle leg-before to end that part of the fun, but captain Darren Sammy promoted himself to number three and made 41 entertaining runs of his own. As had been the case throughout England's group campaign there were twists and turns aplenty. Runs were scored and wickets fell as the teams traded blows without ever really gaining control. Andre Russell appeared to be changing that as he played the big shots while a watchful Ramnaresh Sarwan kept him company.

Their 72-run stand for the seventh wicket took West Indies within 22 runs of victory. They would get only three closer as England fittingly ended their group stage – and, still possible at this point, their whole campaign – in suitably dramatic style.

Russell became Tredwell's fourth victim, pinned lbw, before Swann had Sarwan caught at short leg and Kemar Roach smartly taken by a tumbling Tremlett at mid-off. Sulieman Benn then inside-edged the ball to third man and attempted a second run that existed only in his mind to be run out by a yard and hand England victory by 18 runs.

Bangladesh didn't get within 200 runs of South Africa's 284-8 and India held off West Indies by 80 runs. England had not only qualified, they had finished third in the group behind only sensible South Africa, who had won all their games before and after England's Chennai heist, and favourites India. England had two wins and a tie from their three matches against fellow qualifiers, and two defeats and a solitary win against the three teams eliminated.

England's one-day cricket had touched heights rarely seen before and plumbed depths that had never previously been explored. It's a wonder that beating South Africa straight after the Ireland game didn't give them the bends.

England were flawed, England were knackered, England were hugely entertaining. The number of truly exciting games in the 42-match group stage could barely have extended into double figures. England had played in six of them.

Having played six exciting games in the dull and predictable group stage, England then played a dreadfully dull and predictable quarter-final in the exciting knockout stage.

Maybe they just wanted to go home. Few could truly blame them. Says Strauss: "There were some bright moments at that World Cup but [before] the quarter-final against Sri Lanka we had a week in Colombo leading up to that game twiddling our thumbs having been away from home for six months. We had a World Cup quarter-final which was a massive event, but at no stage did I feel really confident as captain of that side that we were going into that with the right frame of mind.

"I think we were completely mentally shot, on all sorts of different levels. I think being in a hotel room for six months, having gone through a very emotional Ashes series, and a number of very emotional games in the tournament up to that point, both high and low. Being together for long periods of time with a lack of time away from cricket. And, to be fair, going to Colombo against a Sri Lankan team that knew the conditions well and not reading the race. We thought our score was a decent one when in fact it was miles off."

England, notes the *Wisden* match report, paid "too much attention to history and possibly even punditry" in pacing their innings against Sri Lanka in Colombo "as though 240 would be enough".

They didn't even get that far, reaching 229-6 from 50 overs. The six wickets is almost as damning as the 229, pointing to resources left unused in compiling such a meagre total. While 229 all out may not be what you want, one can at least understand why and how it might happen from time to time.

Sri Lanka won by ten wickets with more than ten overs to spare. "They played their percentage cricket," says Lawrence Booth, "getting 240 at the Premadasa in the belief that par scores would win the important games. It wasn't the catastrophe that 2007 was, but it was annoying for other reasons."

After a rollicking, freewheeling, sometimes enthralling and occasionally embarrassing World Cup campaign, England had finally gone all sensible and played to their percentages. They had looked at the data. And it wouldn't be the last time.

2015 World Cup

England's Greatest Hits

S O this was it. Everything England have ever done – or not done – at the Cricket World Cup was just laying the foundation for 2015. It was a Greatest Hits compilation, and there is definitely a lost consonant there somewhere.

All the old favourites were here. The 1996 party piece of failing to beat a single other Full Member nation. The 1999 and 2011 last-minute changes to personnel. The 2007 trick of adopting an outdated game plan completely at odds with all the more successful sides and appearing to be genuinely astonished to discover that the game has moved on without them.

England were thrashed by the best sides, threw it away against the mid-range ones, and scored meaningless victories over the associates from which not even the media-trained players could truly claim to extract any significant positive. So wretched was England's performance that their second – and last – victory of the competition, over Afghanistan, came with the earliest possible exit already confirmed. And this in a tournament with a format specifically designed to assist England and the rest of the 'Big Eight'.

Even allowing for the World Cup's bloated schedule, England had been eliminated after just 28 days. Just 28 Days' Data. This, says *Wisden* editor Lawrence Booth, "is the World Cup that should really get England fans angry". Because it was all so predictable, and it was all so avoidable.

Between the 2011 and 2015 World Cups, England managed to reach the number one spot in all three formats – they were even the number one seeds for the World Cup thanks to the ICC's underrated comedy timing meaning the ranking cut-off point arrived during a period at the end of 2012 when England were briefly atop the ODI tree. England's one-day rise from their 2011 disappointment was built chiefly on home results, where they hit upon a strategy that for two years paid rich dividends. They should have won the 2013 Champions Trophy on home soil, as they should have in 2004. They allowed this modicum of success to blind them to what was happening all around them.

The seeds for England's 2015 disaster were sown in the Ashes double-header of 2013/14. There was some sense behind the revised calendar; playing the World Cup straight off the back of Ashes tours had been a huge contributing factor in the failures of 2003, 2007 and 2011. Win or lose, the Ashes had left the players spent by the time the one-day showpiece came along. Moving the Ashes forward by 12 months allowed England the luxury of a winter spent solely in coloured clothing; the only Test tour of 2014/15 would be to the Caribbean and it would come after the World Cup.

But it was to prove disastrous. Whatever was gained from the move never came close to making up for the damage it caused. "They split up the World Cup and the Ashes precisely to avoid this kind of scenario," says Booth. "And all that happened was they split the misery over two winters. They lost 5-0, and then lost the World Cup. They could've got it out of the way in one winter, like they usually do."

The toil of ten Ashes Tests in a row – and there can be little doubt that playing the away games second made it tougher – hastened the end of the international careers of Graeme Swann, Jonathan Trott, Kevin Pietersen and Matt Prior. At least two of those, with careful management and less pig-headedness, could have made a difference to the 2015 World Cup.

But in one-day cricket, the Ashes fallout was perhaps felt most keenly not in who was lost but in who remained. The real impact came in the doubling down of the top brass's support for Alastair Cook as captain in both Test and ODI cricket.

It was a dubious decision at the time and soon became indefensible. The stubborn streak that made Cook one of the finest Test openers of his generation was counter-productive here as he clung to the job while the suits who had staked their own continued employment on English cricket's golden boy continued to pledge support until the very last possible moment.

Cook faced a near impossible task. After the Ashes humiliation, working to rediscover his Test form and impose himself as leader of that side were more than enough to occupy even a man as iron-willed as Cook. One-day cricket, both batting and captaincy, were an unwelcome and unnecessary distraction, if only he and those in charge had seen it.

"They were stubborn," insist Booth. "And Cook's a stubborn guy himself. I do think it verged on the selfish from Cook, because he was holding back the one-day team, anyone could see that."

In a form of the game that did not come naturally, he was unable to justify his place in the side as either batsman or leader. Still the management refused to make any move.

When they did, it was already too late. While England would finally go to the World Cup led by a man with an instinctive feel for one-day cricket in Eoin Morgan, they managed to hand him the job so late in the day that the chance for material change to England's approach was already gone.

Cook had taken over the one-day captaincy immediately after the 2011 World Cup, as England followed a post-World Cup path they knew all too well.

Andrew Strauss stood down, to be replaced by the man ideally suited to eventually replace him in the Test job. As with Michael Vaughan, Cook was given the one-day captaincy as a dress rehearsal for the big job, the one that mattered to England cricket, rather than because he was the man best suited to this particular role. It could charitably be described as succession planning, but it once again left little doubt over where one-day cricket stood in England's Big Plan.

Clearly, the selectors were hoping Cook could perform the same trick Strauss himself had managed, taking the talent and temperament that made him a fine Test player and using them to become an effective option at the top of the order in the shorter form of the game.

Then when Strauss was ready to give up the Test job, Cook would seamlessly take over the full captaincy from his opening partner and all would be well.

But in one-day cricket Cook was required to take off from a standing start. Before taking the captaincy, Cook had played a total of three ODIs since November 2008. And those three appearances only came because he was standing in for Strauss as captain on the 2010 Test tour of Bangladesh and was chucked back into the one-day squad to captain that too.

Yet despite his lack of recent exposure to the format and a mediocre record, the early signs were hugely encouraging. Cook made 119 and 95 not out in his first series as full-time ODI skipper against Sri Lanka in England, and made four half-centuries in home-and-away series against India. In early 2012 Cook made 137, 102 and 80 in consecutive innings against Pakistan in the UAE. Another century followed that summer against West Indies.

From his appointment as skipper until the end of October 2012, Cook made 1,263 ODI runs in 30 innings at an average of 46.77 and a strike-rate of 85.74. He made four hundreds and eight half-centuries. All looked good. Cook had not become an overnight dasher, but he was finding a way.

But the end of October 2012 is not an arbitrary cut-off point. 30 October marked the latest implementation date for the ICC's regular tinkerings with one-day cricket.

The ICC's latest attempt to prevent ODI innings featuring 30 dull overs in the middle, where the batting side are happy enough to score five an over and the bowling side happy enough to let them, led to a change ostensibly designed to help the batsmen. Instead of five fielders allowed outside the 30-yard fielding circle, there would now only be four. The idea, fairly obviously, was to make it easier to hit boundaries during the two-hour lull between the mandatory PowerPlay and late-innings charge.

For Cook the change was less welcome. The nurdler's nurdler, his game was built on working the ball around and finding gaps. Suddenly those gaps became harder to find. That captains had largely been unwilling to attempt this tactic against Cook before it was forced upon them speaks volumes for the formulaic leadership that can blight the limited-overs game, but it had a significant effect. With Cook's accumulation supply lines cut off, his limitations were once again exposed in white-ball cricket.

After the fielding restrictions changed, Cook never scored another ODI hundred. He managed just six half-centuries in 36 more innings that brought 1,083 runs at an average of 31 and a strike-rate of 73.22. His highest score was only 78. The runs didn't completely disappear but it was the drop in strike-rate that really hurt.

Because Cook being Cook, he was still scoring runs. Still contributing. But he was doing it far too slowly in a team that in 2013 already had Jonathan Trott not only playing the anchor role but playing it far better.

England could have moved as early as 2013 to remove Cook from both the captaincy and the team, but there was a big reason to hold on. The Champions Trophy was to be held in England, before the Ashes, in the slot at one time slated to host the oft-touted but still-to-materialise World Test Championship.

The Champions Trophy remains a largely unloved competition, but it does have its merits. Chief among them is brevity. With only eight teams in two groups, the Champions Trophy took only 18 days to get through its 15 fixtures. It may only ever receive a limited welcome, but at least the Champions Trophy is in no danger of outstaying it.

It was more significant for Alastair Cook and his side than most. For England, in England, the Champions Trophy represented a golden opportunity to finally win a global 50-over title, even if it remained very much the League Cup of international cricketing silverware.

"We haven't won a global 50-over tournament, as everyone keeps reminding me," said Cook before the final against India. "So we're desperately keen to try and change that. It would be a great achievement if we can win and one which we will cherish."

England qualified for the semi-final impressively enough, with big wins over Australia and New Zealand either side of a defeat to Sri Lanka.

The semi-final against South Africa was perhaps the high point of Cook's one-day reign as the Proteas were dispatched by seven wickets. James Tredwell and Stuart Broad took three wickets apiece as South Africa made just 175 in 38.4 overs. It was a perfect run-chase for England's Test-geared team, and Trott helped himself to an unbeaten 82 to complete a facile victory.

But the final, like the 2004 event, proved to be an astonishing missed opportunity as England once again contrived to lose from a position where the game appeared won.

For much of the day, it appeared there would be no final at all. Persistent rain at Edgbaston looked sure to leave the spoils shared in an unsatisfactory conclusion. Remarkably there was no reserve day in place for the ICC's second most important 50-over competition.

In a brilliant fudge of the playing conditions that appeared in an attempt to save the blushes that not having a reserve days would have caused, the time allowed for the game to be completed was extended by 75 minutes in order to squeeze in a 20-over game. So England were left to try and claim their first global 50-over title by winning what amounted to a T20 with a top three of Alastair Cook, Ian Bell and Jonathan Trott. Had they failed miserably, there would've been some sympathy. England were locked into the team because the toss had already taken place when the match was still due to be 50 overs a side. Circumstances had conspired against them.

Yet England restricted India to just 129-7 on a pitch that turned square and held up for those who took pace off the ball. Ravi Bopara took 3-20 in four overs.

Even on a difficult pitch and with a batting line-up better suited to Tests than T20s, England should still have got home. Especially when they reached 110-4 in the 18th over with one-day specialists Ravi Bopara and Eoin Morgan both going well.

Then Ishant Sharma, India's most expensive bowler on the day, removed both set batsmen in successive balls. Morgan contrived to miscue a slower ball to midwicket, Bopara hoiked a full-toss to deep square leg.

Jos Buttler fell in the next over, before England almost managed to lose three wickets in one ball. Tim Bresnan might have been lbw, while either he or Broad could've been run out. Bresnan slipped, and he was the man to go. "All it needed," wrote Jarrod Kimber on *ESPNcricinfo*, "was an actual banana skin."

A run-chase England had under complete control somehow in the end came down to Tredwell needing to hit the last ball of a bizarre game for six. He swung, he missed. England lost by five runs. Alastair Cook's ODI reign would never know such good times again.

"We should have won the Champions Trophy," says coach Ashley Giles. "I can still see it unfold. We needed 19 off 16 balls I think it was. We lost back-to-back wickets, Morgan and Bopara, and cocked it up. We should have won it.

"In that moment India coped better with the pressure. Bopara and Morgan had played beautifully to get us into a position where we would win the game and then we just had a mad over. In that situation, you need a cool head, but you still need to score. We needed 19 runs, it wasn't like we needed 10 off 16 balls. Morgan would still back himself, the field came up a little bit, and it was 'right, now is my moment, now I can kill him'. Probably with Eoin Morgan eight times out of ten he would."

England won only one of their next six one-day international series, and that a 2-1 success in the West Indies when a Cook-free T20 squad under the leadership of Stuart Broad was preparing for the World Twenty20 in Bangladesh.

England's climb to the top of the ODI world rankings in 2012 had come on the back of a stunning run of form for both the team and the skipper. By the end of the 2012 English summer, Cook's side had won 19 and lost just nine of 31 ODIs since the 2011 World Cup.

It was an excellent record but the fixture list had been kind. 21 of those 31 games (and 14 of the 19 wins) were at home, with another in Ireland, where England's steady approach proved largely effective. Their overall run-rate in this period was 5.29; on a completed 50 overs, that's a score of 264. And that is precisely the sort of totals England would make. Again and again. Remarkably, in a 31-match run – a run where England won two-thirds of their completed matches – they didn't reach 300 once. England's highest score was 298-4 in Mohali; India chased it down on their way to a 5-0 series victory that hindsight paints as a clear indicator of where England really stood in one-day cricket away from the green, green grass of home. And this was before the game would change again with the amendments to PowerPlays and fielding restrictions that produced a further shift in favour of the big hitters.

%, %, %,

The Champions Trophy final was a disappointment of course, but England were playing to a plan and playing to their strengths in the years leading up to it. While they struggled overseas, at home England remained a force and with the 2013 Champions Trophy a legitimate focus.

Things were looking good. Cook had formed a promising opening partnership with Craig Kieswetter. The World T20-winning keeper-batsman's recall also at least hinted at England moving on from the default position of attempting to solve any problem by just shoehorning more Test players into the side.

England's first ODI series under Cook's leadership was a 3-2 victory over Sri Lanka in the summer of 2011, the highlight of which was a thumping ten-wicket win at Trent Bridge, as England skipped gaily to 171-0 on the back of a startling 75-ball unbeaten 95 from the skipper. A win in Ireland under the leadership of Eoin Morgan was followed by a 3-0 victory over India. In truth, it's a scoreline that flatters England after a September series plagued by poor weather. Not one match was played out over the full distance.

In the opening game, England were 27-2 after 7.2 overs in pursuit of India's 275 when rain ensured there would be no result. While England were by no means out of the game, it's hard to contest *Wisden*'s claim that the tourists had "taken charge" in bowler-friendly conditions at Chester-le-Street.

There was little more joy with the weather at the other end of the country in Southampton for the next game, which was reduced to 23 overs per side. But England scored a memorable victory and, as at Trent

Bridge, it owed much to a Cook innings that suggested he could indeed follow Strauss' path to one-day success.

India made 187-8 from their 23 overs, but Cook made light of that total and a mockery of thoughts that he should leave himself out of the side for such a shortened game by seeing his side over the line with 80 not out off 63 balls. The innings contained his second ODI six and an actual reverse-sweep for four.

England made it 2-0 with a Duckworth-Lewis victory in the third match, before the calculators were again needed in a tied game that secured the series for England.

England led the series 2-0, but India could argue with some justification that it could easily have been at the very least 2-2.

The fifth game did nothing to ease the tourists' frustrations, as their imposing 304-6 was Duckworth-Lewised down to 241 from 34 after Cardiff joined in the wet and wild fun. England got home with time to spare thanks in large part to a bold 41 not out from 21 balls on debut from Jonny Bairstow.

It completed a disastrous tour for India, who had lost ten games and 11 players to injury during three chastening months in England and Wales for the newly-crowned world champions.

India's revenge would be swift, regrouping in their own conditions to hand England a 5-0 beating before the year was out.

For England, though, it was a temporary blip in 50-over cricket. After a 3-0 Test series defeat to Pakistan in the UAE when their batsmen had no answer to the spin of Saeed Ajmal and Abdur Rehman, the one-day series was won 4-0. Kevin Pietersen was back at the top of the order alongside his skipper, this time with far more success than during the 2011 World Cup, as he and Cook collected two centuries apiece in a near-flawless campaign. Cook was named player of the series. The final match featured an England debut for Jos Buttler, who made a two-ball duck as a specialist batsman.

That win in the Emirates began another impressive year that would complete England's rise to the top of the rankings. They beat West Indies 2-0, before thrashing Australia 4-0 in a standalone series – because who wants an English summer without yet another visit from Australia? By now England had won their last ten completed ODIs.

So well were things going for Cook and England that much was made of their apparent new approach. Here was an England side suddenly playing one-day cricket with freedom, with a new no-fear attitude. Things were different now. Mark Nicholas, writing for *ESPNcricinfo*, was moved to observe that "Captains Cook and Strauss and their merry men have got something going that is the envy of just about everyone else.

"England are winning 50-over matches," Nicholas went on, "because their minds are in the fun house." This was a "confident, cocky, charismatic England, where the culture changed and so did the results."

This is no slight on Nicholas, but more a warning from recent history that England making startling, intoxicating improvement at the start of the four-year World Cup cycle is nothing new. There is every danger that England's most recent successes are just another false dawn.

In reality, by the time Nicholas was extolling the virtues of England the Cook ODI honeymoon was already coming to an end. He had by now scored the last of his one-day international centuries, and the one-day series against South Africa in late August and early September 2012 ended all-square.

With Andrew Strauss the third England Test captain seen off by South Africa's apex predator Graeme Smith, Cook ended the summer in full charge of a side about to embark on a daunting schedule.

"We've got India away and we've got two Ashes series in the next 18 months, so there's a lot of cricket to play and hopefully I can do a good job," said Cook when unveiled as the new Test captain.

There was indeed a lot of cricket to play, and England would look very different by the end of it.

※ ※ ※

As with the one-day captaincy, Cook's full-time leadership of the Test team got off to an astonishing start with a 2-1 come-from-behind series win in India and a stack of runs for the skipper, as well as the successful "reintegration" of Kevin Pietersen to the side after he had ended the 2012 summer outside the set-up for allegedly sending derogatory messages about then captain Andrew Strauss to South African players. And a narrow 3-2 loss in the one-day series that followed was an acceptable improvement on England's previous white-ball efforts in India.

England won a tight one-day series 2-1 in New Zealand – their last series win under Cook – and then lost to the same opponents by the same scoreline at home.

The post-Ashes one-day series was also lost 2-1 in Cook's absence, but after reaching the final of the Champions Trophy and – far, far more importantly – retaining the Ashes, all was generally considered to be well.

But flaws had crept into England's one-day cricket and were already starting to emerge.

In November 2012, Ashley Giles had taken over as coach of the limited-overs teams with Andy Flower keen to reduce his workload. But outside the Champions Trophy campaign, Giles never had the opportunity to pick from the strongest available one-day international squad.

"I don't want to look back at it in any bitter way," he says. "I think it was an interesting experiment with the split roles with me and Andy but I do think to a degree one-day cricket was the poor relation of Test cricket, so it will always suffer a little bit. The argument to that of course is 'well there was a hell of a lot of important Test series with the back-to-back Ashes', so it was going to happen and I accept that to a degree."

Even at the Champions Trophy, injuries robbed him of key men in Graeme Swann and Kevin Pietersen.

Pietersen was recovering from the knee injury that had cut short his tour of New Zealand, and England's cautious approach to his recovery was undoubtedly in part influenced by ten looming Ashes Tests.

Swann was struggling with calf and back injuries and played in just one of England's five games. Again, the upcoming Ashes double-header meant the England camp were in no mood to take any risks.

And Mark Nicholas' "fun house" of 2012 was markedly less evident a year later. While key players were frequently rested or rotated for one-day games – a move only ever considered in the Test team for tours of Bangladesh – the team still appeared more prosaic.

Cook's early dashing as captain had passed, and, where his opening partners had once been the likes of Kieswetter and Pietersen, he was now alongside Ian Bell with Jonathan Trott at number three. Fine players all, but it left England with a one-paced and one-dimensional top three. Again.

England had come up with a plan that might, and very nearly did, get them through a Champions Trophy campaign on home soil, but the game was changing around them and they appeared completely oblivious to it. The one-day series against Australia after the Ashes victory was relegated to little more than an after-thought. Cook was rested, as were Ian Bell, Graeme Swann, James Anderson and Stuart Broad.

BBC cricket correspondent Jonathan Agnew was among the more vocal critics of England's rotation policy. "I got really angry about that particular selection, because it was as if 'England have won the Ashes, therefore the one-dayers really don't matter'. They got that completely wrong. There is too much resting, I've always felt that an England cap is an England cap, be it a one-day international or whatever. And that, if you are tired, and knackered, or a bit spent, well I'm afraid that's professional sport, and if you get injured that's life."

※ ※ ※

The 2013/14 winter and the months of recrimination that followed were an astonishing period in English cricket. It really is hard to overstate quite how bad things became. England had risen to the top of the rankings in all three formats, but were now at their lowest ebb since the darkest days of the late 1990s before the Nasser Hussain and Duncan Fletcher revolution.

ECB chairman Giles Clarke rejected the idea that things were bad when he spoke to the *Evening Standard* in March 2014: "It's utter nonsense to say we're at some sort of massive low ebb." If Clarke meant that he thought things could be even worse then the next 12 months proved him spectacularly right.

Having won the Ashes convincingly only months earlier, England arrived in Australia as favourites to at least retain the urn and perhaps win the series outright.

Before the series, all appeared to be going well for England. They were ready, while Australia captain Michael Clarke was busy naming the England side in one of the stranger press conference performances.

The two-minute display, which Clarke visibly began to regret after about ten seconds, was an exercise in rapidly diminishing confidence. It's painful to watch as Clarke begins by saying he "knows" the XI, to almost forgetting it as he names it, to then saying he's "very confident" and finally "confident" in the selection apparently shared with him by Alastair Cook during a Remembrance Sunday service.

He did get the team right, though. And had he managed to successfully name the team for the fifth

Test before the series began it would have been a truly impressive feat.

Things began going wrong almost immediately for England in Brisbane. Almost, because things actually started rather well.

Stuart Broad took five wickets on the first day of the series and ended up with six for the innings as Australia were bowled out for 295 on the second morning.

Then Mitchell Johnson happened, and one of England's best ever teams ceased to exist in an instant. All the optimism and hope evaporated. It seemed not just the match but the series had been lost there and then, such was England's utter capitulation to the pace and fire of Johnson and Ryan Harris at the Gabba.

Jonathan Trott left the tour after the first Test, Graeme Swann retired after the third. These were hammer blows to the Test team, but also robbed England of two key performers in their one-day side.

England's strategy of always getting to around 260 or 280 in ODIs and very often winning relied heavily on both men, but particularly Trott who remains the most consistent run-scorer England have ever had in one-day cricket. There are still only five men in ODI history with a better average and four of them – AB de Villiers, Michael Bevan, Hashim Amla and Virat Kohli – are undisputed greats of the one-day game.

By the time the Test series had been played out to its grimly inevitable 5-0 conclusion, England were a broken team who had simply had enough.

But there was still a one-day series to get through. By the time a beleaguered, battered and bruised England fell 3-0 down, Cook's resolve to lead the side in both forms appeared to be wavering. "English cricket needs a little bit of a change," he suggested.

A win can make things look different, though, and that's what England finally managed to get in their next match to avoid going through the entire tour without a single victory over the old enemy, but that was the only win England secured during a woeful Australian tour.

Cook's resolve strengthened with that W on the board. The change that had been needed five days earlier was suddenly no longer necessary after a dead-rubber win in Perth. Indeed, any such move would in fact be far too risky. "I spoke what I was feeling, sometimes you probably shouldn't do. I think, what I've learned over three years as one-day captain, it would be wrong so close to the World Cup to change."

This may have been a message for the selectors as much as anybody else. Because behind the scenes, battle lines were being drawn, and English cricket was about to be engulfed in a bitter feud.

Despite Cook's renewed swagger, the facts were he had led England to a 5-0 Test series defeat and the one-dayers had gone only very slightly better, ending in a 4-1 loss. Whether he wanted to continue as skipper or not could very well have been moot.

Before the Ashes defence in Australia had begun, changes were already afoot. In October 2013, the ECB had announced that the former England wicketkeeper Paul Downton would be replacing Hugh Morris as managing director from February.

Few could have anticipated then just what he would be walking into. But this was, quite literally, a safe pair of hands. Not only a former England keeper who had enjoyed a successful county career in an excellent Middlesex side, but a man who had gone on to have a career in the City after a freak eye injury ended his playing days. When Downton's appointment was announced his former Middlesex team-mate Simon Hughes was in no doubt that his friend was the man for the job. "As a playing colleague for 12 years and a good friend for 30, he has always been Mr Nice Guy," Hughes wrote in *The Daily Telegraph*. "Gracious, encouraging, unfailingly polite, a diplomat. The kind of chap, I once suggested, who would offer the bailiffs a glass of sherry if they turned up unannounced."

His first act upon taking up his new position, in admittedly trying circumstances, was to watch one Test match and decide to sack the team's best batsman.

In so doing, and with head coach Andy Flower shuffled sideways to Loughborough, Downton and England were also swinging fully behind the captain. Pietersen was gone, and Cook would continue to lead in both Test and one-day cricket.

Not since David Gower was dropped for the 1992/93 tour of India has a decision caused such recrimination. England's cricket throughout 2014, on to the World Cup, and beyond was all played out against the increasingly bitter and unpleasant backdrop of the ECB v Pietersen.

Few emerged from it with much credit. Pietersen had been "reintegrated" into the team barely a year earlier and was now being removed again, except this time there was to be no hope of a return. "I will continue to play but deeply regret that it won't be for England," said Pietersen in a prepared statement.

Downton, having held meetings with Cook, Flower, one-day coach Ashley Giles and national selector James Whitaker, insisted this was a necessary change. "We have decided the time is right to look to the future and start to rebuild not only the team but also team ethic and philosophy."

In a moment of hopeless optimism, he added: "This decision brings some clarity now for the future of the England teams."

Of course, it did nothing of the sort. While there had been hearsay and rumour about poor behaviour on Pietersen's part, there had been nothing official. He had not been reprimanded during the tour. There was talk of "dossiers" listing Pietersen's "misdemeanours". When details of these offences started to emerge, they were almost indescribably petty. Whistling after getting out, or staring out of a window.

Now, the apparent collapse and failure of the "team ethic and philosophy" appeared to be pinned on one man. That this man was England's leading international run-scorer and most watchable, entertaining batsman and the reasons so unclear meant the decision would not – could not – be accepted without some further justification.

But the ECB had hamstrung themselves. In the agreement to cut short Pietersen's central contract there was a confidentiality clause. Neither side could speak publicly about the reasons for Pietersen's axing until October.

Maybe the ECB thought any fuss would have long since died down by then. Certainly they appeared unprepared for the fact England cricket fans wouldn't just move on and accept the end of such a fine career without further explanation. It was a boneheaded stance. When Pietersen had been jettisoned for the first time in 2012, the furore only died down with his recall several months later – and that time everyone had some idea about what he'd supposedly done wrong.

With nothing official forthcoming from either side, the vacuum was filled with rumours, reports, hearsay and Twitter. Pietersen's cheerleader-in-chief Piers Morgan used the platform provided by his vast social media following to attack the ECB's decision.

The subject of much of Morgan's ire was the role played by Matt Prior in arranging a players' meeting after the fourth Test in Melbourne, when Andy Flower's headmasterly style of leadership came in for criticism. Views aired by Pietersen and others at the supposedly private meeting made their way back to Flower, with Morgan adamant that Prior had stabbed Pietersen in the back.

Bound by that confidentiality clause in their agreement with Pietersen and frustrated at the way Morgan had been able to set the agenda, the ECB – in a joint statement with the Professional Cricketers' Association – attempted to calm the situation by pouring a load more petrol on to the raging fire.

The astonishing statement, which still sits on the ECB's website, was released on 9 February, four days after Pietersen's sacking. It remains a staggering, mystifying misjudgement. It was bad enough that the ECB had previously believed Pietersen's departure would require no explanation, worse still that someone, anyone, thought this statement would help.

While there had been plenty of adverse reaction to the Pietersen decision and opaque reasoning behind it, it was clear that it was Morgan – the loudest voice on the largest platform – who had vexed the ECB. He had criticised Cook, Prior and Flower, and in so doing shared information the ECB felt was not only dubious but should not in any case have been his to share.

With Morgan the obvious target of the statement, it was a grave error not to mention Piers by name. Perhaps they didn't want to give him the satisfaction.

Instead they said of his inflammatory, accusatory tweets: "Allegations have been made, some from people outside cricket, which as well as attacking the rationale of the ECB's decision-making, have questioned, without justification, the integrity of the England Team Director and some of England's players."

There it was. Outside cricket. Not 'outside the England team', but outside the very sport itself. It was immediately clear to whom this none-too-subtle epithet referred, but equally clear to any England fan that this wide-ranging description (use of the word 'people' rather than 'person' seems important here) applied also to them. Whether you agreed or disagreed with Morgan, he was and is an England cricket fan. If he was outside cricket, so were you. So were we all. You can buy the Sky subscriptions and the £100 tickets and £45 replica kits and flat lager at £5 a go, but you're not in the gang. You're not inside cricket.

In one clumsy statement, the ECB had managed to not only widen the existing divide between the decision-makers and supporters, they had also given the pro-KP lobby a catchy name and managed to make

Piers Morgan look like the victim. It was a remarkable effort.

And it wasn't the last farcical statement made on the subject. The ECB chairman Giles Clarke would emerge, apparently from 1953, to describe Alastair Cook and his family as "very much the sort of people we want the England captain and his family to be". After genuine attempts – successful ones too – at modernisation, English cricket's leadership was drifting desperately out of touch.

In May, Downton made another attempt to justify what increasingly appeared to be the unjustifiable and made a mess of it. Appearing on BBC's *Test Match Special*, Downton described Pietersen as "distracted" and "disinterested" during the fifth Ashes Test in Sydney. Pietersen denied the claims, with the ECB and Downton forced to issue a humiliating and grovelling apology for breaching that pesky confidentiality clause.

It was clear that England had acted in haste when axing Pietersen so swiftly after the Australia tour. If Downton was correct in his assertion that there was "not one supporter" for Pietersen in the England set-up, then he was most certainly not asking the question at a time when careful, sober judgements could reasonably be sought. He was new in the job and England had just endured one of the most difficult and demoralising tours in their history. It would be surprising if there were not some strong polarised opinions being expressed. One a more basic level, the scale of England's defeat left everyone on the defensive, fearing for their own future and perhaps sensing in these questions the opportunity to pass the buck.

Downton seemed to place an amazing amount of stock in an opinion that he formed in a matter of days of taking up his role as the man in charge of the England cricket team. There was little evidence throughout his time in the job that this confidence in his own decision-making abilities was in any way justified.

English cricket, so often slow to react to what was happening, had this time moved too fast. There was a reason for it, and that was the upcoming World Twenty20 in Bangladesh.

The squad announcement was due, and it would be impossible to simply leave Pietersen's name off the press release and hope nobody noticed. Although it must have looked a tempting option at one stage.

Pietersen, man of the tournament in the 2010 victory, had already missed the 2012 World Twenty20 during his previous spell outside the team, but there was no doubt that a full-strength England squad with serious designs on winning the Bangladesh event would include him.

A decision had to be taken, even if that meant the decision being taken by a managing director who had not yet got his feet under the desk, an outgoing head coach, a captain who was fighting to preserve his own job, and a limited-overs coach seeking promotion.

The World Twenty20 campaign was a disaster. A stunning Alex Hales-inspired victory over eventual winners Sri Lanka apart, England didn't really compete. In England's last game they were thrashed by the Netherlands to put a final nail in the coffin of Giles' spell as coach and effectively end Stuart Broad's career in the format. Although not officially replaced as T20 skipper until 2015, the Netherlands defeat remains Broad's last T20i appearance. It's hard not to feel sorry for Giles. At a time when plenty of guilty men were keeping their jobs, he was on his way out after trying to do his with one arm tied behind his back.

When England announced their new head coach, it was a further hammer blow to any hope Pietersen had of returning to the fold. England could not have sent any clearer message than reappointing Peter Moores, the one coach absolutely guaranteed to have no temptation to call again on England's great batting maverick.

Moores and Cook. The ECB's kind of people.

There is an argument that Moores deserved his second chance. Since his first spell with England, he had enjoyed further success in county cricket, winning the 2011 Championship title with Lancashire (and, it should be noted, getting relegated the following year).

Moores was and is a fine coach and a very good man, and it was reasonable enough to expect he had learned lessons from his first spell in charge and another stint in the county game. But it's hard to imagine any other sport where England would return so readily to a man who had failed so conspicuously once before. Steve McClaren is unlikely to be the next England football manager, while Stuart Lancaster is unlikely to get a phone call from the RFU.

Downton didn't help by referring to Moores as "the outstanding coach of his generation", immediately providing social media with another catchy stick with which to beat both the coach and the men who appointed him. Throughout his time with the ECB,

Downton would remove his right foot from his mouth only to immediately replace it with his left.

England were a side in flux and under pressure, but Moores came into the job with eyes open. "Obviously I knew more the second time having done it the first time," he says. "Both times I took it on, I knew that you don't go through transition without it being hard because you're going to be inconsistent and suffer some losses because you're rebuilding something.

"What you often find when you first go in at that situation, is that people who've been through a period of loss normally, because you've lost games to cause the transition, they're all a bit defensive. They're in survival mode, you know, trying to keep their positions in the side and they're not really expressing themselves as players."

Despite some encouraging individual performances, the 2014 summer got off to a bad start. England lost both Test and ODI series to Sri Lanka. Even the ODI series' one big bright spot – an England record 61-ball hundred from Jos Buttler – came in defeat at Lord's. If you have a guy scoring the fastest hundred ever made in an England shirt and you still go on to lose the game you know things aren't going your way.

With feelings still running high from Pietersen's axing, Cook was under serious pressure. He wasn't scoring significant runs, and his captaincy was coming in for criticism. By now it wasn't just his one-day leadership under threat, but his Test captaincy as well. But he continued to receive unswerving support from above. And when Cook's batting form started to return in a 3-1 Test series win against an increasingly dispirited

India side, it was confirmed he would be retained as skipper for the one-day series that followed.

Having turned that Test series around from a 1-0 deficit, and overcome every other obstacle placed in front of him during his career, Downton and co decided to keep the faith.

England, once again, were using red-ball form to justify white-ball decisions. In a *Test Match Special* discussion on England's one-day approach, former captain Michael Vaughan said: "We've made the same mistake now as we did in my time – five, six years ago – and in the 1990s. We're picking one-day squads on Test form. English cricket has always had Test cricket at the pinnacle, but the games are so different. England are looking too much at these new white balls. The other teams have gone power at the top and all the way through. It's a completely different era because of T20."

The changes were significant, and England were missing them. In 2014, England scored their ODI runs at 5.14 runs per over. For comparison, eventual World Cup winners Australia scored at 5.40 an over in the same period. England reached 300 once in 15 innings – Australia did it four times in 13. If England needed further evidence that the game had changed, then three scores in the 290s that yielded only one victory should have provided it.

One-day cricket was no longer about either going big at the start or the end; it was about packing the side with power players throughout. By the end of the World Cup, 400 was the new 300.

Graeme Swann, only eight months into retirement, echoed Vaughan's sentiments. "The good Test form has made it easier for the selectors to have a more conservative selection than most people want to see.

"Alastair Cook is the most stubborn man in the world. He has almost backed himself into a corner where he's got to carry on. I don't think we've got a cat in hell's chance of winning the World Cup.

"I used to sit in the changing room and I always felt we were so far behind other teams because we play such an old-fashioned brand. Some of my best mates – Cook, Bell, Ballance – are not one-day players who are going to win you a World Cup. Alex Hales is going to win you a World Cup; James Vince, Jason Roy, Jos Buttler, Eoin Morgan. They're players I wouldn't want to bowl at, who can build a total of 360–370. I love Alastair Cook dearly but I don't think he should be bothering playing ODI cricket anymore."

Moores admits that England had been slow to spot the signs. "The game changed, didn't it? We changed to four people out rather than five, which made quite a big shift in the game and I think that sort of shift – it took time for it to really land with the players, to work out how to get the most out of it. The actual 2015 World Cup, on very good pitches, started to really show how people could really attack the last 10 or 15 overs of a game, with two new balls and they're still quite hard. It's very difficult for bowlers to stop them scoring at a rate somewhere in excess of 10, 11, 12 an over."

But it was Cook and the old approach for the series against India, who, after the first match was abandoned, promptly hammered England three times in a row to take the series. A Joe Root-inspired victory at Headingley in a series that was already lost was scant consolation. India won by 133 runs, six wickets, and nine wickets. In the fourth ODI, England made 206 all out from 49.3 overs and they only got that many because of a 50-ball 67 from Moeen Ali at number seven. India chased it with almost 20 overs to spare.

Even England's sole victory at Leeds highlighted their limitations. Even when the batting plan worked – a top-order batsman, Root in this case, making a run-a-ball hundred and everyone else chipping in around him – they only made 294. At a time when 300 was becoming a baseline for other sides, it remained England's ceiling.

England weren't just using outdated tactics. They were using them badly. Until the success at Headingley, none of England's top six had scored a 50 in the series. Had Jonathan Trott still been around averaging 50 at a strike-rate of 80, their tactics might have had some chance of success. Old-fashioned ODI cricket was about building a solid base with wickets in hand and accelerating at the end. But England weren't doing that. Instead, England were scoring slowly and losing wickets in the process. Without Trott, they had been bowled out for less than 250 six times in 17 innings. In his last 25 ODIs, around the time of England's rise to number one and the Champions Trophy campaign, it had happened just once in 25.

Cook's position was by now untenable. He was in charge of a losing team and had made one half-century all summer. It was by now 39 innings and over two years since he'd last made it to 80 in ODI cricket.

"The management's continued insistence that they believe he is the man to lead the ODI side forward in the face of all logic and evidence," wrote *ESPNcricinfo*'s George Dobell, "is beginning to resemble those who deny climate change."

England now had a maximum of 12 games left before facing Australia in the opening match of the 2015 World Cup. Seven of those would be in Sri Lanka. If there was to be change, this was the last chance for it to have any real effect.

But Cook was backed once more. National selector James Whitaker insisted that Cook still retained "100 per cent support" – although as it later came to light that Cook was kept on only after lengthy discussions ("Nearly a week kicking the tyres and working out were we best to stick with Alastair," as Downton put it during the Sri Lanka series) that 100 per cent would appear to be more of a Win Predictor 100 per cent than the traditional mathematical version.

Whitaker went on, sounding like a man desperately trying to convince himself as much as anyone else. "Leadership is unique and it takes time to develop. We believe Alastair still has the skills, the drive and enthusiasm, which are all great qualities, to instil the right direction and control of the players. He's fully respected within the group and, more than anything, we believe he is a very constant person."

His own form and the team's results were certainly constant. But Moores insists there was still a case for retaining Cook even at that late stage. "He was in a period of lost form and under huge amounts of pressure – in all forms of the game. But what I do know is in those big global tournaments you need your big players, so you need stability along with flair because you're going to be under a lot of pressure because the eyes of the world are upon you. We needed a top-order player who could still knock it around.

"The task for the selectors was to try and find balance, some stability and some new faces going into a World Cup knowing we wouldn't be settled because we'd just lost our two main one-day batters in Jonathan Trott, who'd been a mainstay, and Kevin Pietersen, an aggressive player. They'd both gone. And one of our big wicket-takers in the middle overs was Graeme Swann, and he'd gone. So you've lost a real core of the team, and you're going into the World Cup where you don't really want to be, which is in transition. You're trying to find that balance."

England, though, were falling further behind and appeared dangerously blind to what would eventually await in Australia and New Zealand. Whitaker was still talking about a "subtle blend" of players to reach totals of "280–300". In Sri Lanka, England would only reach 280 once, in the first game of the series. England got 292 in that one. Sri Lanka, sadly, had already got 317.

England's two wins in a 5-2 defeat came in a Duckworth-Lewis 35-over chase and a game when the bowlers were able to restrict Sri Lanka to 239.

England were bowled out for 185, 202 and 215. After the 292, they only once reached 250. There had been no progression. They were still playing the same way as they had during the summer, and they were still doing it badly.

The bright spots were Joe Root's continued pro-gress down a seemingly inevitable path to all-format greatness, and some chutzpah from Moeen Ali, who had been promoted to opener and hammered an 87-ball 119 in the opening defeat. But once again, that innings in a total of 292 showed the sort of things that had to go right for England to reach the sort of totals that were becoming routine in 50-over cricket.

Perhaps the biggest find for England was James Taylor. Coming into the side after three games, he made 90 and 68 batting at three. Here, potentially, was the Trott replacement England had searched for in the top three. And Taylor had more range to his game if he was still batting in the final ten overs.

"As James has moved up the levels I think he's shown he can bat three, he showed that for England in Sri Lanka, and he's a very adaptable cricketer," says Moores.

At least England had got something from the tour. But Cook made just 119 runs from six innings, with a highest score of 34.

After series defeat was confirmed in the sixth game of the series, Downton once again reiterated his support for Cook. "I would be very surprised if he was not captain at the World Cup. He's not captain forever, of course. But to the specific question: who is the best person to take us to the World Cup? The discussion we had in September, it's Alastair Cook. It hasn't helped that he hasn't scored any runs yet because this question keeps coming up. But I've got to think that form will turn."

Four days and one final defeat later, Cook was sacked. Downton yet again made a fool of himself when he opened his mouth. To the end, Cook still believed himself the right man to lead England in the World Cup, even as his most ardent backers lost the faith. "He had a dream to lead England at the World Cup and it's been taken away from him a month away from its fulfilment," Downton said at the time. "He still believes he's the right man for the job but the selectors had to make a decision in the best interests of English cricket."

Eoin Morgan, short of form himself, was given the captaincy with only four or five games in a tri-series against India and Australia to prepare for the World Cup.

England now also had three different captains for three different formats, with Broad still officially T20 captain in absentia having not played since the 2014 World Twenty20 exit.

While it was clearly the correct decision to put a stubborn but proud Cook out of his one-day misery, England had left it far, far too late. At the very least, Morgan should have had the Sri Lanka series to get his feet under the table. It was the right call made at the wrong time. One of the classic England pre-World Cup moves.

"They sleepwalked into disaster with sacking Cook so late on," says Lawrence Booth. "Cook should've gone the previous summer. Morgan was handed Cook's team essentially and had to work with a coach he didn't necessarily see eye-to-eye with. So Morgan was made to look a fool, and that was unfair on him."

For his part, Moores insists that he and Morgan had no issues and that the new captain's approach was not so very different from his departed predecessor's.

"We got on very well, I think we saw the game pretty much from the same point, and it wouldn't be far different from what Alastair Cook saw either, not as far as people would think. Just because Alastair plays an accumulative role as a batter doesn't mean he doesn't want to see people in his side play an expansive game.

"To me, take the build-up to our World Cup, in that time we had Jos Buttler score the fastest ever one-day hundred by an Englishman at Lord's against Sri Lanka. That would be difficult to happen if it was a regime where we were saying don't go and play your shots. Moeen Ali opened the batting and played an expansive, aggressive game all the way through every game he played.

"When Eoin came in [as captain], I was really conscious that it was really important that Eoin could put his stamp on the team quickly. But it was tough for Eoin as well because it is difficult, a settling-in period for a captain getting to know his players in a different light, and them to know him and what he wants. That's not an easy process to go through. And it's definitely not ideal changing your captain that close to a major event."

The Carlton Mid Tri-Series in Australia was England and Morgan's last chance to prepare for the World Cup. And it didn't go too badly. England may not have exactly looked like they were about to stun the world, but nor did they look like a side about to be humiliated.

Two impressive wins over India took England to the final, where they lost for a third time in the series against Australia.

Ian Bell was the leading run-scorer in the series with 247 at better than a run a ball, James Taylor impressed again in Trott's number-three role, and there was even a welcome century for Morgan the skipper in the first game, although he subsequently added only two further runs in four innings.

The wins against India both came chasing low totals, and England failed to defend another bat-around-one-player-and-get-300 effort. But it was too late to change their tactics now even with a new skipper, and there were at least legitimate signs that while the tactics remained outdated they were at least being deployed slightly more effectively.

With Steven Finn, Chris Woakes, James Anderson and Moeen Ali all doing an effective job with the ball, England had at least stumbled on a team that could compete.

Then came the first game at the World Cup, against Australia again, and England decided to shuffle everything.

In came Gary Ballance at number three, having been out of the side since the previous summer. James Taylor, after batting at three since the start of the Sri Lanka tour, dropped down to number six in place of Ravi Bopara.

England had done it again. Having stood by a failing captain for at least six months too long, they had now made wholesale changes to the team for the start of the tournament.

"James had batted at three and done a good job for us," says Moores, "but we also knew James was an excellent finisher of games who batted at four and five for Notts, been there at the end of games a lot. He's got this really very good tactical nous, and he's a really good player under pressure. We felt that, to win the World Cup, that we would need that sort of quality. We'd have liked to have tested it out before, but everything was being done pretty fast because of the amount of games we'd got.

"And Gary's a fantastic one-day player. He played the one practice game we had against Pakistan and got 57, played well. It wasn't a flippant decision, or something we thought of on a whim. We thought, actually if it's Gary here we can use James at six, we get some real finishing power in that lower middle order. Now what happened then was that the press I think really quite unfairly had a real go at Gary's position there. That put Gary under a bit of pressure when he didn't do well early on and unfortunately it didn't work out."

Against Australia, Taylor at six did work out. He made 98 not out from 90 balls. Unfortunately, by the time he began his innings England were 66-4 in response to Australia's 342-9. An England team geared up to accelerate towards 300 was already out of the game before Taylor arrived at the crease.

A failure of the Decision Review System protocols, which resulted in England's last man James Anderson being given run out after Taylor had overturned an lbw decision, brought the game to a farcical end.

The initial decision to give Taylor out meant the ball should have been regarded as dead when Glenn Maxwell subsequently ran Anderson out. The error unfairly denied Taylor the chance of a first ODI century, but could do nothing to mask the extent of

England's failure. Australia had won by 111 runs, and England's safety-first approach had been made to look very risky indeed.

In another change, Woakes had earlier been relegated to first change having taken one of the new balls all winter as Australia got off to a flying start.

The Sun's John Etheridge points to a "common trend" in England's World Cup performance. "These are quite significant tactical changes being made just a matter of days before the World Cup starts. This is a common trend, a common thread throughout all the World Cups really. It's just a lack of planning, always a feeling of trying to play catch-up, and other teams thinking more radically and more inventively and being a couple of years ahead of England in terms of their game plan and their thinking and their execution."

And things were about to get worse. In one of the most astonishingly one-sided World Cup games in history, England's rejigged side were shot out for just 123 by New Zealand. Tim Southee removed both openers, and then returned to annihilate the tail and end with figures of 7-33.

Remarkably, that represented the high point of England's day as an outrageous Brendon McCullum assault sent New Zealand racing past the finish line in just 12.3 overs. McCullum made 77 off 24 balls before being bowled by Woakes, who had now been relegated to second change. Finn's two overs cost 49 runs, while Broad went for 27 in 14 balls.

McCullum's 18-ball fifty was the fastest ever in the World Cup, Southee's seven-for the third best World

Cup bowling analysis. It was England's heaviest ever ODI defeat in terms of balls remaining, and 123 their lowest ever World Cup total having chosen to bat first.

In a World Cup format specifically designed to assist the big teams, England could perhaps point to an unkind fixture list. It's a fairly flimsy straw to grab after so many self-inflicted wounds, but England's frailties after their last-minute changes had been exposed by what would prove to be the two best teams in the competition. New Zealand would beat Australia in a one-wicket thriller in the group stage, before Australia would land the decisive blow with a comfortable win in the final.

While England could point to having got their two hardest group games out of the way, they could hardly be said to have taken anything positive from them.

To scrape through the group stage, England now needed to win three of their last four games. Despite everything, they would still have expected to do it with Scotland, Bangladesh and Afghanistan on the fixture list.

Scotland came first, and England got their first win on the board. Even here, though, their game plan remained the same. Moeen Ali scored a swashbuckling century, and everybody else chipped in with a few here and there to get England to 300. Ian Bell crawled to 50, and Ballance failed again.

The 303 England accrued proved more than enough to keep Scotland at bay, but England were about to receive yet another lesson in modern one-day cricket as they returned to Wellington, scene of the New Zealand fiasco, to take on Sri Lanka.

Once again, their game plan worked perfectly and got them to the 300 mark. This time it was Joe Root with the well-paced century, while Bell, Morgan, Taylor and Jos Buttler chipped in to nudge the total over 300.

Sri Lanka chased the target for the loss of one wicket as Lahiru Thirimanne and Kumar Sangakkara helped themselves to unbeaten centuries in a partnership worth 212 in 28.2 overs.

England's 309-6 was their sixth 300-plus total since the beginning of 2014. The biggest of those was 316, and England won only three of the six matches.

England were persisting with a strategy that required everything to go right in order to reach a total that was still only sufficient half the time.

With three defeats from their opening four games, it was make-or-break time for England. Defeat to Bangladesh would end their tournament even before the final group game against Afghanistan.

Gary Ballance finally made way after failing to pass ten in any of his four innings leaving the decision to recall him for the first match of the World Cup to look very silly indeed. Back into the side at number three came Alex Hales, the big-hitting T20 gun who had so far failed to impress in the 50-over game.

In the end, Bangladesh beat England at their own game. Mahmudullah scored a hundred to steer his side to 275 in Adelaide. England, despite contrasting half-centuries from Bell and Buttler, fell 15 runs short.

"We thought 275 was chaseable. We'll have to look at the data," said Moores on the BBC afterwards. Or rather, didn't. What he actually said was "we'll have to look at that later". But by then it was too late, a

317

meme was born. It seemed to strike at the very core of England's problem. Whether Moores said data or later – and there was another interview, on Sky, when he did mention data – the point was that he was unable or unwilling to pinpoint where England might have gone wrong in a chase that slumped from 121-2 after 26 overs to 132-5 by the 30th.

Moores' reputation for a stat-obsessed approach is perhaps unfair. "During my time as England coach, I was trying to unpick some of the analysis that had gone on because the game had moved on, certainly one-day cricket," he says. "Any analysis with five-men-out, the four-men-out rule would've changed anyway because the game moved so fast.

"Also it's frustrating, because my trademark as a coach has been to try and help people become independent, thinking people. Not institutionalised, robotic-type people who work to formulas, because sport isn't like that."

During that World Cup England's captain Eoin Morgan, an intuitive, shrewd and calculating one-day cricketer, had hidden behind data to avoid laying blame at the feet of his players. "After Sri Lanka chased down 300 in Wellington," remembers Etheridge, "Morgan said at the post-match press conference that we'll have to look at the data to check the areas in which the bowlers bowled, if they bowled in good areas or bad areas. And of course he didn't need to look at the data. Anybody watching the game knew straight away that they'd bowled very badly."

If England were not obsessed with stats, there were at best mixed messages. The references to data and stats in press conferences didn't help, and nor did subsequent attempts to distance themselves from the stat-heavy approach they had been accused of adopting. So fraught had things become, that England's stats man Nathan Leamon at one point even threatened to go home if he was not required.

England's problem, then, was perhaps less the use of stats and data in itself, than the manner in which they were used.

Clearly, the numbers weren't helping, and the game plan England were using wasn't working. While they had at least one accumulator too many in the top three to start the tournament, they still had players like Moeen Ali, Joe Root and Jos Buttler who were capable of scoring freely, not to mention the captain himself. Root, Buttler and Morgan would all go on to prove just what they were capable of only a few months later.

"Moores was probably not as obsessed with historical analyses as people have said and probably written," says Etheridge. "But he'd say to the players, 'go out and express yourselves, play with freedom, don't worry about getting out, but remember that teams that lose three wickets in the first PowerPlay lose 80 per cent of the games', so he'd sow a slight seed of doubt based on data."

For Ashley Giles, the late changes to crucial personnel were the foundation of England's failure. "I went to India first as coach and then to New Zealand [in 2013]. In New Zealand we had a strong side, we didn't have Kevin Pietersen, but we had a strong bowling line-up and we beat them 2-1. The first time we had beaten them there in 20 years or something. You look two years on from that and we had a different coach, a different captain, a completely different batting order and the Kiwis had almost exactly the same line-up. They planned. They were consistent for that World Cup and very nearly won it, and we weren't."

Wherever the blame lies for England's failure at the 2015 World Cup, and the truth is that very few involved shouldn't step forward to accept their share, it marked the lowest point in a bleak and damaging period for the England team.

The relationship between the team and the fans had been damaged, careers had been prematurely ended, the Ashes meekly surrendered and another World Cup opportunity discarded.

England's final game against Afghanistan was a sombre affair. Rain interrupted Afghanistan's innings three times before eventually cutting it short altogether at a stuttering 111-7 from 36.2 overs.

The target for England was eventually reduced to 101 from 25 overs, and they eased home by nine wickets. Bell helped himself to another half-century to massage his tournament stats, but like England he could not hide from the data.

Those meaningless, forgotten runs for Bell against Afghanistan lifted his tournament average above 50, but his strike-rate of 77 runs per 100 balls was from an era of one-day cricket that simply no longer existed. Of the 26 men to make more runs at the tournament than England's leading scorer, only William Porterfield of Ireland and Pakistan's Misbah-ul-Haq did so at a slower rate. Half of those above Bell, including the four at the top of the list, scored their runs at better than a run a ball.

By the end of the World Cup, England's batting was miles behind the best. After England's exit, Downton finally seemed to have noticed that things had changed. His comments made in the aftermath of England's exit about T20 cricket having made all the difference in the last year or so was at least an admission of England not playing with the right tactics, but it exposed just how far behind they had fallen. It wasn't in the last year or two that T20 had started a revolution in ODI cricket, the change had happened earlier than that.

The World Cup had been merely the continuation of a trend to which England had been oblivious. Perhaps they needed to look at the data more, rather than less.

"Downton came back from the World Cup and said it was interesting to see how much T20 had influenced the 50-over game," notes Booth. "That was a hand on forehead moment, because the rest of the world realised that about seven years ago. And the man in charge of English cricket, it had just dawned on him after a disastrous World Cup."

The biggest frustration of all was that England did not have to play the way they did. They chose to. They chose to persist with their old-school tactics, but the players were there. The clues were there. The data was there in the efforts of Moeen Ali at the top of the order, in the scoring efficiency and growing maturity of Joe Root, in the T20 record of Alex Hales, in the freakish talents of Jos Buttler. Even in that World Cup squad, England had the players to play the game differently. They had the players to make that World Cup a very different event. But those inside cricket only realised when it was all too late.

The future's bright, the future's solar red

"THE best thing that happened out of that World Cup: if you fail badly enough it causes a reaction and this World Cup has done that."

Peter Moores is such a relentlessly positive man that one suspects he could find the positives in anything up to and including ITV's Saturday night schedule. But, even for someone with as sunny an outlook as Moores, it's impressive to locate the positive for England from the 2015 World Cup. Incidentally, it says much for Moores' character that the positive he found specifically includes his own departure.

There can be little doubt that he's right, either. The 2015 World Cup was such a disaster at the end of such a damaging and divisive 12 months that it shocked English cricket into action. A month after the World

Cup, the ECB managing director and the head coach were gone. Coaches may come and go, but when the ECB moves so swiftly and decisively to remove one of the suits you know something big has gone down. Giles Clarke, for instance, is still at the ECB.

Downton's failure, though, had been so absolute that not only was he no longer the ECB managing director but now nobody else would be. The "managing director" was no more.

Although it was his disastrous management of the senior men's team that led to his downfall, Downton's remit extended much further. He was responsible for the whole of English cricket; even someone competent would have struggled.

Downton's job was replaced by the oddly-named but more tightly focused role of Director, England Cricket. The new man would be responsible for the "long-term strategy of the England men's cricket team and for developing the right coaching and management structure to support it."

As with Downton's own arrival as both lord high executioner and kingmaker in the aftermath of the Ashes a year earlier, the swiftness of his eventual departure owed much to decisions made earlier but only now coming into effect.

Downton had been appointed as managing director in October 2013, but hadn't even officially started the role when making his decision about Pietersen's levels of interest during a Test match at Sydney in January 2014.

Tom Harrison was appointed chief executive of the ECB in October 2014 in place of the retiring David

Collier, but only took over the following January. In April, Colin Graves was elected, as expected, as the new chairman.

Harrison in particular gave the ECB at the very least a more progressive outward appearance. Still only in his mid-40s and looking remarkably like Michael Sheen playing Tony Blair, Harrison was a new broom at the top of the English board.

Harrison had a brief first-class career with Derbyshire, but had worked at the ECB before. He had worked on the first deal that brought home Test cricket exclusively to Sky from the 2006 summer onwards, before leaving for sports marketing agency IMG. His work there – especially his experience of dealing with the Indian market around the IPL – was seen as crucial to the ECB's desire to reform the domestic county structure.

That, in truth, was the change Harrison was brought in to facilitate. Restructuring county cricket and making it more lucrative, reconnecting with the grass roots of the game and reversing the fall in attendance and participation.

Only a few months into the job, Harrison was overtaken by events and forced into a bigger, more immediate change.

It was certainly bold to remove such a senior figure so early in his tenure – especially as Giles Clarke had not yet officially finished his term as chairman when his man was removed.

Unlike Downton's hasty actions in scapegoating Pietersen the year before, there could be little doubt Harrison was making the right call.

Downton was making an impossible job look even more difficult than it needed to be. Harrison's remodelling of the job specification required someone with better, more recent, more cricket-based credentials than Downton possessed. The new job would carry responsibilities more akin to football management than business management. Downton had only just spotted that T20 was affecting the game. He had to go.

It seemed clear that the new job appeared best suited to one of the assorted former England captains now working in the media. Nasser Hussain ruled himself out; Michael Vaughan ruled himself in and was the early favourite. He used his *Daily Telegraph* column to outline his vision, and said: "For the first time since retiring six years ago I am open to a conversation with the ECB. I am passionate about English cricket. I love the game and I always want England to move forward and be successful."

He was approached but withdrew his interest when told he would have to work with the current coach Peter Moores, leaving the way clear for Andrew Strauss.

Concerns that Strauss, only three years retired and still only 38 years old, may have been a move too far in the other direction – a man too close to the England team and modern cricket rather than too distant – were outweighed by his impeccable credentials.

Strauss was an England captain who had won the Ashes home and away and led the Test team to number one in the world, and had done as well as anyone else, and far better than most, in the last 20 years in the one-day team as both a captain and a batsman.

The ECB's slick new era did not get off to an auspicious start. The announcements of Strauss' arrival and Peter Moores' departure were bungled, with both bits of news eventually rushed out as Harrison and Chris Haynes, the board's new director of communications, were wrong-footed by news of Strauss' appointment and with it Moores' imminent sacking being broken during a damp one-day international against Ireland in Dublin.

As Moores sat in a Malahide changing room, the world knew what he did not: that his time as England coach had come to an end. Harrison had planned to tell Moores early the following week and then have Strauss' arrival confirmed at a press conference. That was always going to be a tough task given the English cricket media were all gathered together in Dublin for a game that had low news value even before the rain arrived. It's no surprise the news got out, and it was clear that Moores deserved better than to find out about his departure in such a cruel fashion.

With the news of Strauss coming in and Moores going out confirmed in a pair of hastily written press releases on the Saturday, the day after the Malahide ODI, it was an uncomfortable start for the new man.

And things got more awkward still for Strauss when his unveiling and first press conference were overshadowed by Kevin Pietersen, who, with the exquisite timing only the greats possess, was busy making a triple-hundred in the County Championship for Surrey.

Colin Graves had made an ill-advised attempt to finally end the Pietersen saga once and for all by calling the batsman's bluff. Graves had challenged Pietersen to return to county cricket and make runs if he wanted his England place back. Pietersen had sacrificed his IPL payday to pick up the gauntlet that had apparently been thrown down.

So Strauss was forced to spend his first press conference explaining the Moores decision and reiterating that there would be no final England hurrah for Pietersen.

While the Pietersen sideshow continued, another Strauss decision outlined that day was perhaps more significant. Eoin Morgan would continue as England's one-day captain despite the World Cup disaster, and would also now lead the T20 side on a full-time basis. Until then, Stuart Broad remained in nominal charge of a team he had not represented in over a year.

It would have been very easy to discard Morgan on the back of the World Cup. He had been given a hospital pass when handed the captaincy but he was far from blameless for the failure, and had scored few runs in Australia and New Zealand. Retaining Morgan was not the straightforward decision the rest of that summer would make it appear. Lawrence Booth calls it "one of Strauss' very good decisions this summer".

With the one-day leadership staying with Morgan and Cook by now secure in the Test job, the next big decision was the identity of the head coach. One Australian edged out another, with Trevor Bayliss preferred to the man who had brought the County Championship title back to Yorkshire, Jason Gillespie. Bayliss' greater white-ball credentials perhaps tipped the balance.

The new coach was arriving just before the Ashes were due to start, but Strauss pointedly namechecked some very different events in the press release announcing Bayliss' appointment. "His expertise in the shorter forms of the game will be vital as we build towards three major ICC events over the next four years; the ICC World T20 tournament in India in 2016 and the ICC Champions Trophy and ICC Cricket World Cup which will be staged in England and Wales in 2017 and 2019 respectively."

Another tick against Bayliss' name was his previous working relationship with England's assistant coach Paul Farbrace, who was popular with the players and would be staying on to work under the new head coach. The pair had worked together with Sri Lanka, and Bayliss said: "I am also looking forward to working alongside Paul Farbrace once again as we have a similar outlook on the game, get on well after two years working together and have kept in touch."

Strauss now had his team in place for one-day cricket, and he is clear that England must treat the white-ball game differently.

"You can't sleepwalk your way into any one-day series and in particular a World Cup," he told us. "And that means we have to have a lot of people in the one-day set-up that are completely focused on one-day cricket. That starts with the captain, and that means we identify one-day specialists and put games and experience into them.

"We are not trying for all of our players to be all-rounders that are playing all forms of the game, although some will."

This idea of the Test and one-day teams becoming more separate, with one-day specialists embraced and encouraged, is perhaps the biggest shift in thinking. Going all the way back through 20 years of failure, England's errors in one-day cricket came so often in erring on the side of the Test player. Nasser Hussain in 1999. Matt Prior in 2011. Gary Ballance and Ian Bell in 2015. "It is easy to say a no-fear brand of cricket but actually you have to select the right players who do that as a matter of course," says Strauss. "You can't ask an Alastair Cook or an Andrew Strauss to score at over a run a ball in one-day cricket because we are not built that way, it is not something that is easy for us to do. You have got to pick players that can do that."

With the one-day game against Ireland in Malahide representing the soggy end to the second Peter Moores era, England's first series in their brave new world would come against New Zealand.

Moeen Ali was rested with the Ashes in mind, but otherwise England were as good as their word. While the squad contained only one uncapped player, Kent keeper-batsman Sam Billings, only seven of the 14-man party had been part of the World Cup squad a few months earlier. James Anderson, Gary Ballance, Ian Bell and Stuart Broad were gone. Long-term, only Ballance has any prospect of returning to the one-day set-up, although Broad was a late replacement when injuries hit the ODI squad in South Africa in early 2016.

In hindsight, England could have had no more perfect opponent for that first series than New Zealand. Brendon McCullum's side were everything this new

England wanted to be. They were fearless, they were bold and they were brilliant.

And, crucially, they would not attempt to stifle or contain. McCullum's attacking instincts ran through his whole team. They would meet any English aggression head on.

In the first match of the series, England scored 408-9. It was their first ever score of 400, and only their second over 350 in a 50-over one-day international. This was in their very first completed game after a humiliating World Cup, and against one of their chief tormentors.

By the end of January 2016, England would post 350 or more a further four times. Some context for those numbers. At the end of the 2015/16 tour of South Africa, England had played 664 one-day internationals. In their first 645, they reached 350 twice (and needed 55 overs to do so in one of them). In England's next 19 games, they reached 350 five times. That's five of England's seven highest ODI scores of all time, in the last three per cent of their total games.

Individual records have tumbled too. Jos Buttler smashed his own record for England's fastest ever ODI century, taking just 46 balls to reach the landmark against Pakistan. He now has England's three fastest hundreds ever in this form of the game.

Maybe it is right that the 2015 World Cup should, as Lawrence Booth has it, be the one that makes England fans angry. Certainly, England playing the kind of cricket so many had been calling for in the *very first* completed ODI after the World Cup made you want to scream. But perhaps they should also be grateful.

England's previous World Cup failures always drew a response, but no failure had ever been so absolute as 2015's and no response had ever been so dramatic.

The shift in the dynamic of England's one-day team is absolute and it feels permanent. We have been here before, but it is somehow harder to see England slipping back to their bad old ways now. They will not always be the best in the world, but they seem far likelier now to at least be the best they can be. Never again constrained by old-fashioned thinking or muddled ideas. No longer aiming for 300 when 350 has become so achievable. Although, this being England, there will probably be some reason why consistently scoring over 350 runs has become old hat and somehow detrimental by 2019.

It is the 2015 World Cup that has given England their freedom. Things had got so bad that anything England did other than more of the same had to be an improvement. Change was not just needed but demanded, and people bought into it. That New Zealand series was a triumph of thrilling and memorable cricket. England won it 3-2 but that almost seems unimportant. England lost to Australia by the same scoreline later that summer but continued to play in the same vein that had won back the fans against New Zealand.

If there is a note of caution, it is that the improvement in the batting has not yet quite been matched by the bowling. As Peter Moores says: "We're producing very exciting one-day batters at the moment, but we're still not producing many outstanding one-day bowlers. Maybe even just that the one-day bowling you need in this country is not what you need in other countries. So we don't produce the pace, the out-and-out pace. That's very valuable in one-day cricket and so is top-flight spin. That's two areas that we're not quite producing enough of that's really affected our one-day cricket and might still affect our one-day cricket going forward."

It may just be natural variation. It may be that England just happened to have a bunch of young, attacking batsmen ready to go and the bowlers will appear later.

Or perhaps the knock-on effect of the change in English one-day batting will be to change the bowling required to counter it. If England are scoring 400 in an ODI in June, perhaps the old ideas about what works in English conditions will change too.

Either way, the bowling looks more of a long-term project than the startling and instant results the batting line-up has so dramatically achieved.

If one-day specialists – or, at least, one-day experts – picked and backed for their ability and willingness to play 21st-century one-day cricket is the first big change in the way new England tackle the game, the shifting stance on the IPL and other Twenty20 tournaments is the other.

For years, Kevin Pietersen was dismissed as a vainglorious, egotistical mercenary for extolling the virtues of the IPL and its imitators. His arguments about the merits of those events, about the lessons to be learned from playing with and against the world's best, in packed stadia full of noise and atmosphere, were dismissed as excuses. He was in it for the money.

Strauss and England have at last, damagingly and desperately late, come to realise he and the rest of the world might have had a point.

"It is what I argued for for so long, and yes, it does bring a smile to my face," says Pietersen. "Playing with other players around the world helped me. I mean, Rahul Dravid, who has been a huge help in my career, that only came through franchise cricket. But unfortunately the regime in England before this new regime, they put a spin through the media that it was money, money, money because it was just me going and I was earning a hell of a lot of money, so it was an easy target. Whereas actually, I knew. I said, yeah, if my career finishes tomorrow, you've got to make all that you can because I ain't a lawyer and I'm not working until I'm 65, I've got to do what I can to earn my money but also, I understood and knew what guys in different dressing rooms were doing for my game."

England players, for so long bit-part players in the big T20 leagues, may now get the same chances that others have enjoyed for almost a decade.

While the IPL's place in the schedule alongside the start of the English season is a problem, it is not insurmountable. Strauss knows England's approach has to change, and also highlights the benefits of putting players under the extra pressure that comes with being an overseas player expected to produce big performances.

He says: "The challenge of the IPL is that it is in our domestic season where Big Bash and some of the other leagues aren't. I think the IPL is a good opportunity at the right time for the right people, but it is more of a general thing about getting some of that domestic T20 experience into our players as an overseas player. If you go to one of these leagues as an overseas player you are under pressure to perform, you are the go-to person to win the game for the team. You are going to bowl the difficult overs, you are going to bat at the more difficult time and you are going to play in front of big crowds in tournament-style conditions. One of the things we most need to learn, and every team needs to do this, it isn't particular to England cricket, is to play under pressure, to react in the right way playing under pressure and those tournaments give our players a great opportunity to do that."

The evidence is already there. The 2016 IPL is a "good opportunity at the right time" for the likes of Sam Billings, Eoin Morgan and particularly Jos Buttler. All are outside the Test team and have taken the opportunity to head to India with the ECB's blessing.

More striking still is the case of Adil Rashid and the Big Bash. Having made his Test debut in late 2015 against Pakistan in the United Arab Emirates, he was then left out of the squad to tour South Africa over Christmas and the New Year.

Rashid was England's second spinner in the UAE, and there was almost no chance the team would include two frontline spinners in South Africa. With Moeen Ali the incumbent first-choice spinner, Rashid would have most likely spent two months wearing hi-viz bibs and ferrying drinks. Tasks he must now be as familiar with as any cricketer in history.

But England had a different plan. He was "dropped" from a Test squad to which he could easily have been recalled at any time had the situation required it, and instead spent his time in Australia's Big Bash with the Adelaide Strikers.

"Adil Rashid showed plenty of promise in the UAE but the conditions in South Africa make the likelihood of playing two spinners extremely remote," said England selector James Whitaker when the squad was announced. "Although he would have been selected as a back-up spinner we feel there is an excellent opportunity for him to spend some time developing his white-ball skills in the lead-up to the ICC World T20 in March."

It helped that the Strikers were coached by Rashid's Yorkshire boss Jason Gillespie. But even so it's hard to imagine even 12 months earlier England taking such a decision as leaving their second-choice spinner out of a hugely important Test tour so he could go and play franchise T20 cricket in Australia.

Rashid was a huge success Down Under, ending the tournament second on the wicket-taking list with 16 from nine games at an average of 14. He was one of the tournament's standout stars, with the sound of Australian commentators talking in hushed tones about the unplayable English leg-spinner a curious sensation for those more accustomed to hearing those roles reversed.

And none of it would have happened had Rashid spent that time sat in training kit and a bib in South Africa. Rashid is not the first England player to perform in a franchise T20 league, but his successful spell in Australia feels like a watershed. Sending him to the Big Bash was a pragmatic decision, where the minimal loss to the Test squad was weighed against the huge potential benefits for the T20 squad – and the player himself. A decision was made for what was the greatest benefit for England, regardless of the format.

Maybe a time will come soon when a player is rested from the final Test of an already-won series rather than the one-day games that follow. For now, though, it is enough that England have men in place in the key positions that will value one-day cricket at all times, rather than only in the immediate "something must be done" aftermath of one World Cup disaster or just as they, as Strauss put it, "sleepwalk" into the next one. You cannot care about one-day cricket only once every four years and then be surprised when you're rubbish at it.

While achieving them over the long term may not be simple, Strauss' goals for England are relatively straightforward.

"We need better planning so that we don't do what we did in 2007 and 2011 and change things the day before the tournament. We need to play a method and a style of cricket that consistently puts opposition teams under pressure so if we come off we have a good chance of winning the game.

"We have one of the greatest opportunities that English cricket has ever had with the 2019 World Cup in this country. If we don't start focusing on one-day cricket now we are idiots. We have paid lip service to it, we have said one-day cricket is important when deep down we have never believed that. Now is the time for us to believe that."

What is hardest to believe is that it has taken England quite so long to reach this point.

Epilogue

Redemption (almost)

THE 2016 World T20 represented the conflation of two things England hadn't had at the same time in limited-overs cricket since 1992. The first was a plan constructed a long way out from a world event and then persevered with. The second was being at the cutting edge of limited-overs tactics.

In the lead-up to their appearance in the 2013 Champions Trophy Final England had a clear plan about how they would play, but it was success borne out of old-fashioned cricket that was only really going to work in early season in England. It would have won them the whole thing but for that ridiculous over from India's Ishant Sharma in the final.

From the very beginning of Andrew Strauss' reign as the head of English cricket there has been a focus on the white-ball game that has never really existed before. Not since the time when Adam Hollioake was taking a ragtag band of bits-and-pieces cricketers to Sharjah in late 1997 has there been a set of players that were primarily a limited-overs squad. There are some players who also play Test cricket – Joe Root, Ben Stokes, Moeen Ali and Alex Hales – but the majority of the 2016 World T20 squad were specialists.

Of all the teams competing at the event none was more attacking in its batting approach than England. Even a West Indies team featuring Chris Gayle and his big-hitting team-mates were not as committed to the Energizer Bunny approach to batting as England. By the final few matches of the tournament, England batted down to eleven. They kept going and going and going and going and going and going and going and going and going and going and going. The only player in the team without a first-class hundred was Chris Jordan, who has a highest score of only 90 in that format. David Willey, a man who has made a 40-ball T20 hundred opening the batting for Northamptonshire, was coming in at nine or ten.

This balls-out batting did have an impact on the bowling, and there was some consternation at the omission of James Anderson and Stuart Broad from the squad. People seemed to think that England should be picking their best bowlers regardless of the format, but that is a mistake hopefully consigned now to the past. Anderson played at the 2015 World Cup, and is England's leading wicket-taker in ODI cricket, but he hasn't played a white-ball game for England since. He hasn't played a game of T20 cricket for England since

2009; he was in the squad for the 2010 World T20 but didn't play once.

The same is true of Stuart Broad. England have decided his skills are better suited to Test cricket. He hasn't been in the reckoning for a first-choice spot in the white-ball teams for England since the end of the World Cup, and only played two ODIs against South Africa in early 2016 because Steven Finn was injured. Broad has not played a game of T20 cricket for England since captaining the side at the 2014 World T20. He has only played one domestic Twenty20 match in that period. England have moved on and, even as their bowlers struggled to keep things tight in the matches against South Africa immediately before the World T20, they did not stray from their chosen path.

England had looked at the cricketers they had available, at the way cricket was being played around the world, and devised a method that could see them compete at a world event. After all England's sustained success in the build-up to this tournament – winning six in a row before the two defeats in South Africa – going back to Anderson and Broad at the first sign of trouble would have been making the same old mistake that England have made so many times before. This time they held firm.

It is a frightening thing to say, but maybe they have finally got it.

※ ※ ※

The first match of England's World T20 was to take place in Mumbai against the West Indies and England stumbled. Having set themselves up as a side where batting was all that mattered they seemed to rein in their attacking instincts. They started scoring at nine an over and never really accelerated. They made 182 at the Wankhede Stadium where the pitch was flat, the outfield was fast and the boundaries were short. It wasn't enough.

"We would have liked 200," Eoin Morgan said in the post-match press conference. "At no stage did we really get going. Guys got themselves in but never got away from West Indies, but I thought they showed a little bit of experience with the ball in getting in and out of overs, and being a little bit smarter against us. One-eighty was competitive but 200 was where we were aiming."

England may have felt 180 was competitive, but Chris Gayle made an absolute mockery of that target. He blasted a 47-ball hundred that propelled the West Indies to their victory target in 18.1 overs. England's bowling weaknesses were brutally exposed. Reece Topley's left-arm fast-medium bowling was marmalised by Gayle. David Willey and Ben Stokes did not fare any better. Only Chris Jordan exerted any kind of control; the rest not only failed to execute their plans, they failed to demonstrate that one even existed.

The mistake they made wasn't in the make-up of the side, or in believing that batting was their strength. It was that they didn't back that up on the field. They didn't get into fifth gear and then into overdrive with the bat, and that was why they had lost. It wasn't a mistake that they made again.

In the next match against South Africa those same problems with the bowling were evident once more. South Africa batted first, having been put in by England, and got off to an amazing start. In the batting PowerPlay South Africa made 83 for no loss. Reece Topley was belted out of the attack and out of England's side when he conceded 33 runs in two overs. Writing for *ESPNcricinfo*, Arun Venugopal summed up Topley's disastrous evening:

"England's Reece Topley made it through the evening like a sloppy stand-up comedian lapsing from one flat joke into a more disastrous one. The scorer in the media box accurately summed up Topley's night when he erroneously mispronounced his name as 'Topple'."

Hashim Amla and Quinton de Kock put on 96 runs in 43 balls and when de Kock fell the rest of the batting line-up kept up that all-out attack approach as South Africa made 229-4, their third highest score of all time. For all of England's planning, for all of the focus on white-ball cricket, for all of the renewed hope they had generated since the embarrassment of the 2015 World Cup, they were on the verge of almost certain group-stage elimination from the World T20 after just two matches.

England needed 230 to win. England's highest ever score in T20 internationals was 214-7 made against New Zealand in 2013. They would need to make their highest ever total, batting second, in unfamiliar conditions against a side that had beaten them in T20 internationals a few weeks earlier. If you were to Google adversity you would probably get a description of this scenario. England found their fifth gear. They managed to not only match South Africa's PowerPlay performance but exceed it, making 89 runs but for the loss of three wickets. Jason Roy made 43 runs at a strike-rate of 268, but the real star was Joe Root.

Root has long been England's best batsman; if he continues on his current trajectory he will become the best all-format player England has ever produced. His innings of 83 from 44 balls against South Africa involved six fours and four sixes but didn't include a single slog. A truism often heard from T20 commentators is that even amidst the mania of T20 you can still score quickly with "proper cricket shots". Joe Root is embodiment of that vision. His innings was brilliantly measured and England made achieving their highest ever total look easy. They needed just one run to win going into the last over having eased down the home straight rather than sprinting for the tape. They could have chased more, and they had kept their tournament alive with one of the more exhilarating run chases in the history of T20 cricket.

They were still in the tournament but realistically they had to win both of their remaining fixtures to get out of the group. First it would be qualifiers Afghanistan and then it would be current world champions Sri Lanka.

Somewhat perversely England would have been more concerned about Afghanistan than Sri Lanka. They have previous for losing to associate nations at the global events. They had lost to the Dutch at the World T20 in both 2009 and 2014 and the Irish at the 2011 World Cup. If they were going to make a mess of things there was every chance it would be against an Afghanistan team with absolutely nothing to lose.

It was an afternoon match. England elected to bat first but struggled to adjust to the Delhi pitch having played their opening two fixtures in Mumbai.

"Starting was difficult on that wicket and it was very different from what we have been playing on in Mumbai," Morgan said after the match.

England certainly made it look difficult. In the tenth over England were 57-6 and made a slight recovery to reach 85-7 in the 15th over when Chris Jordan was dismissed. Then a partnership between Moeen Ali and David Willey extended England's total to 142-7, a position that looked way out of reach for much of their innings.

In the match against South Africa, it had been the ultra-aggressive top order that had rescued England; against Afghanistan it was the long tail that came to their aid. Moeen had made six single-figure scores in a row before his 41 against Afghanistan. Willey had barely had a chance to bat in his previous matches. Together they took England to a winning total, plundering 25 runs from Amir Hamza in the 19th over.

Willey followed up his 20 runs from 17 balls with two early wickets including that of the dangerous Mohammad Shahzad to a ball that swung into his pads and dismissed him lbw. Without him Afghanistan had little chance of the start they needed to push England close. After looking like they were going to lose for the second time in two games England had turned it around and pulled off a victory.

With the way results had gone in the rest of the group, mostly the West Indies winning each of their first three group games, an England win against Sri

Lanka would guarantee Morgan and his men a semi-final spot. This wasn't the same Sri Lanka that had won the World T20 two years earlier. They were without both Mahela Jayawardene and Kumar Sangakkara, and losing those two is the equivalent of misplacing your vital organs. On top of that they had lost the services of Lasith Malinga, whose pinpoint yorkers have served Sri Lanka so well for so long in limited-overs matches. He had failed to recover from a knee injury in time to take part in an event where he was supposed to be captain.

He was replaced as skipper by Angelo Mathews, and it was the stand-in captain who almost knocked England out of the tournament. England batted first and made a very creditable 171-4 thanks to a brilliant innings from Jos Buttler. He got off the mark with a reverse-sweep that he drilled for four and finished on 66 not out off 37 balls. Sri Lanka's successes in the 2016 World T20 had come with the ball not the bat so it should have been more than enough for England to win comfortably.

England had the game won when Sri Lanka stumbled to 15-4 at the end of the third over. So certain was an England victory by this point that the "Win Predictor" on the TV coverage had them as 100 per cent favourites. While this was evidently an embarrassing rounding error it wasn't so very far removed from the sides' respective chances at that point. What the mathematics of the Win Predictor had not taken into account was the *cojones* dangling between Angelo's legs.

When mere mortals are thinking about giving in, Mathews is thinking about getting started. His 73 not out was remarkable and it took Sri Lanka from having no hope to being favourites at the start of the 19th over. Take that, mathematical TV gizmos. Mathews' team needed 22 runs from 12 balls, and he had Dusan Shanaka batting with him. They may have been six wickets down but Shanaka is no traditional number-eight batsman – he has scored two domestic T20 hundreds in his career.

Two wickets in that over put England back in front, but it still wasn't over. At the beginning of the final over Sri Lanka needed 15 to win with Angelo Mathews on strike. It was a tough ask, but not impossible. Ben Stokes then bowled a fantastic over that began and ended with dot balls as England won by ten runs. Those final two overs by Stokes and Chris Jordan were the most accurate and most important the England team had produced at the World T20. From the end of the third over of Sri Lanka's innings until the start of the 19th England had been woeful, but those last two overs that went for just 11 runs secured England a semi-final.

New Zealand had been England's opposition right at the start of this road to white-ball redemption and it would be the Black Caps they faced in the semi-final in Delhi. It would be England's first game of knockout cricket since the 2013 Champions Trophy Final. England were marginal underdogs yet again, New Zealand having won all four of their Group B matches, judging conditions perfectly along the way. Their spinners were conceding less than a run a ball while in Martin Guptill and Kane Williamson they had two of the form batsmen in T20 cricket.

While Williamson and Guptill had made runs it was New Zealand's bowlers who had got them this far, while it had been England's batsmen that were chiefly responsible for their semi-final spot. It would be a clash of approaches in some ways, but the gung-ho swing-from-ball-one method that England have made work for them was borrowed from Brendon McCullum's New Zealand playbook. Even with McCullum now retired, his influence remained.

It was England who won a vital toss at the Feroz Shah Kotla and put New Zealand in to bat with the possibility of dew making it hard to grip the ball later in the innings. It was a perfect start, but England were already ahead when it came to preparations. Whereas New Zealand were playing at their fifth different venue in as many matches, England had played at just two. This was their third consecutive match in Delhi having played two matches in Mumbai before that. By the time they took the field for the semi-final the Kotla must have felt like home.

Having stuck the Kiwis in, England decided it was time to put together their most complete bowling performance for over a year. Willey had Guptill caught by the wicketkeeper early, but Williamson and Colin Munro put together a partnership of 74 to see New Zealand reach 91-1 in the tenth over. Williamson was dismissed by Moeen Ali for 32, and from that point onwards England dragged things back brilliantly. Once again Chris Jordan was parsimonious and he combined with Ben Stokes to produce some astonishingly successful death bowling.

At the end of the 16th over New Zealand were 136-4. Scoring at ten an over between the 17th and 20th overs should have been the minimum target for the

Black Caps from there. It would have given them a total of close to 180, a formidable total in a high-pressure game. In the end, the New Zealanders only managed half that.

The final four overs of their innings cost England just 20 runs and they took four wickets in the process. Stokes and Jordan were immense, between them delivering 23 dot balls in eight overs. New Zealand managed a paltry 156-8 in their 20 overs having been looking set for a great deal more than that at both the halfway stage of their innings and before the start of the death overs.

That left England chasing a sub-par total on a decent pitch in conditions they were used to and in which they had tasted success in the very recent past. They were big favourites to win the game, but all too often it has been in these situations where England sides have contrived to make an absolute mess of things. Not this lot, though. All that baggage from the past is not part of the psyche of the current group of players. They won and they made it appear effortless.

Jason Roy and Alex Hales started off like elephants in musk charging though the savanna. At the end of the PowerPlay England were 67-0 and the required rate was down to a run a ball. From there it just needed steady heads and England were in a World T20 final. Hales departed in the ninth over to leave England on 82-1, but Jason Roy carried on as he had begun. He finished on 78 from 44 balls – his highest score in T20i cricket.

When Roy went and Eoin Morgan followed to the very next ball, there was a chance for New Zealand to come back into it, but, once again, this wasn't the

England side of old. Root and Jos Buttler took a few overs to gather themselves and get set, and then Buttler smashed three sixes to finish things off with 11 balls to spare.

It was ridiculously easy, a complete performance from an excellent team where every player knew their role, had planned meticulously and had absolute faith in himself and his team-mates. They would be playing the West Indies in the final; a team that had already beaten them at this World T20 but one they would fancy were not invincible. One more win and the fairytale turnaround would be complete.

※ ※ ※

It didn't happen. It probably should have happened, but it didn't. The final against the West Indies came down to the final over. The victory target was 19 runs away. There were six balls left. Even after they had stumbled with the bat to set an underwhelming 155-9 off their 20 the English went into the final over of the tournament as favourites.

Ben Stokes was given the ball and, having performed brilliantly in the death overs against both Sri Lanka and New Zealand in the two previous fixtures, he would have felt confident of defending 19 runs against the West Indies' number eight batsman, Carlos Brathwaite. But Brathwaite was no tailender. He had made a first-class hundred and scored a belligerent 69 in a Test match against Australia. His fast-medium bowling and big hitting had generated enough interest at the IPL auction to earn a salary of $635,000.

Going into this innings, Brathwaite had 25 runs in T20 international cricket in four innings, but 18 of those runs had come in sixes. He had not had much opportunity to show off what he could do on this stage, but what came next wasn't a complete surprise. Well it was, but it wasn't as if England would have been surprised to discover Brathwaite could hit a long ball.

Stokes' first ball was too short and speared towards the legside. Brathwaite hoiked it over square leg for six. Thirteen runs needed, five balls left.

The next ball from Stokes was an attempted yorker. He had been putting them in the blockhole for fun, but he missed the length. It became a half-volley that Brathwaite blasted over long-on for six more. Seven needed from four balls.

In the space of two balls England had gone from big favourites to massive underdogs. Stokes couldn't quite believe what was happening and a long conversation took place between bowler and captain. Whatever they discussed it made no difference to the outcome.

The third ball of the over was another failed yorker, another half-volley and another six, this one over long-off. The scores were level, the West Indies bench were dancing and Stokes was distraught. The England all-rounder was on his haunches, close to tears. The scores were level and the West Indies needed just a single to win with three balls left. The game was over barring a miracle involving three dot balls and a Super Over.

Of course Brathwaite didn't do it with a single; he smacked Stokes over midwicket for a fourth consecutive six. He finished on 34 not out and had secured his place in cricket folklore. Maybe next time he is up for auction at the IPL he will get even more money.

※ ※ ※

The final was much more than just those four balls. It was a truly remarkable game that really put paid to the idea that only Test cricket can produce such dramatic swings of fortune. England were put into bat, the tenth time in succession that West Indies captain Darren Sammy had won a coin toss. They got off to the worst possible start when the remarkably consistent Samuel Badree dismissed Jason Roy with the second ball of the match when he played inside a googly that bowled him.

Things got even worse when Alex Hales tried to pull a short ball going down the legside for four and only succeeded in scooping it into the hands of Badree at short fine leg. England were 8-2, and that became 23-3 when Eoin Morgan edged a ball from Badree to Chris Gayle at slip.

Morgan had a terrible tournament with the bat. He managed just 66 runs in five innings with two golden ducks in the process. While he struggled with his form he brought so much more to this team. Of all the people that had been responsible for the turnaround in England's one-day cricket Morgan's role was every bit as significant as those of Andrew Strauss, Trevor Bayliss and Paul Farbrace. This is Eoin Morgan's team built in his image. For that he deserves plaudits and some forgiveness for underperforming with the bat in India at this World T20.

While Morgan was gone Joe Root was still at the crease, as was Jos Buttler. The two men have become the bedrock on which England's limited-overs success has been built. Root is the first England batsman since Kevin Pietersen to master all three formats of the game, and is well on target to outstrip even his achievements. Root's 54 runs consolidated and accelerated at the same time. He lost Buttler along the way but Root was unperturbed. He manoeuvred England into a position where they could have set a really impressive total, but this ridiculous match gave us another switch in fortunes.

England lost three wickets for a single run in just four balls to put them in trouble. That long batting line-up game to the rescue once again. David Willey and Chris Jordan combined to take England past 150 and to the point where they had a chance. Chasing in a final can do funny things to a batsman.

This proved to be true when that man Root surprisingly took the new ball and picked up two wickets in the second over, including danger man Chris Gayle. The West Indies were 5-2 as Gayle departed and that became 11-3 when Willey dismissed Lendl Simmons lbw for a duck. England were on top, but the West Indies, as they had proved against India in the semi-final, had plenty of match-winners in their batting line-up.

One of those men was the pugnacious Marlon Samuels. He could well have gone for 27 when he edged a ball from Liam Plunkett through to Buttler. The England keeper was convinced the catch had carried, and Samuels had almost made it off the field when he was called back after the replay indicated that Buttler had not got his gloves underneath the ball. It was a marginal call, but the right one. If Samuels had gone at that point, the West Indies would have been 37-4; as it was he would be there until the very end, finishing on 85 not out and in the best seat in the house for Ben Stokes' final-over suffering.

Samuels' partnership with Dwayne Bravo was painfully slow at first, and had put West Indies a long way behind the game. Samuels accelerated brilliantly towards the end of the innings. He reached his 50 off 47 balls and then added another 35 runs in just 19 more.

It was Samuels who rescued the West Indies and then set up the win. It was Brathwaite who finished the job in the most spectacular fashion with four sixes that will be talked about for years to come.

England had lost the final but they played a big part in one of the finest games of cricket you will ever see.

%% %% %%

A World T20 victory would have been the Hollywood ending to a year of limited-overs discovery for England, but the point had been proven. Giving the white ball the focus it deserves produced brilliant cricket that helped England win cricket matches. Maybe the message has got through. Maybe they have finally realised that it doesn't have to be Test cricket or one-day cricket. Maybe this is the start of something truly special for England in the limited-overs formats.

England have led us down this path before and let us down. This time, though. This time it feels different.